3D EDITION

LET'S TALK BUSINESS

JEAN H. MICHULKA

Associate Professor Emerita
Drama and Speech
The University of Texas at El Paso

Published by

E92 **SOUTH-WESTERN PUBLISHING CO.**

CINCINNATI   WEST CHICAGO, IL   CARROLLTON, TX   LIVERMORE, CA

ISBN: 0-538-05920-6

Library of Congress Catalog Card Number: 86-63174

5 6 W 2

Printed in the United States of America

PREFACE

It is exciting to welcome you to the Third Edition of *Let's Talk Business*. With helpful insight from teachers and students who have successfully used the earlier editions of this book, we invite you now to study a thoroughly reviewed and revised text. In addition, the publisher has designed a fresh new format to make the book more attractive and easier to use.

The basic arrangement of the text, however, remains the same. Ten chapters of text material provide the "why" of communication; each of the ten chapters concludes with a workshop section to provide the "how to." Because just reading about oral communication rarely changes communication behavior or improves speaking and listening skills, these workshops are filled with practice materials: exercises, individual and group assignments, case studies, sample speeches, illustrative outlines, problem-solving and discussion activities, speaking assignments, and evaluation sheets to focus your learning. Each chapter sets up specific objectives as student goals. Each chapter includes a summary of the text material. To make finding activities easier, the table of contents lists the workshop activities for each chapter.

As a student, you bring a wealth of communication experience to this book. Now you are challenged to examine and to improve this experience as you prepare for a career in business. Successful businesspeople are skillful communicators. But skill in communication doesn't just magically happen. It is the result of deliberate effort to learn about oral communication and to practice the things you learn. You are expected to do four things:

1. Study the chapter material.
2. Ask questions and participate in class discussions.
3. Involve yourself in group activities.
4. Prepare and present individual speeches and assignments.

Groups of students have provided careful evaluations of the text material and of the activities. I owe them my grateful thanks. And this edition contains an even greater number of examples of student work. Special gratitude goes to Patricia Aguilar, Ernesto A. Baca, Phyllis Caves, Robbie Chavez, Shari J. Dorris, Orlando Fonseca, Sherry Gray, Sandy Igoe, Steven Jones, Susan Law, Lillian Lazavick, Debra R. Lobato, Pat Lopez, Beth Lux, Mark McGurk, Ron Montgomery, Chuck Munoz, Ronnie Ng, Estela Rascon, Romelia Ramos, Letitia R. Rueda, Beverly Ruiz, Eddie Salazar, Lynn Scherotter, Carol A. Siefker, Therese Stadnisky, B. Kent Straughn, Phil Swegler, Peggy Willis, Reba Woodward, and Brenda Yeager. I acknowledge also the contributions and willing help of the following friends and colleagues: Margaret Barry, Madeline Brand, Dayton Ballenger, Penny Byrne, David Harlan, Harry Mallo, Edward Salazar, R. W. Sims, Ray Spitzenberger, and J. Henry Tucker. It is good to have a panel of experts working with you.

As a student, you have high hopes of being successful in your chosen field. Whatever that field is, your communication skills will contribute to your success. I hope this book and all it offers will have a direct impact on your future. My good wishes go with you, and now *Let's Talk Business*.

JEAN H. MICHULKA

CONTENTS

CHAPTER 8 LET'S TALK ABOUT THE BUSINESS OF DELIVERING YOUR PRESENTATION 251

WORKSHOP ACTIVITIES

CHAPTER 9 LET'S TALK ABOUT THE BUSINESS OF COMMUNICATING ONE-TO-ONE 289

WORKSHOP ACTIVITIES

CHAPTER 1

Let's Talk About the Business of Presenting Yourself as a Communicator

Welcome to the world of business speech communication. This textbook is designed to introduce you to the principles of communication used in talking business. Speech is a remarkable skill, often taken for granted. This chapter will introduce you to speech communication and suggest ways to use speech more effectively on the job and in your personal life. After you have read and discussed this chapter and participated in the workshop activities, you should be able to do the following:

Chapter Objectives

1. Feel comfortable in a friendly classroom situation.
2. Recognize the need to improve speech communication skills.
3. Understand how speech fits into the total communication process.
4. Identify the elements of a communication model.
5. Recognize barriers in the communication process.

Suppose you awoke tomorrow morning to find that everyone had suddenly lost the ability to speak—no friendly voice on the radio, no telephone messages, and none of those important oral exchanges that make you feel good about being alive! Imagine the obstacles the business world would face if people could not talk. The whole process of producing, buying, selling, transporting, storing, supervising, and managing would be handicapped. More than 12 million business firms in the United States engage in manufacturing, wholesaling, retailing, or performing services for the public. Each of these businesses is cemented together by many kinds of people who have different skills and a variety of goals. In this dynamic, complex world of business, the primary means of working with and through people is speech communication.

"Speech is civilization itself. The word, even the most contradictory word, preserves contact—it is silence which isolates."

Thomas Mann

This book is designed to help you as a business student and as a speech communicator. As a future employee, you are studying to improve your business skills with an eye toward advancement. For example, knowing computer languages, accounting procedures, or marketing techniques will advance you in business. Equally valuable are your communication skills. Understanding how to give instructions, how to listen, or how to organize and deliver a presentation will help you too. The primary concern of this book, then, is to help you make effective adjustments in the way you use speech. No one can make changes in the way you present yourself. You are the only one who can apply the principles of this book to your work relationships.

COMMUNICATION

Let's begin by looking at a big picture of how communication works. The *two major functions* are output and input. What you say is **output**; what you receive from the world outside yourself is **input**. In order to function as both a speaker and a receiver, you are equipped with five senses for responding to stimuli, a brain for processing the incoming information, and a voice and body capable of expressing what your brain creates. So, communication functions in two ways: within you as *intrapersonal communication*, and between you and others as *interpersonal communication*. Let's define these terms.

Intrapersonal communication—perceiving sound and light stimuli and creating mental images within yourself by blending the new stimuli with past experience; thinking.

Interpersonal communication—recreating your mental images by translating them into sounds—speech—and movements—gestures—that call up similar images in the minds of others.

Communication—A Process

A **process** is an ongoing, continuous activity or a dynamic series of changes that are constantly occurring. Communication is an ongoing, continuous process. It takes place within you and between you and others. All that you think, do, and say is part of the continuous communication process. For instance, thinking is the process of communicating with yourself. Smiling or shaking hands is the process of communicating through movement. Speaking to another person is the process of communicating a message through oral language. Thoughts, actions, and speech are bits and pieces of the whole communication process.

Even when you are silent, your face and body convey nonverbal (wordless) messages to others. You may stop speaking, but your face may communicate that you are listening. Or you may pretend to listen, but your body sends the message that you have gone off on a private mental journey. Even without words, you are able to communicate such messages as:

concern	or	indifference
enthusiasm	or	boredom
approval	or	anger
friendliness	or	irritation

The communication process is more than just speaking and listening. It includes messages that you send consciously and unconsciously. Therefore, we call communication a process because it is going on all the time; speech is only one part of the process.

Variables of Communication

Another way to think of communication is to consider a number of variable factors which affect the communicative act. Some of these variables are:

How you see yourself—the picture you have of yourself as a person, a worker, a customer, a supervisor, etc.

How others see you—the picture others have of you based on their experiences with you at the moment or in the past.

How you feel at the moment—how you feel toward the person with whom you are talking, or toward the subject with which you are dealing.

How you think—your assumptions, beliefs, attitudes, and values, which are based on your own life experiences.

How you behave—your facial expressions, gestures, voice, eye contact, and physical distance maintained as you talk to others.

Even without speech, people receive messages about you. Your total communication message includes your clothing and hairstyle; your personal possessions such as your car, your home, and your jewelry; your activities; the way you spend your time; and the people with whom you associate. In its broadest sense, then, communication deals with the information you consciously or unconsciously reveal about yourself.

SPEECH—ONE PART OF A WHOLE PROCESS

"In giving a speech, remember that surveys reveal the ways the audience pays attention to your talk: 50 percent to how you speak, 42 percent to your appearance, 8 percent to content."

Dorothy Sarnoff

The study of speech cannot be separated from other aspects of behavior that send messages to people. The presentation you make of yourself as a total package determines how effectively you will communicate. If people are attracted by what they see, they often pay close attention. If they like what they see, they often listen better. A neat physical appearance, direct eye contact, and a pleasing voice and manner add dimension to speech messages. Communication, then, is a series of activities and responses; and speech is part of the process.

Need for Speech Communication

Throughout the ages, people have had to communicate with one another. From smoke signals to semaphore to sonar, humans have designed symbolic codes to carry messages. Probably the most satisfying and useful of these communication devices is human speech.

You probably can think of many reasons for using speech. It is a means of getting to know and understand others. It is the way you tell others what you think and believe so that they can understand you. Speech also is the basis for talking business. In your business of earning a living, you use speech in four major ways:

1. **To make contact with others.** You use speech to:

   greet people
   exchange social conversation
   chat about the weather
   report on people and events
   establish personal relationships
   find common ground for discussion

2. **To exchange information.** You use speech to:

   explain an idea
   clarify a difficult point
   illustrate with examples
   extend ideas by relating to others
   ask and answer questions

3. **To influence others.** You use speech to change attitudes and beliefs. You try to:

   stimulate feelings
   present new viewpoints
   convince through basic appeals
   encourage open communication
   counsel or give advice
   share a conviction

   You move others to action with speech messages that:

   appeal to emotions
   motivate through persuasion
   reason with logic
   present evidence
   describe through personal experience

4. **To solve problems.** You work with others through speech communication to:

   identify problems
   specify causes
   consider alternatives
   propose and select solutions

"No man is an island entire of it-self; every man is a piece of the continent, a part of the main. . . ."

John Donne

Speech communication is essential to your personal and business life. In fact, you use speech in so many ways that it is your primary means of maintaining contact with others. Think of the times you use speech to express your feelings or opinions. Think of the ways you influence or adapt to others through speech. Often you say, "If I could just talk to her" or, "If they would just listen to me." The ability to speak and listen is your bond to others.

Speech Communication Terms

The following are terms that can be used to talk about speech:

Sender—originator of a verbal or nonverbal message.
Speaker—sender of an oral message; words accompanied by face and body movements.

Encoding—the act of a speaker who translates an idea into a verbal code or language.

Message—sounds or words carried by sound waves and/or nonverbal movements which are communicated by light waves.

Receiver—person who hears or sees the message being sent.

Decoding—the mental process by which a receiver translates a received, coded message into meaning.

Feedback—verbal or nonverbal response to a message.

Channels—media through which messages flow—air, telephone lines, etc.

Barriers—obstacles that block communication.

Speech is the means by which people interact with each other. **Interaction** occurs when two people are sending and receiving, acting and reacting, interpreting messages and responding to each other. Moreover, interaction occurs when both people are aware that they are jointly participating in the communication act. Speech is the interpersonal bond through which people share meaning. Let's try to stop the action and label what occurs. (See Figure 1-1.)

FIGURE 1-1   A speech communication model.

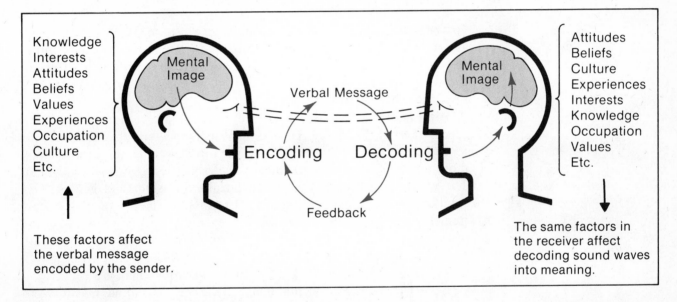

Speech Communication Model

Each of the people represented in Figure 1-1 has a mental image that is based on a variety of personal experiences. Each person brings to a communication transaction unique experiences that have shaped the individual's attitudes, beliefs, values, and behavior. However, even with common experiences, mental images may be different. For instance, the words *apple pie* probably conjure up one image for you and a different image for me. However, we can still talk to each other and understand one another. Thus, oral communication is as effective as the ability of the sender and the receiver to transmit mental images to each other via words, or language symbols, which are traveling as sound waves.

Keep in mind that speech is not an alternating process in which two people take turns speaking and listening to each other. True, we are all receivers who are capable of sending and receiving messages; but unlike a two-way radio which cuts off reception when sending a message, the human being is capable of encoding a message while decoding nonverbal feedback—*all at the same time*. As a sender speaks, that person checks to see if the receiver is listening and to see what clues to understanding the message the receiver is giving. As the receiver decodes a verbal message, that person sends nonverbal signals, such as a shrug of the shoulders or a nod of the head, to respond to the speaker. Feedback occurs while the message is being sent. Transmission is almost simultaneous! In a transaction between two people, each serves as the sender and the receiver of messages.

> **Transceiver**—a combination transmitter and receiver housed in a common cabinet and employing some common circuit components for both transmitting and receiving.[1]

Thus, speech communicators are like transceivers. Human beings are capable of sending and receiving messages at the same time. These are called transactions.

DESCRIPTION OF A TRANSACTION

One person translates an idea or mental image into words that are produced as sound waves traveling in many directions. If another person is within receiving distance of the sound waves, he or she can hear the voice, listen to the words, translate the sounds into a similar mental image, and feed back a response. This is a **transaction**.

In Figure 1-1 there is a speaker, or message **source**, and a **verbal message** spoken by the source. There is also a person who is the **receiver** of the verbal message. The receiver listens to the words, watches the face and body movements of the speaker, and then recreates the message in his or her mind. The verbal (words) and nonverbal (facial expressions and gestures) responses sent by the receiver are called **feedback**. These responses are extremely useful to the speaker because they give clues that tell whether the message sent is being received favorably, unfavorably, or perhaps not at all.

The term **encoding** is used to describe the way a speaker translates a thought into oral language. The sound of the words, then, is a coded message that symbolizes the mental image in the speaker's mind. Of course, to communicate effectively through speech, the speaker and the receiver must know, use, and understand a common language.

Decoding is the way a receiver makes sense of speech and turns a message into meaning. In other words, the receiver interprets the word sounds, creates personal meaning, and recreates the speaker's original idea. The receiver makes use of more than just the words to decode a message. For example, words, plus vocal tones, plus nonverbal clues such as facial expressions and gestures, are all helpful in the business of decoding. So, the receiver uses eyes as well as ears to receive oral messages. Light and sound waves serve as channels to stimulate these senses.

"It takes two to speak the truth . . . one to speak and the other to hear."

Henry David Thoreau

"In a good transaction, it is difficult to determine which one is the sender and which one is the receiver."

Dr. Fred Craddock

---

[1] Editorial and Technical Staff of Radio Shack, *All About CB Two-Way Radio*, 1976.

Limited Transactions

If you speak to someone on the telephone, you limit the messages you receive, because you cannot see the person to whom you are talking. Your translation of the message, therefore, depends on the words and the sound of the voice that is delivering those words. These clues are known as **paralanguage**.

For instance, words may convey certain meanings, but the paralanguage—the tone of the voice, the inflection, the rate of speech, etc.—may indicate a conflicting meaning or message. Someone might say to you, "I'll be happy to work overtime"; but though the words may indicate "happiness," the sound of the voice may indicate "unhappiness" with regard to the situation. The message you receive, then, will depend on the message to which you choose to pay attention.

Face-to-Face Transactions

When we talk about **nonverbal** messages, we generally mean body language. You are probably quite adept at reading messages that are not at all related to the spoken words. If you watch a speaker, you note the directness of eye contact with the receiver, the tension in the body, the hand movements, the shrug of the shoulders, or the shifting of weight. All of these actions send messages that alert receivers.

Another characteristic of communication messages is the use of **space**. Most of us feel a need for personal space, which has been compared to an invisible bubble of air that surrounds each of us. We also like to choose the people who enter our space. For example, your choice of a seat beside someone may communicate your interest in him or her and your willingness to talk. If someone enters your personal space and this action makes you uncomfortable, you are likely to back off. People discussing private matters will often move close together, while strangers are more likely to maintain space between each other. People who share a close relationship often share the same space. They do not mind sitting or standing near each other, and an intimate relationship may include a great deal of touching.

Our use of **time** may also send messages about ourselves. For instance, do you tend to put off things you don't like to do? Are you late for events that don't interest you? Can you always make time for things that are really important to you? You are communicating through your use of time.

One other area of communication that sends messages is **personal appearance**. A speaker once advised a group of business students that upon obtaining jobs, they should dress like the people who are on the next rung up the organizational ladder. His contention was that if you communicate through the way you dress that you are ready for a promotion, chances are you will be considered for one.

We have been talking about a number of channels of communication which are illustrated in Figure 1-2. Note the zigzag lines marked "Barriers." This is a communication term indicating anything that interferes with the speaker's intended message or that gets in the way of the receiver's accurate reception of the message.

"A breakdown in speech communication is what happens when a barrier works."

Penny Byrne

FIGURE 1-2   A speech communication model showing message barriers.

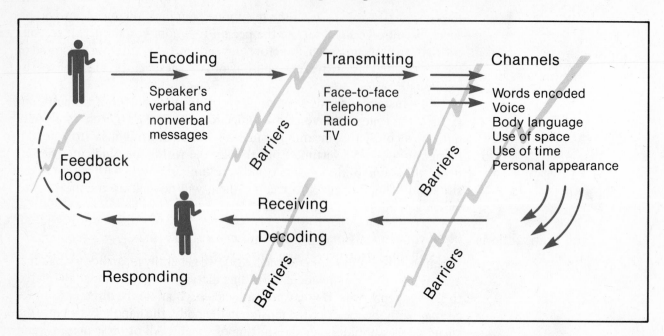

COMMUNICATION BARRIERS

Communication barriers prevent understanding and can appear almost anywhere in the speech communication process. Consequently, when a message is not understood as a speaker intends, there is some kind of barrier existing in one of the following places:

1. Within the sender or receiver
2. In the encoding or decoding process
3. In the message itself
4. In the channel through which the message is transmitted
5. In the feedback process

Let's look at some of these barriers more closely.

Perception Barriers

Perception—the process of absorbing, organizing, and interpreting messages from the world outside—is different for every individual. You live in an environment that showers you with sound waves, odors, light waves, and other stimulating sensations. You react to some of these stimuli. Others you are not aware of or simply ignore. You also live in a world of people—a personal world and a business world. These people bombard you daily with carefully designed speech messages. You pay attention to some of these messages and ignore others through a process called **filtering**. Your own senses, interests, and needs let some of these messages through and filter out others.

As you receive sensations from the world outside, you blend them with those you have already stored up from previous experiences. You select, identify, organize, and interpret the messages you receive, and you create your own mental images. Since no other person will ever select and interpret in exactly the same way you do, barriers can occur between you and your listeners or within you as the speaker. Chapter 2 will help you understand how to work around these barriers.

Language Barriers

Spoken language is a unique blend of sounds. To receive a message accurately, the listener must of course be able to understand the language in which it is sent, whether English or French or Spanish or Japanese. But even within your own native language, there are specialized languages—medical language, legal language, and the vocabulary unique to different businesses and industries. If you don't understand the terminology that the speaker is using, there may be barriers in the communication process.

Ideally, the use of language should result in the images in one person's head being duplicated in the head of another. However, even when two people speak the same language, they may not communicate precisely. Because no two people have exactly the same experiences, each may have a somewhat different understanding of words used by a speaker. For example, if your supervisor says, "This must go out immediately," does this mean that you must drop everything and perform the task right away? Or does it mean that you should finish the work you are doing before completing the request? Language is symbolic. Words may have different meanings to the speaker and the listener. We will discuss how to overcome language barriers in Chapter 4.

Listening and Feedback Barriers

Your ears are designed to hear. However, listening requires an active mental process. You must be tuned in to the communication message so that you can decode accurately. Words fall on deaf ears if no one listens. But listening is more than just turning your ears on. Specifically, it is a partnership with the speaker. We will work on listening skills in Chapter 3.

Feedback, too, is an area where barriers can occur. You may be aware that something is blocking your speech transaction and you may ask your listener, "Did you hear me?" Now your receiver can tell you, "I heard you but I don't understand you." Frequently we fail to eliminate the barrier by not asking that question. Instead we rely on nonverbal feedback (often facial expression) for clues that our messages are getting through—or failing to get through. Feedback is expressed both verbally and nonverbally. We will discuss getting and giving feedback more accurately in Chapter 3.

"A good listener is not only popular everywhere, but after a while he gets to know something."

Wilson Mizner

Stage Fright—A Speaker Barrier

Because you were born into a speaking society, you quickly picked up the skills of oral communication. You delighted your parents by imitating the sounds you heard. As you related the word sounds to objects and events, you developed a language vocabulary. You learned to speak from those who loved and cared for you. However, beyond this initial stage, you probably had little training in speaking.

Unless something goes wrong with your physical mechanism—a bad case of laryngitis, for example—your speaking voice operates well. Yet speech may desert you in an unfamiliar situation. Feelings and attitudes within you may reduce your confidence in speaking before a group of people. This barrier is called *stage fright* and we need to talk about it now—before you are asked to get up and speak in front of the class.

Stage fright is a universal problem that can plague the presentational speaker and hinder performance. The problem recently has been called *communication apprehension* or *speaking anxiety*, and it is recognized as a very real fear. In 1973, the London Sunday *Times* reported the results of a survey in which 3,000 people in the United States were asked, "What are you most afraid of?" Forty-one percent responded, "Speaking before a group."

Stage fright is powerful enough to make people refuse opportunities to speak or to prevent capable people from advancing in their professions. So, if going to an interview, taking part in a discussion, or speaking in front of a group is a problem for you, you are certainly not alone.

When human beings are threatened by something perceived as harmful or potentially harmful, psychologists tell us that their natural instinct is to fight or take flight. Most of us believe that because speaking is something we have been doing all our lives, it is something we should be able to do as well as the next person. Hence, we are not likely to run away from the experience. If we accept the challenge, prepare for it carefully, and face it, we are more likely to stay and fight. We will see it through. But we would rather not worry about it so much—if possible.

It *is* possible to reduce your anxiety level! First, you need to understand what happens inside the body when a speaking situation looms ahead.

1. The brain, that clever human computer, alerts the body exactly as if it had a physical danger to fight off.
2. The brain signals the *adrenal-medullary system* to release chemicals that stimulate the body.
3. These chemicals increase the heart rate, elevate the blood pressure, and raise the level of fatty acids in the blood.
4. As the blood flows away from the digestive tract, we have that strange sensation of butterflies in the midsection of the body.
5. The oxygen in the blood tenses the muscles of the body so that we suddenly are aware of tight shoulders and wiggly feet (the body is getting ready to fight or run).
6. Blood circulating rapidly warms the hands and feet, which, as they perspire, feel clammy and unnatural.
7. The senses become keener and more aware.
8. The breathing rate accelerates, and we may not be able to control the breath needed for speech.
9. The mouth becomes dry. (Many speaker stands are provided with a pitcher of water and a glass.)
10. Poisons are removed from the body more speedily so that toxicity and fatigue are reduced.

As a result of all these physiological changes, we suddenly possess a tremendous amount of energy—energy with which to deliver a dynamic, forceful presentation or energy that becomes nervousness indicating that we cannot cope. Knowing what is going on inside yourself may help to explain the above symptoms, but it does not help to convert your fears into a source of power that can be directed toward being a poised, successful speaker. Let's look a little further.

Psychological Attitudes Causing Stage Fright. Why is a speaking situation so frightening? Your job probably does not depend on it, nor is your position in the company likely to suffer because of it. However, while there is no physical threat to your well-being, there *is* a psychological threat. You may worry about what people think of you. Because your self-image is related to the way people respond to you, you may feel that you are laying your self-image and others' opinions of you on the line. This is frightening! The opinions of your boss and your co-workers are important to you. You want to appear competent, skillful, and interesting to them. Feeling that you won't is a great personal threat.

Speaking situations also are frightening because of inner conflicts. You may be required to give a speech you don't want to give. Your resentment may cause communication anxiety. You may feel your knowledge of the subject matter is inadequate. Your worry produces anxiety. The size of the audience or your unfamiliarity with the group may cause apprehension. The conflict between what you have to do and the way you feel about doing it can make the speaking situation very threatening to you.

If any of these reasons is the basis of your stage fright, the following are some suggestions that will change your mental state.

Suggestions for Reducing Stage Fright. Perhaps not all of these ideas will work for you, but some of them should help calm your platform jitters.

1. **Carefully select the topics you discuss.** Speak on issues you care about, information you know well, or ideas to which you are committed. Know how the topic relates to your audience.
2. **Concentrate on your speech.** Do justice to the message you are to deliver.
3. **Remind yourself** that you have carefully planned this message for a specific group with special needs and interests.
4. **Keep the tone of your presentation conversational.** Stiff or unnatural language keeps you remote from your audience rather than drawing you closer. Treat your audience as business associates and maintain frequent eye contact with them.
5. **Be prepared to handle mistakes.** If you stumble, don't call attention to it. Go right on and let the group forget it. If you lose your place, take a second to put yourself back on the track.
6. **Use the power of the pause.** This gives you a chance to gain poise and provides your listeners with the opportunity to reflect. Use pauses to give your points a chance to be understood, to win agreement, or to recapture wandering attention.
7. **Focus the listeners' attention on visual material.** Give the listeners something else to look at besides you. Visual impact will be discussed further in Chapter 7.
8. **Be prepared by practicing orally.** Practice your speech orally at home. Stand up and use your note cards as if you were really speaking to an audience. Ask a friend to listen to you and to time your speech. Be sure it fits your allotted time. Don't deliver your speech without practicing beforehand!

Finally, remember that your confidence increases if you practice speaking in nonthreatening situations with groups you know well. If you are in doubt about your readiness to speak, ask yourself if you will be disappointed if you are *not* called on to deliver your presentation. You will want to speak if you have spent adequate time preparing. Be glad you care enough to feel the symptoms of stage fright. Use the energy provided to control these symptoms, not to eliminate them. Think on your feet, focus on your ideas, and say what you have prepared with passion and concern. You will forget you ever had the jitters, and your audience will be so impressed they will not notice your nervousness.

"The mind is a wonderful thing— it starts working the minute you're born and never stops—until you get up to speak."

Anonymous

"An able speaker is an able person, in a good emotional state, with a good attitude toward himself and toward his audience."

Lew Sarett and William T. Foster

PHOTO 1-1

Focusing the listener's attention on visual material can reduce a speaker's stage fright.

STEPS TO IMPROVEMENT

Barriers in communication break the flow of human contact and, as a result, misunderstandings, hurt feelings, and poor relationships develop. People may stop speaking to each other; or they may fail to communicate at all. Communication is a fragile encounter between people.

In the workshop activities which follow this chapter, you will be working with others in small groups or speaking in front of the class. Here are some suggestions for preventing barriers in communication when you talk in a small group:

1. Find common ground.
2. Define your terms.
3. Establish eye contact.
4. Speak clearly and directly.
5. Check listener's feedback.
6. Adjust messages to feedback.

When you are listening:

1. Listen open-mindedly.
2. Decode openly—repeat what you hear.
3. Ask questions.
4. Ask a speaker to define terms.
5. Give honest feedback.

These suggestions are also useful when you are speaking before a group or when you are a member of the audience. Next are further tips for your presentational speaking:

1. Don't just say it—show it. Use at least one visual aid in each presentation. (Write on the board, use a chart, hold up an object, etc.)
2. Use note cards with your key ideas jotted down as a memory aid.
3. Write out your opening and closing statements so you'll feel secure.
4. Stand up and practice the whole speech beforehand as if you were in front of the class.
5. Look at your audience as you speak.
6. Strive to be conversational and comfortable.

As a member of the audience:

1. Listen courteously and openly.
2. Focus your attention on the speaker.
3. Put yourself in the speaker's shoes.
4. Give deserved recognition and praise.

As you progress through this book, you will become aware of your communication habits and begin to recognize potential barriers to communication. Eventually you will become a more skillful communicator by working toward the goals of this course—to understand speech in a communication context; to apply the techniques presented here; and to extend your communication skills to business encounters.

CHAPTER SUMMARY

This chapter has introduced you to communication and more specifically to speech communication. Communication functions in two major ways—intrapersonally and interpersonally. In the first way, you communicate within yourself as you receive sensations through hearing, seeing, smelling, tasting, and touching. As you process, organize, and interpret incoming information, you put together mental images through the thinking process. You use speech in your interpersonal communication when you translate your mental images into sound waves for others to hear. You use speech for your transactions in face-to-face encounters or telephone conversations.

Messages flow through a number of channels—vocal sounds or paralanguage, body language, physical appearance and behavior—and through the use of time and space. You are a receiver and a sender simultaneously. You transmit and receive messages both consciously and unconsciously. Your feedback or response may be verbal or nonverbal.

You have learned that barriers to effective communication can arise at many different points—in perception, language, listening and feedback, or within the attitudes of the speaker or listener. Stage fright can be a barrier to presentational speaking, but it can be recognized and controlled. Many steps can be followed to reduce or prevent communication barriers when you speak and listen.

WORKSHOP ACTIVITIES

PRESENTING YOURSELF TO A SMALL GROUP *(Group Activity)*

Purpose: To share information about yourself. To learn about others.

Briefing: As your teacher reads the following list of topics aloud, check the ones you would like to discuss with others. The teacher will divide the class into small groups. Gather with other class members into a comfortably seated group. Now select ten of the topics the group would like to talk about. Tell the members of your group the information asked for. Try to remember what the others tell you. If there is time, go on to the unchecked topics.

_____ 1. State your full name and spell it. Tell what you would like to be called in this class. Make sure the group remembers your name.

_____ 2. Share a description of the area or region of the world you know and like best.

_____ 3. Describe your favorite fantasy vacation trip.

_____ 4. Talk about the one sport you like best and why.

_____ 5. Identify the automobile you would choose to drive if you could own any one.

_____ 6. Share information about the person you feel closest to in your life. (No names are needed.)

_____ 7. Discuss the music you would most like to hear playing in a dentist's office.

_____ 8. Tell about the most wonderful gift you've ever received.

_____ 9. Name your all-time favorite movie or television show. Explain why.

_____ 10. Rate the President of the United States on his performance based on a scale of 1 (poor) to 5 (superior). Tell why.

_____ 11. Discuss the most exciting thing that has happened to you in the past two weeks.

_____ 12. Identify the size of the group you prefer to work with—three to four people, more than five people, or alone—and why.

_____ 13. Cite the magazine or newspaper you read most frequently. Why?

_____ 14. Describe your behavior with others. Is it usually competitive or usually cooperative?

_____ 15. State what you would order for your last meal on earth.

_____ 16. Describe your feelings about being in school this term.

_____ 17. State the first thing you would buy if you won a million dollars in a lottery.

_____ 18. Identify your honest feelings about giving a speech in front of an audience.

_____ 19. Discuss your favorite way to spend leisure time.

_____ 20. Speculate as to the words you'd most like to see engraved on a trophy presented to you.

SAMPLE RÉSUMÉ *(Individual Reference)*

Romelia Ramos   Phone: (915) 555-9325
9603 Kentucky
El Paso, TX 79930-1245

JOB OBJECTIVE
To become a computer operator.

EDUCATION
19-- to present: University of Texas, El Paso, TX 79931-2465
                        Curriculum: Business Administration
                           Degree: Bachelor of Business Administration
                          Courses: Computer Information Systems,
                                     Accounting
                      Grade Point: 2.9

19-- to 19--:   Austin High School, El Paso, TX 79933-2111
                        Curriculum: General Education
                           Degree: High School Diploma

WORK EXPERIENCE
19-- to present: Coronado Bank, El Paso, TX 79931-2444
                      Commercial Teller
                      Work Responsibilities: Customer transactions, handling
                      money paid out or received.

19-- to 19--:   Handi-Pac Products, El Paso, TX 79932-8431
                      Clerk/Bookkeeper
                      Work Responsibilities: Bookkeeper and computer operator in
                      charge of payroll, inventory, sales, and billing.

MEMBERSHIPS
Alpha Phi Omega sorority   Student Advisory Board
Student Council Representative   Senior Executive Board

OTHER INTERESTS
- computer games
- handcrafts
- volleyball

SPECIAL SKILLS
Operating and programming computers (IBM with emphasis in Lotus 123), 10-key by
touch, typing 55 wpm, bookkeeping, accounting. Reliable, hardworking, and
accurate.

REFERENCES
Excellent references available.

PRESENTING YOURSELF AS A BUSINESS COMMUNICATOR *(Individual Résumé)*

Purpose: To collect and organize information about yourself.

Briefing: A résumé describes your qualifications for a job. Refer to the sample résumé on page 16. Then write the information needed to complete your own résumé on this page. Type a copy of your résumé on 8½" x 11" white paper. Turn this copy in to your instructor.

NAME: PHONE:

STREET:

CITY, STATE, ZIP:

JOB OBJECTIVE (State the type of job you would like and the type of business or industry you prefer:

EDUCATION (In reverse chronologic order, list the college you attended, curriculum studied, degree, applicable courses, grade point average. Next list the high school attended, curriculum, degree received. List the dates you attended all institutions):

WORK EXPERIENCE (In reverse chronologic order, list place of employment, job title, and work responsibilities):

MEMBERSHIPS (List school or community organizations):

OTHER INTERESTS (List hobbies, special talents, etc.):

SPECIAL SKILLS (List job-related tasks):

REFERENCES (Type "Available upon request."):

SAMPLE SPEECH OUTLINE *(Individual Reference)*

Introduction to the Thesis

Attention Step   **A.** Red lights flashing, the sound of sirens . . .

Involve Audience   **B.** You have probably experienced . . .

Establish Credibility   **C.** I only know that car accident changed my life.

Thesis: Because of the accident, there are three things I want you to know about me.

Development of the Thesis

Transition (The first thing . . .)

Main Point   **I.** I am now aware of how precious life is.

        A. Appreciation for . . .

        B. Feel more deeply . . . laugh more readily, etc.

        C. Stop to smell the roses . . . (Visual—Show rose)

Transition (The second way the accident changed . . .)

Main Point **II.** I try to take nothing for granted.

        A. The opportunity to study . . .

        B. My family . . .

        C. My friends . . .

        D. My puppy . . .

Transition (The third way I am changed . . .)

Main Point **III.** I try to live life to the fullest.

        A. Listen more carefully . . .

        B. Lend a helping hand . . .

Transition (In conclusion . . .)

Conclusion

Summary **A.** I have told you that a car accident changed my life because I am now aware of how precious life is. I take nothing for granted. I try to live life to the fullest.

Focus   **B.** I hope you have learned a bit more about me . . . Reba Woodward.

PRESENTING YOURSELF TO THE CLASS *(Individual Speech Outline)*

Purpose: To introduce yourself to the class in a brief, well-structured speech.

Briefing: Use this sheet to plan your speech. Use note cards when giving your speech. Write your name on the board before you begin to speak.

Introduction to the Thesis   (To get the audience ready)

Attention Step   **A.**

Involve Audience   **B.**

Establish Yourself **C.**

Thesis: There are three things I'd like to tell you about myself.

Development of the Thesis   (Body of speech)

Transition (First . . .)

Main Point   **I.**

A.

B.

Transition (Second . . .)

Main Point   **II.**

A.

B.

Transition (Third . . .)

Main Point **III.**

A.

B.

Transition (Let me summarize what I have told you . . .)

Conclusion

Summary **A.** (Repeat the three things.)

Focus   **B.** (What do you want the audience to remember?)

Name _____ Class _____ Score _____

CRITIQUE SHEET FOR FIRST PRESENTATION *(Instructor's Evaluation)*

Purpose: To provide you with direct feedback after you make your first speech.

Briefing: A critique is an evaluation based on some established guidelines. Tear this page out of your book and hand it to your instructor before you begin your speech. You will not be graded on this first speech, but you will be evaluated on the following guidelines.

	Average	**Good**	**Superior**
1. Did the introduction catch attention, get the audience involved, and make us want to hear the speech?			
2. Was the speech built around the thesis statement?			
3. Did the speaker move smoothly from one point to the next?			
4. Was the speaker's voice loud enough to hear easily?			
5. Did the speaker control nervous mannerisms, stand confidently, and maintain eye contact with the audience?			
6. Did the speaker bring the presentation to a smooth ending with a summary and a focus?			
7. Were the goals of the assignment met?			

Comments: When your teacher gives this sheet back to you, jot down below some of the things you plan to do better on your next speech.

BARRIERS *(Group Activity)*

Purpose: To give and receive instructions in a speaker/audience situation. To set up barriers to communication and to note their effect on the communication results. To eliminate barriers; to provide for two-way communication. To compare the results between one-way and two-way communication.

Briefing:

1. Materials needed: box of paper clips; paper and pencil for each student.

2. Each student is given one paper clip to use as a pattern for a design which a speaker will describe. The design will be an arrangement of five paper clips.

3. One volunteer is needed to be the message source. This student will follow these instructions:

   a. Stand with his or her back to the audience.
   b. Arrange five paper clips in a pattern on a flat surface.
   c. Describe the paper clip design so that each member of the audience can draw the pattern described without seeing it.
   d. Not look at the audience. Not use gestures. Not answer any questions.
   e. When finished, check the students' papers and count the number of students who have drawn the exact design you have described.

4. A second volunteer may repeat the experiment using these instructions:

   a. Stand facing the audience, but arrange the paper clip pattern (making a different one) so that it cannot be seen.
   b. Describe the paper clip design so that the students can draw the pattern described.
   c. The second volunteer may use gestures; may watch the audience while talking; may *not* answer any questions or correct errors.
   d. When finished, check the number of accurate designs.

5. A third volunteer may repeat the experience using these directions:

   a. Stand facing the audience but arrange a different pattern in a position where it cannot be seen.
   b. Describe the new pattern. Use gestures. Encourage the students to ask questions. Answer questions. Watch their efforts and help them. Check the papers for accuracy.

Debriefing:

1. Identify the barriers existing between the speaker and the audience in each round.

2. What feelings did the barriers cause when you were the speaker? one of the receivers?

3. What differences are there between one-way and two-way communication? Which seems most effective?

4. List specific barriers of which you became aware.

BUSINESS COMMUNICATION PROBLEM *(Small Group Discussion)*

Briefing: Work together in a group of four to five people. Read the following case aloud; follow the suggestions for discussion at the bottom of the page.

A Problem in Presenting Herself

Raintree College has a number of students who are called work-study employees because they work part-time at school jobs. The positions are awarded to students on the basis of financial need. Linda Turner is a work-study student who is employed in the Library Annex with seven other work-study employees, two librarians, and the assistant head and the head of the Documents Department.

Linda's supervisor is a librarian named Nancy Spires. Mrs. Spires delegates the work to the work-study students and outlines their tasks for the day. One afternoon Linda overheard Mrs. Spires speaking to the other librarian, Don Baxter. Mrs. Spires said she often wondered if Linda was satisfied and comfortable with her job, because each time Linda was invited to a library employee gathering, such as a party or picnic, she did not attend. Mr. Baxter replied, "I believe Linda does not associate with her employees as much as you would like because she is very shy." Mrs. Spires closed a drawer firmly but made no verbal response.

Several days later, Mrs. Spires reported to the assistant head of Documents that the subject of lack of communication with Linda was making her angry. "If it wasn't for her signature on the time sheet," Mrs. Spires stated, "I wouldn't know when Linda works." The assistant head of Documents suggested that since Mrs. Spires was Linda's supervisor, it was up to her to take care of the matter. Mrs. Spires called Linda into her office and told Linda to report to her in person each time she arrived at work and when she left for the day. Mrs. Spires also suggested to Linda that she speak to the other employees more often.

1. Role play the parts of Linda, Mrs. Spires, Mr. Baxter, and the assistant head of Documents. (Talk out the parts; try to speak as you imagine each individual would in this particular situation.)

2. Use these questions for discussion.

   a. Who has the greater communication problem in the incident described above? Why?
   b. Is the solution chosen by Mrs. Spires going to solve the communication problem?
   c. What may be some of the causes of the problem?
   d. What specific actions do you recommend Linda take in order to present herself more effectively?

3. Record the results of your discussion and report to the class.

THE BUSINESS MOST NEEDED IN OUR AREA OF TOWN *(Group Oral Report)*

Purpose: To find common bonds. To work together on a group task. To present a report before the class.

Briefing: You are to work with a group of three to four students who live in the same general area of town. Follow these instructions:

1. Identify your general geographic area of the community. List the areas on the board (east-west, lower valley-upper valley, etc.).

2. Move into groups according to the geographic location in which you live. Groups larger than five or six may be split into two smaller groups. Small groups may merge to include a larger area.

3. Spend a few minutes reviewing each other's names and exchanging information. You will need to feel comfortable with each other as you discuss the topic.

4. Topics for discussion:

   a. What type of business is needed in our particular area? Why?
   b. Where is a good location for this business in our area?

5. Present a report to the class on your conclusions.

   a. Identify your geographic area and the names of your group members.
   b. Identify the type of business you have chosen and present the reasons for your decision.
   c. Show the proposed location of the business.
      (1) Draw it on the board in advance, or
      (2) Use a city map large enough to be seen, or
      (3) Prepare a chart and bring it to class.
   d. Identify a similar business that is successful in some other city.
   e. Predict the chances for success for your business, or explain why this type of business has not already been established in your area.
   f. If possible, describe how the business would be financed and managed.

6. Be sure that each member of the group has a part of the oral report to present to the class. Divide the information to be reported.

Debriefing: After each group has given its oral report, meet again with your small group and evaluate the discussion experience. Select one member to record the information for the teacher. (Start with the geographic name of the group and the names of the members of the group.)

1. What common bonds did you discover as you began to talk?

2. What were the factors that helped create a good climate (atmosphere) for your group's discussion?

3. Did any speech communication barriers prevent good communication during the discussion?

4. How effective was your group oral report to the class?

EVALUATION SHEET FOR GROUP ORAL REPORT *(Instructor's Evaluation)*

Briefing: Your group will be evaluated on the following points for your oral report to the class. Before you speak, one member of the group will fill in the names of the group members and turn this sheet in to the instructor. The total points will be recorded for each member of the group. Use this sheet to help prepare the oral report.

AREA OF TOWN: _____

NAMES OF THE MEMBERS OF THE GROUP:

_____

_____

_____

_____

_____

POSSIBLE POINTS: 50   (Each question: 10 points)

1. Was the oral report carefully planned with a beginning, a middle with clear transitions, and a strong ending? (Leader could introduce each speaker, or speakers might introduce each other.)   _____

2. Were the visual aids neat, clear, and visible, and were they handled well by the speakers?   _____

3. Did each speaker carry an equal part of the speaking load?   _____

4. Were the speakers loud enough to be heard and enthusiastic about their material, and did they maintain eye contact with the audience?   _____

5. Were the goals of the assignment met?   _____

Total   _____

Instructor's Comments:

Name _____ Class _____ Score _____

CHECKLIST OF COMMUNICATION TERMS *(Quiz)*

To communicate effectively with each other, we need to speak the same language. Check your understanding of the terms presented in this chapter by matching each definition with the appropriate term. Write the correct number in the blank preceding the definition. Note there are more terms than definitions.

Definitions

a. _18_ The response to a message—whether verbal or nonverbal.

b. _8_ The act of translating an idea or mental image into a verbal message.

c. _19_ Verbal and nonverbal messages are communicated through these.

d. _4_ Made up of word symbols which can be spoken or written and which provide a common bond between speakers and receivers.

e. _1_ Any obstacle that results in miscommunication or interferes with or blocks understanding.

f. _12_ Making sense of a coded message.

g. _5_ A speaker condition that gets in the way of speaking before an audience.

h. _11_ The sound of the voice, which includes rate, quality, pitch, and volume or intensity.

i. _20_ A human being capable of both sending and receiving messages may be compared to this.

j. _15_ The originator of a message.

Terms

1. barrier
2. transaction
3. verbal
4. language
5. stage fright
6. process
7. receiver
8. encoding
9. space
10. intrapersonal communication
11. paralanguage
12. decoding
13. perception
14. nonverbal
15. speaker/source/sender
16. personal appearance
17. message
18. feedback
19. channels
20. transceiver
21. filtering
22. output
23. input
24. interpersonal communication
25. interaction

CHAPTER 2

Let's Talk About the Business of Presenting Yourself in a Business Environment

This chapter explains why you are unique and how perception affects your communication in the business environment. After you have read and discussed this chapter and participated in the workshop activities, you should be able to do the following:

Chapter Objectives

1. Explain the steps in the process of perception.
2. Identify various filters in perception.
3. Cite ways to check the accuracy of your perception.
4. Describe the structure of the business environment and its effect on employee communication.
5. Inventory your oral communication strengths.

You are a unique, complex bundle of feelings, attitudes, beliefs, and values which have accumulated throughout your life. Like a sponge, you absorb impressions from every event. You sort and store these impressions to create your personal view of the world. No other human being is exactly like you. No one else sees things exactly as you do.

Your personal view of the world, or your perception, lays the foundation for speech communication. **Perception** is the ability to receive sensations through the ears, eyes, nose, mouth, and skin and to process incoming information into mental images. Thus, the brain blends sensations from the outside with stored memories and responses already inside. Assumptions are made, attitudes evolve, and beliefs and values are established through perception. The result is speech (talking) and action (behavior). Consequently the study of speech communication begins with perception.

This chapter discusses: (1) the phenomenon of perception and those factors that link or separate people; (2) how perception affects speech interactions; and (3) how organizational structures affect business speech communication.

THE PROCESS OF PERCEPTION

A baseball umpire makes a call on a close play. The people in the stands roar disapprovingly because they saw it differently. You attend a movie with a friend and enjoy it fully; your friend, however, was unimpressed. Why do people experience the same event in such varied ways? Isn't reality the same for each person?

Sources of Incoming Information

Reality is never the same for each person. Your view of "what's out there" is your own exclusive creation. A friend who attends a movie with you creates his or her own set of mental images. These mental images may be vastly different from yours. But until you share what you are experiencing, you are not aware of these differences.

The sensations that you receive come from two different sources. The first source is **reality** or the **empirical world** in which things can be heard, tasted, touched, smelled, and seen. You know this world through observation and experimentation.

The second source of incoming information is the **symbolic world**, which is generally based on the agreement between people that a **symbol** will represent or stand for something else. For example, regardless of the language printed on the sign, an octagonal red sign located at a crossroad is internationally agreed upon to be a stop sign. Similarly, words, as symbols, must be agreed upon as a means of communication.

Some examples of the symbolic world are:

Photographs—images that are produced on photosensitive paper and represent people or places.
Written contracts—papers that represent specific agreements between people.
Maps—lines and markings on paper that represent geographic territory.
Spoken words—sounds that represent mental images in the speaker's mind or the mental images created by the listener as the sounds are heard.

So, the empirical and symbolic worlds serve as sources of information. You provide word symbols that tell someone about your perception of reality, and you demonstrate your meaning by showing the real thing or a picture (symbol) of it. Moreover, you receive messages from the empirical and symbolic worlds through your senses. You convert these messages into mental images, and your brain creates your view of reality.

In Figure 2-1, Sue may be tired and very much aware of the smell of coffee brewing. She may feel the ice-cold blast of the air conditioner as she wonders if someone will answer the ringing phone. Meanwhile, Sue's customer may be getting some of her input through the symbolic world—the sign identifying the Jewelry Department and the sign that says "Sale Priced." Both can shift the focus of their attention from moment to moment, changing what they are perceiving.

FIGURE 2-1 Physical senses enable people to receive input from the world around them. People filter these stimuli and either accept, reject, or ignore them, depending upon their needs or interests at the moment.

Description of the Perception Process

The process of perception can be compared to a business operation. A business receives goods and information by selecting from a wide variety of each and ordering what it needs. The company stocks and stores what it receives, inventories the stock, and makes company decisions on policies and procedures. It also predicts sales and verifies the accuracy of its predictions. Finally, a business frequently updates its operation in order to continue profitably. Like a business operation, your perceptual process is composed of several departments:

"We may think of this mental model as a fantastic internal warehouse. . . ."

Alvin Toffler

Receiving Department—Your five senses take in information from the outside world.

Purchasing Department—You choose which information you will receive.

Warehousing Department—You sort out, categorize, organize, and store mental images in your memory bank.

Administrative Department—You relate the information you receive to the information you have on hand—thinking—and arrive at policymaking decisions about what you will do or say.

Quality Control—You verify your perceptions and assumptions to ensure that you are as accurate as possible.

Let's now examine each of the steps in the perceptual process as if each were indeed a separate department. Of course, they are not separate, but this analogy will clarify what goes on in your internal warehouse.

Receiving Department—The Senses. From fingerprints to voiceprints, each individual is physically distinguishable from others. However, a common factor links all of us—we are housed in similar equipment. Our bodies have comparable receiving departments—the five senses. If you are lucky, you can see, hear, smell, taste, and touch. You take in information about the empirical and symbolic worlds through sensations. Your eyes respond to different light waves, and you see differences in colors. You hear sounds and can distinguish between the voices of friends. You are aware of textures, temperatures, and stimulating touches on your sensitive skin. And when, for example, you see a round, red object, which from previous experience you know is edible, you pick it up, feel it, smell it, and taste it. You use several senses to verify or check out the real world.

You also receive stimuli from the symbolic world. For instance, signs along the highway like those in Figure 2-2 provide clues about the road ahead: no left turn, slippery road, deer crossing. You learn what the signs represent and you create meaning from them. You read print—black marks on white paper. If the symbols are familiar to you, you give meaning to them from the information stored in your head. You hear familiar speech sounds and realize that you share a common language with someone else. You are also aware of sensations from inside yourself such as pain, strong emotions, or discomfort.

Think of yourself as locked inside your physical body. Your senses— your receiving department—open you up to the world around you.

Purchasing Department—Selective Perception. Like a business, you order what you like. The physical process of receiving information through your

FIGURE 2-2

Familiar messages from the symbolic world.

senses allows you to acquire a storehouse of impressions. But each store-house does not contain the same things. Indeed, you are capable of selecting the stimuli (things that affect the senses) to which you pay attention. This is called **selective perception**. Unlike a photocopy machine which makes clear, exact duplicates of the original material, your senses do not record precise pictures of the external world. There is too much happening. Your senses are peppered with sights, sounds, and smells from the empirical world. You also are bombarded with stimuli from the symbolic world, such as signboards, television, and spoken and written language. But your human nervous system is limited in the amount of information it is programmed to accept. You do not, and cannot, pay attention to everything at once. Only a small portion of these stimuli reach your level of awareness. You choose the details you want. Your perception is selective.

What do you choose to put into your mental warehouse? Your nervous system responds to stimuli by **abstracting**—selecting some sights and sounds and disregarding others. You notice a familiar face in a crowd of strangers, or you hear your name spoken amid the chatter of voices. Like a photographer focusing a camera, you concentrate on a particular person or object and filter out other details. For example, when your favorite song is being played on the radio, you focus on the music and blur the sounds around you into the background of your consciousness. This process of selective perception can happen consciously or unconsciously. When you look at the picture in Figure 2-3, you can shift the focus of your perception as you like, seeing by turns a vase and two profiles facing each other. You filter in some stimuli and filter out others.

You are physically able to adapt to a constant stimulus and endure it for long periods of time. Workers in a noisy manufacturing plant, for instance, can become so accustomed to the roar of a production line that they block out the sound of it.

FIGURE 2-3

Which figure do you see? It all depends on your focus.

You tend to perceive what you are trained or conditioned to perceive. You may have a difficult time getting used to the metric system when you have learned another system of weights and measures. You are more likely to notice and anticipate details with which you are familiar than those that are unfamiliar to you. You choose what input you perceive.

Selective perception is an asset because it permits individual choice in abstracting (selecting) information from the environment. You now can appreciate and understand why human beings perceive differently and why you are not a passive receiver of sensations but an active participant in the perceptual process.

Warehousing Department—Organizing and Labeling. If you work in the warehousing department of a company and accept a consignment of goods, you have to decide what to do with the goods you receive. In a warehouse, goods are divided into various categories, invoices are checked, and the items are classified and shelved according to a system.

In a similar fashion, we use a **classification** system in the perceptual process. At the same time that your eyes and ears select and receive stimuli, your brain actively converts these sensations into mental images and organizes these perceptions.

Like the classification system in the warehouse, you impose order on the received stimuli by relating them to similar items and then categorizing them. For example, when shelving office supplies, you stack paper according to quality or size, typewriter ribbons according to style and color, and paper clips in a separate category. With perception, you select the characteristics of an item that are important to you and match them to things that seem similar.

Some details, such as loud noises, bright colors, and unusual shapes, frequently scream for attention. Consequently you are likely to focus on the particular detail that engages your attention and blur the rest into the background. As in Figure 2-3, the focus becomes the **figure** and the rest becomes **ground** (background).

Your past experience becomes the basis for comparing details. You might think, "This job interview is like the one I had last January." The details you select to perceive and the relationship you see between what you perceive and what you already know help you to organize present experience.

Language symbols also help you set up categories such as slim, square, tall, metal, manufactured, etc. The **labels** or symbols you select will determine how you *think* about something. For example, an item may be labeled by its function:

ice cream scoop	nail polish	buttonhole
ice pick	toothpick	stopwatch
can opener	screwdriver	trashmasher

A person may be labeled by occupation:

teacher	pilot	pipe fitter
lawyer	doctor	engineer

People frequently are classified according to appearance, race, nationality, skills, etc. The classification system is not static. Any person or item can be catalogued in a number of ways. When new information is received, adjust-

FIGURE 2-4

New symbols are needed to move from one way of perceiving to another.

ments in thinking and mental reclassification are in order. One label will not cover all there is to say or think about any one person or thing. For example, your automobile may be filed in a number of categories depending on your attitude toward it. Try this exercise. Identify the characteristics of your car that are involved when you refer to it as a:

means of transportation	monthly payment
status symbol	ticket to freedom
great trade-in value	constant headache
gas-guzzler	wheels

You classify so automatically that you are often unaware of how well you do it. If, for example, a newcomer walks into your classroom, your sorting and filing process might begin with "human being" and continue with these subcategories:

male/female	student/teacher
young/old	familiar/unknown
short/tall	attractive/unattractive

"We see things not as they are but as we are."

Anonymous

The list could go on and on according to the details you choose to perceive. Remember, you choose the categories and the language. What you can see or hear, what you choose to see or hear, and how you label the details of your perception will make a difference in how you file that image and what you say about your perception.

Another noteworthy point is the human tendency to create organized and simplified mental pictures. People like to have things "make sense." For example, what happens when you see or hear something that does not make a whole picture? You may bridge the gap between what you know and do not know by filling in (thinking) the details. This is known as **closure**. To illustrate, if a friend speaks and you miss some of the words, you may complete the message in your head by using closure to add what you did not hear. And you may be wrong. In Figure 2-5, do you see a circle or a series of lines arranged in circular form? Do you see a triangle or three separate lines arranged in triangular form? It is easy to fill in the gaps and be unaware of doing so. As another example, a handbook for campers may identify the facilities of a particular campsite by this description:

"Htd pool, rec room, plgrd, frwd, swr hookup sites, scenic mtn trls, near frway, boat rntl nrby."

FIGURE 2-5

These are unconnected lines, but closure makes us perceive them as a circle and a triangle.

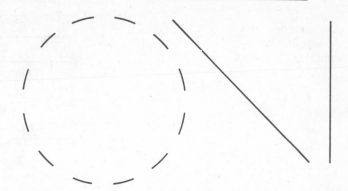

You probably had little difficulty filling in the missing letters, especially if you are a camper. But beware of filling in missing details or lumping together unrelated objects. For example, if you hear information about salary increases via your company grapevine, you need more details before you fill in the dollar amount gap for yourself.

In classifying perceptions, remember not to treat each person or event as if it exists exactly as you perceive it. Selection and organization of perception are highly subjective. You abstract some details, leave out others, focus on some, and link others. This creative and subjective process is a shortcut to understanding. It can be a marvelous asset as long as it remains flexible.

Administrative Department—Interpreting. The interpretation of mental pictures is a personal business too. Administrators of a company frequently set policy which determines the course of action a company will take on one or many issues. Thus, in a business, someone else often makes policy decisions that affect you. But in interpreting your perceptions, you are the policy-maker; you draw your own conclusions. Conclusions based on your percep-

"We are constantly comparing images, associating them, cross-referencing them in new ways, and then repositioning them."

Alvin Toffler

FIGURE 2-6

Are the long lines in this sketch parallel? How can you be sure?

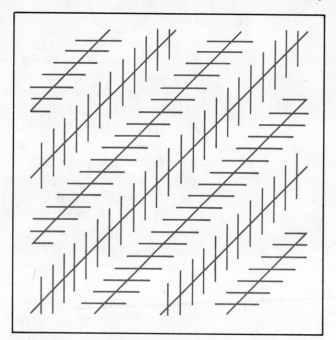

Source: Gail E. Myers and Michele Tolele Myers, *The Dynamics of Human Communication* (New York: McGraw-Hill Book Co., 1980), p. 34. Reproduced with permission.

tion are called **assumptions**. These are like guesses based on previous experience, and accepted as true without proof. Sometimes you guess accurately and your assumption is correct. Sometimes you are incorrect. You might guess that an apple will be as good as the last one you ate—but it isn't. No one guesses right every time. Some assumptions, however, are more likely to be true than others.

You generally collect a huge number of basic assumptions that develop from just the experience of living. For example, you can count on some things:

> Days and nights follow each other.
> Seasons come and go in cycles.
> People live and die.

These assumptions involve little risk. You are safe to conclude that what has been true in the past will be true in the present. But other assumptions may not be as accurate. Perhaps you may safely assume that the chair you are sitting in will not collapse under your weight. You may assume that the electricity will come on when you flip the switch. And unless an earthquake shakes the building or a power failure occurs, you are probably making valid (true, or likely to be true) assumptions. Such assumptions about the empirical world (reality) are often less risky than assumptions about the symbolic world. You normally assume, for example, that other drivers will stop when they come to a red traffic light (symbolic world). But you probably have learned that you are safer if you check first and then proceed defensively through the intersection.

Assumptions about the meaning of speech messages are sometimes risky. When you hear a verbal message, you decode (organize and interpret) the symbols to get the meaning. You use your eyes to check the speaker's facial expressions. You listen to the vocal tones with which the message was delivered. You decide what is meant. You often are right, but sometimes you are wrong.

Assumptions are a necessary and important part of perception. But because things change, a previous policy based on an assumption may not be useful in the present. It is often necessary to verify assumptions before you act.

Quality Control—Verifying. How can you verify or check your assumptions? Traditionally, a business sets standards by which it measures the quality of its product and establishes controls for the items it produces. Similarly, you establish standards for checking the accuracy of your perceptions. If you use such standards to verify assumptions that you make based on what you see and hear, you provide more accurate statements about your perceptions.

First Standard: Discriminate between the empirical world and the symbolic world.

> **Empirical world**—Things which can be seen, heard, felt, tasted, and touched. Things that can be verified through the senses.
> **Symbolic world**—Things which represent objects, people, events, ideas, etc. A symbol is agreed upon through general acceptance and may be verified by checking the acceptance.

"I know you believe you understand what you think I said—but I am not sure you realize that what you heard is not what I meant."

Anonymous

FIGURE 2-7

Are both of these lines the
same length? How can you
verify your perceptions?

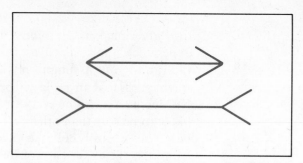

Source: Gail E. Myers and Michele Tolele Myers, *The Dynamics
of Human Communication* (New York: McGraw-Hill Book Co.,
1980), p. 35. Reproduced with permission.

A symbol becomes a symbol only when many people agree that it represents a certain thing. Assumptions based on such agreements make the
symbols difficult to verify. For example, the car ahead of you has its right-
turn signal flashing. You assume that the vehicle will turn right. You may be
correct. But then again, you may not. The car may turn left, or it may not
turn at all. The driver may have forgotten to flip off the turn signal or may
have had a change of mind.

In the empirical world, the flashing turn signal indicates that one particular circuit in the electrical system of the car was working. In the symbolic
world, however, the assumption that the light indicates a turn is based on an
agreement to let other drivers know that a change of direction is planned.
But sometimes it isn't!

You can be more certain of an assumption if you recognize whether it is
based in the empirical world or in the agreed-upon symbolic world. It is
important to note the difference.

Second Standard: Practice specific techniques to check perception.

1. Use more than one sense.

    A small bottle of clear liquid may look like water until you use your sense of
    smell to identify vinegar. (*empirical*)
    Your supervisor's instructions may confuse you as you listen, unless you
    use your eyes to watch for the facial expressions and gestures which ac-
    company the words. (*symbolic*)

2. Repeat the experience.

    The bus you expect to take to work arrives at your corner each morning.
    You check the time and regularity each day before you count on it.
    (*empirical*)
    You verify that you are taking the right bus by reading the route name sign
    on the front each time. (*symbolic*)

3. Compare to previous experience.

    When you write a business letter, you use a recognized standard form
    which has proved acceptable for letters in your past experience.
    (*empirical*)
    The office manager asks you to step into a private office for a moment. You
    mentally compare this request to a previous nonthreatening experience
    and then stop worrying about it. (*symbolic*)

4. Ask questions.

    If you hear a sound you cannot identify, you ask someone if they can iden-
    tify it. (*empirical*)

If you misunderstood the meaning intended by a speaker, ask for clarification or repeat what you understood so that the speaker can clarify. (*symbolic*)

You create your own unique perceptions, but you use the same process of selecting, organizing, and interpreting that others do. You can come close to matching your mental images to the reality of what you perceive by making your assumptions tentative until you verify them.

PEOPLE ARE UNIQUE

Human beings see the world through rose-colored glasses or perhaps blue-shaded contacts. Everyone projects pieces of himself or herself into the perceptual process. Each of us has an individual way of looking at things. For example, a group of visitors standing on the rim of the Grand Canyon for the first time may react to the scenic view very differently:

> "Gee, what a big hole. It makes me dizzy to look!"
> "This is an example of the power of rushing water. The Colorado River moves about 170,000,000 cubic yards of earth a year and has been doing so for millions of years."
> "I'd install escalators, cable cars, and moving sidewalks, and quadruple the revenue on tourist trade volume."
> "What a marvelous blend of colors. It's a feast for the eyes."
> "This is a magnificent example of the wonders of nature."

Each viewer perceives the same thing, but the results are different. Surely the view of the Grand Canyon provides the same light stimulus to the eyes of each observer. Yet each response is filtered through a unique set of human experiences. No two persons have exactly the same experiences, because **filters**—physical, cultural, mental, or psychological factors—affect and shape our perceptions.

Physical Filters

Even if you have 20/20 vision, you cannot see everything that goes on around you. For example, you cannot see through solid objects or around corners. Your hearing may be very acute, but it is likely that your dog has a greater hearing range than you do. Technology has extended seeing and hearing, but your human senses are limited and thus filter the stimuli you can receive. Even if your senses are perfect, you cannot know all there is to know.

Of course, physical senses may not be perfect. Differences in physical equipment may produce differences in perception. If three engineers bend over a blueprint, one may put on glasses to see better, another may adjust bifocals, and a third may remove glasses for a closer look. Failing hearing also may affect perception. Even with a hearing aid, the hearing-impaired person finds that perception is filtered.

One other physical factor that affects perception is the physical distance from the event that is being observed. For example, when you watch a televised football game, cameras located on the 50-yard line, or in the end zone, or high in the stands, or from a blimp above the stadium give different views of the game. Similarly, if you witness a bank robbery, your report will be

"The ant divides the animal kingdom into two classes: (a) the kind and gentle animals such as the lion, the tiger and the rattlesnake; and (b) the ferocious animals, such as the chicken, the duck and the goose. Like I say, it's all in your point of view."

Jimmy Powers

affected by your physical location at the time. Where you are helps to determine what you will perceive. Assumptions based on what you perceive through your physical senses may not be accurate.

Cultural Filters

Your filtering system is shaped by the external environment in which you grew up: your family, community, business and social groups, and nation. Each culture has customs, traditions, and ways of thinking and behaving that are a part of its heritage. You learned your ways because they were a part of your environment. This background provides a framework in which you mold your view of the world. Specifically, cultural patterns are provided for:

religious beliefs	use of leisure time
career choices	ways to celebrate
selection of a mate	etc.

Common backgrounds and shared experiences usually set up a *common frame of reference* for two people. You may say, "Do you remember Mrs. Nolan, our last supervisor?" Your friend may remember her well, but her perception of Mrs. Nolan may not be exactly the same as yours. The common experience, however, makes a subject about which you both can communicate.

Mental Filters

"Habit is a cable. We weave a thread of it each day, and at last we cannot break it."

Horace Mann

Mental filters also affect perception and make you see things differently from others. For example, where did your basic beliefs originate? What is your attitude about work? What possession do you cherish most? What value do you hold so important that you will never change it?

All that you are, you bring to perception; these mental processes do not just happen. Rather, as you respond to your experiences day by day and year after year, you establish habitual ways of accepting information, adjusting to new situations, and adapting to different people. Sometimes set patterns of reaction take root. These attitudes, beliefs, and values become filters through which perception is sifted.

Attitudes—the tendency to respond in positive, neutral, or negative ways to people and things.
Beliefs—the body of information which is accepted as true or untrue, probable or improbable.
Values—those standards of right or wrong, good or bad, etc., by which personal judgments of worth are made.

Every person has a different set of mental filters. To give just one example, some people have warm and loving attitudes toward cats; others can't stand them. This observation points out the differences in people. It says nothing at all about cats.

Psychological Filters

Of course, your personal needs, desires, and interests affect the way you view the world. When you are hungry, your interest focuses on delectable smells from the kitchen. When you are tired, your teacher's lecture seems dull. You and your best friend may not enjoy exactly the same music, movies, or sports events, but you accept each other's tastes. Wouldn't it be a dreary world if we were all alike?

You are not the same as you were five years ago—or five minutes ago. You are changing constantly. As you live through more and more experiences, your **self-image**, your mental picture of yourself, adapts and adjusts. This self-image, based on perception, is another filter through which you view the world.

For example, you accept the reality that you are a living, breathing human being who occupies space on this earth. Empirically you may be five feet seven inches tall, weigh 142 pounds, have brown hair, blue eyes, etc. But your self-image also is based on what you think you are like (from the responses you receive from others—friendly, outgoing, athletic, musical, creative, shy, etc.) and what you would like to be (your dream of achieving your potential).

Your self-image also determines how you behave. When you receive supportive, favorable responses to what you do and say, your **self-esteem** (your feelings about yourself) increases. You feel good about yourself and build confident, secure attitudes about your behavior. On the other hand, your self-image may be shaken when you experience failure or frustration or when others criticize you. You then may respond with derogatory statements about yourself such as:

"I never get anything right."
"I'll never get promoted because I'm not liked."
"It always seems to be my fault."

This filter of a low self-image often keeps you from achieving what you are capable of achieving.

Perceptions about self-image normally come from firsthand experiences in the empirical world. Yet a great many more come to each person from the symbolic world. For instance, you dream about great successes as you communicate intrapersonally (with yourself). You fantasize about your personal attractiveness. You build air castles about the achievements you would like to accomplish. Like every other human being, you dream about the way you would like your life to be. But *if* there is a gap between your mental picture and your experiences, you may feel defeated.

For example, if you yearn to be a poised and interesting speaker but you hate to face an audience, there are changes you can make:

1. Stop saying uncomplimentary things about your own abilities.
2. Examine the causes of stage fright and work to eliminate those causes that bother you.
3. Use every opportunity to talk with others about the things you know and are interested in.
4. Listen to others and find common bonds.

It is quite possible to turn a low self-image into a more realistic acceptance of self. For instance, adjust your dreams and expectations to fit reality. Adjust to reality by recognizing the filters which affect your perception of it. Changes are possible.

Perception also is filtered by the roles each person plays. A **role** is the behavior you perceive to be expected of you in your relationship to someone else. You learn your roles through the expectations that others have of you. Some general roles you are expected to fill are:

"Personality is the name we give to our own little collection of funny ways."

Anonymous

"If you build castles in the air, your work need not be lost; that is where they should be. Now put the foundations under them."

Henry David Thoreau

son or daughter	citizen	employee
taxpayer	consumer	customer

Each person plays many roles every day. Thus, Roberto may be a husband and father when he is not at work, but at his business he fills the roles of:

secretary	friend
receptionist	typist
advisor	payroll supervisor

Roberto is expected to work with people he likes and dislikes, to perform tasks he enjoys and those he finds tedious. He is expected to present a smiling face, regardless of what his feelings are. It is not easy for Roberto or for us to be all the things expected of us, to fill all roles equally well. Each role requires a different behavior and adjustment to others. Indeed, your interests, needs, and desires, as well as your self-image and the roles you fill, filter your perception.

PERCEPTION AFFECTS COMMUNICATION

We have been discussing the way in which perception works and how personal experience affects perception. We are each responsible for what we select to pay attention to. Just as important, we are also responsible for how we think about what we perceive. Each of us has the wonderful capacity to think for ourselves. This quality makes us human. Thinking is our own personal creation. No one can think for us. Nor can anyone force us to think something we don't want to. This is important because all of our feelings and behaviors—including how we speak and listen—come directly from our thoughts.

Perception Shapes Behavior

You work with people who are different from you. Each of us has a personal style, strength, and motive for getting work done. You deal with others using a particular style of behavior that you have found comfortable. These behaviors reflect a style that you believe works best for you. Do you see yourself in one of the following descriptions?

1. **Team Player Style.** This person's dominant style is trusting, responsive, idealistic, and loyal. This individual does the best at whatever task is assigned. He or she sets high standards for self and for others and is highly receptive to others' ideas. This person is cooperative and helpful.
2. **People-Oriented Style.** This person's dominant style is enthusiastic, flexible, and tactful. This individual is charming to everyone. He or she never makes enemies, is sensitive to what people want and feel, and modifies the approach to each accordingly. This individual is open to new ideas, is stimulating to fellow workers, and enjoys the spotlight.
3. **Dependable Computer Style.** This person's dominant style is methodical and precise. He or she analyzes the best ways of doing a job before performing it. This individual makes the most of existing resources, is thorough and practical, and although often reserved, does a predictable, efficient job.
4. **Assertive Leader Style.** This person is a go-getter who acts quickly, expresses self-confidence, is persuasive and very competitive. This individual requires very little supervision.

Chapter 2   Presenting Yourself in a Business Environment

It is important to recognize that each style of behavior has a place within any operating unit. Each is different, but there is room for many ways of getting the job done.[1]

Perception Forms the Basis for Speech

How you decide to think is one of your most important choices in life. Because we categorize and label incoming information, we must be careful. This very process can get us into trouble. If we put people or events into categories and then refuse to change or adjust our thinking, we become rigid thinkers. If we pop people into mental categories such as young/old, attractive/unattractive, friendly/unfriendly, similar to me/different from me, then we may use these labels as convenient excuses for avoiding or rejecting people. This kind of divided thinking places people or ideas into rigid either/or categories. We then see the world not as it is, but as we choose to see it.

Let's look at some examples:

1. **Stereotyping**—generalizing about a group based on limited examples.

   "All Indians walk in single file; at least the one I saw did."

2. **Closed-mindedness**—unwilling to accept new information.

   "I've always voted Democratic and I'll continue to do so regardless of the candidate."

3. **Inaccurate observation**—unwillingness to see what is really there.

   "Well, I didn't see the 'Do Not Disturb' sign on the door."

4. **Distorted perception**—accepting only what the speaker wants to see or believe.

   "My friend would never pass on gossip."

5. **Rigid system of behaving**—unwilling to change past ways of doing or thinking about things.

   "I'm not going to wear a seat belt in spite of the new law."

6. **Either/or attitude**—limiting the possibilities of other choices.

   "America—love it or leave it."

7. **Faulty assumption**—presupposing that because something was true in the past, it will continue to be true.

   "We are supposed to get paid today. We've always received our checks on the first and fifteenth of the month."

8. **Jumping to conclusions**—making evaluations without sufficient data.

   "He's not wearing a wedding ring so he must not be married."

9. **Low self-image**—unwilling to take personal credit for accomplishments.

   "I guess I could have done better on the exam—but the math always throws me."

---

[1] From "Getting Your Team in Tune," *Nation's Business*, March, 1975. Copyright 1975 by *Nation's Business*, Chamber of Commerce of the United States.

10. **Know-it-all attitude**—speaking as if it were possible to know everything and say everything about a subject.

"Well, I've described the accident in detail and that's all there is to say about it."

11. **Failure to verify**—making an assumption without checking to be sure it is correct.

"I got a grade of 52 on the exam. All the grades must have been low."

"Speech is the index of the mind."

Seneca

These ways of thinking result from perception barriers or a lack of clear thinking. Rather than being guilty of speaking this way, we might try saying, "I just don't know enough about it to make a judgment." Thinking before speaking often prevents interpersonal misunderstandings.

Perception Influences Listening

Why do you listen to one person more thoughtfully than you would listen to another? Why do you accept what one individual says rather than what another says? Your perception of a person affects your willingness to listen, to accept, and to retain information. You catch faint or fleeting impressions from a combination of cues such as voice, body movements, behavior, and words. Consequently your judgment of the person's character and knowledge sets the stage for the listening you do. If you judge the speaker favorably, you are more likely to accept his or her message as credible (believable).

Perception Determines Feedback

You may often feel scared or inadequate when you face an unfamiliar environment, a difficult job, or a person whose behavior makes you defensive. When you perceive a threat to your self-image, you often put on a mask and guard against disclosing yourself (revealing what you really think or feel). You may not feed back (respond) honestly.

"We grow shells to protect ourselves. Too often the shells become us."

Eli J. Schleifer

One way to reduce defensive feedback is to use empathy. **Empathy** is the ability to see the other person's point of view. This perception permits you to appreciate the other person's feelings without losing sight of your own. Thus, your feedback can be less defensive and more open.

Ways to Present Yourself More Effectively

- Check your observations carefully and use all your senses to verify what you see and hear.
- Recognize that your personal filters may distort your perception.
- Admit the possibility of error and check again.
- Report what you actually see rather than what you *think* you see.
- Try to be open-minded and tentative in your conclusions by recognizing that other people perceive differently.
- Look more carefully at the differences between people who are categorized as the same. For example, Customer 1 is not the same as Customer 2 or Customer 3.
- Refuse to stereotype people by placing them in a rigid category with a label. Accept people as human beings who fill different roles and are different from all others.
- Recognize that there are more alternatives than just a simple choice of either/or. Things are not clear-cut; a number of options are available.

Chapter 2   Presenting Yourself in a Business Environment

- Realize that you are fallible (can make mistakes), that things change, and that people and situations change.
- Try being specific when you report what you see, rather than being general and vague.
- Withhold your judgments until you have as much information as possible.
- Refuse to display a know-it-all attitude and be aware that you cannot know all or say all there is to be said.
- Verify your assumptions before you make positive statements or take action.
- Refuse to prejudge. Permit each person or situation to provide new insights or information.
- Maintain an empirical attitude (check perceptions in the real world when possible) and a symbolic attitude (realize that everything cannot be proven). Use the appropriate attitude to fit the situation.
- Accept yourself with your strengths and weaknesses. Recognize that all human beings are a mixture of both.

In summary, each person thinks, speaks, and acts on the basis of individual perception. In presenting yourself to others in business, it is wise to be aware of how others perceive you and how you look at the world in which you work. Ths business environment is a symbolic and an empirical world that surrounds each worker. Let's examine the effect of this environment on speech communication.

SPEECH COMMUNICATION IN A BUSINESS ENVIRONMENT

The business environment is composed of people who work together to accomplish specific goals. Speech communication serves two important functions in business. First, it serves to get the job done. For example, in business, you may speak to:

1. Provide information
2. Explain a procedure
3. Sell a product
4. Ask a question
5. Justify a decision
6. Order equipment or supplies
7. Conduct a meeting
8. Report on progress

You may also perform numerous other tasks in which speech communication is necessary to keep a business functioning toward its goal.

"Speech was made to open man to man; to promote commerce and not to betray it."

David Lloyd

Second, and equally important, people establish and maintain working relationships through speech communication. You speak to let others know you appreciate their work, to acknowledge their contributions to your work, and to create a climate of cooperation and harmony on the job.

Good communicators know how to adjust their speech skills to meet the particular requirements of a business situation. They successfully participate in one-to-one meetings, in small group conferences, or in presenting ideas on company products and services to audiences of fellow workers or customers. People do not talk at random in business. Speech is used purposefully, precisely, clearly, and effectively to accomplish business goals.

PHOTO 2-1

The Structure of the Business Environment

When the owner of a store was getting his business established, he hired his first employee, a salesperson to wait on customers. As the business grew, the owner hired another salesperson and later hired a delivery person. Communication was simple because employees could talk to each other directly. As sales increased, a bookkeeper was hired and then several more salespersons. When there were six salespersons, one of them was asked to supervise the work of the others.

When people work together toward a specific goal, dividing the duties improves efficiency. Each person brings special talents to the enterprise. Through organization of the tasks and the human resources, the efforts of all are coordinated toward common goals. The responsibility is shared among the employees. Organization makes it possible for human talents to be used in special ways to contribute to the business goal. However, communication throughout the organization is the vital link that keeps the whole structure together.

Business structures are carefully designed blueprints for achieving business goals. Such organizational plans result from:

1. Dividing groups of specialized workers into special departments.
2. Delegating specific work.
3. Designating authority or responsibility for tasks.
4. Setting up a formal organizational structure.

Horizontal Structure. In a horizontally organized business, the operating tasks are separated into departments with equal responsibilities. Thus, our store owner's business became divided into sales, delivery, and accounting departments. Each department had specialized work; each was equally important to the business. Because people in the same department are located close together, they can consult with each other on a daily basis. When there is a need for communication between departments, the organization deter-

FIGURE 2-8

Business is a complex network. Communication is its lifeline.

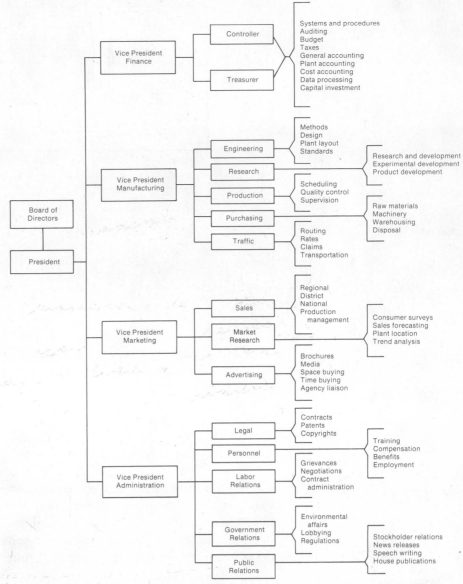

Source: From Powell, *Career Planning Today*, copyright © 1981 by C. Randall Powell. Reprinted with permission of Kendall/Hunt Publishing Company.

mines methods of communicating such as memos, work orders, shipping orders, telephone calls, etc.

Vertical Structure. Another way of achieving business goals in an organization is through a vertical structure. When there are many employees in one department, a supervisor is needed to assume responsibility for the employees and their work. A manager is responsible for the work of a number of supervisors. At a higher level, a vice-president may take responsibility for a number of managers. This structure depends on the concept of managerial authority. The *span of management* means the number of subordinate people that one manager can effectively supervise.

Since many managers see good communication as the biggest single contributor to business success, the company finds ways of keeping information flowing horizontally between departments and vertically between the various levels.

FIGURE 2-9

Horizontal communication
channels.

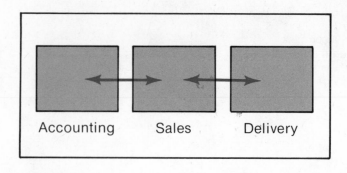

FIGURE 2-10

Vertical communication
channels.

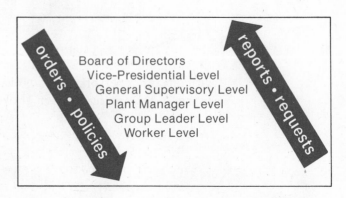

Formal Channels of Communication

Instructions and policy decisions normally flow downward from supervisors to group leaders to workers. Information about the finished work flows upward from workers to group leaders to supervisors. These channels of information are called **formal channels of communication**.

Information passed between several people at different levels, however, may result in communication problems. When the same message is reproduced several times and passed through the sending and receiving equipment of a number of people, the message may be changed. For example, details may be omitted or sharpened, information may be changed or condensed, and the language may be altered. Thus, communication problems are likely to result. Unfortunately some messages fail to reach their destination. Or there may be a lack of sufficient information to understand a message. For example, a worker may be given a task, but may not be told why she or he should do it. Furthermore, workers may use a language different from that of management. This may cause communication problems.

Problems such as these can overwhelm employees and can result in inefficient production. In trying to prevent this loss of efficiency, many companies have set up ways to encourage better upward communication, such as *open-door* policies or *private lines* which permit employees to ask questions or discuss matters of concern.

Improved communication within organizations pays company dividends in:

1. Improved relationships between superiors and subordinates
2. Improved attitudes toward the company and the job
3. Increased efficiency
4. Decreased turnover and decreased absenteeism
5. Increased performance and profits

Communication Networks Within Groups

Within a department or work group where members can communicate with each other, there are a variety of patterns of communication networks. Some of these are shown in Figure 2-11. The patterns can be determined by asking yourself this question: "Who talks to whom and through what channels and with what effect?" People who do not have direct access to others for communication in their work environments may experience low morale. It has been found that people tend to develop leadership skills, solve group problems, and interact more freely in communication networks where each person can interact with several others. Study Figure 2-11. Are some of these networks more limited than others?

Imagine that each colored circle in Figure 2-11 is an employee. Because of that employee's position, he or she is able to communicate with others along the lines shown by the arrows. Some individuals communicate only with one other person; for example, the individuals at the ends of the wheel or the "Y." Does the position of the individual in the center make a difference in the amount of power that person can exert? Which arrangement would make for the greatest communication?

Because unexpected and novel problems develop in today's business environment, the need for direct and rapid problem-solving information has caused changes in organizational structures. Shortcuts in communication which bypass the older systems have been explored in offices and factories. Sometimes a *task-force unit* is brought together to solve a particular problem; that is, workers with different types of training or skills work together on a specific task for a limited time. This requires side-by-side or horizontal communication. Since the teams are composed of people with a variety of professional skills, background, and training, team members must be skilled in human relations. Consequently sideways communication in this situation requires communicators who can work through the barriers of specialized languages. In addition, the communicators must be able to cooperate in solving problems and in accepting other people as team members.

FIGURE 2-11

Patterns of communication networks.

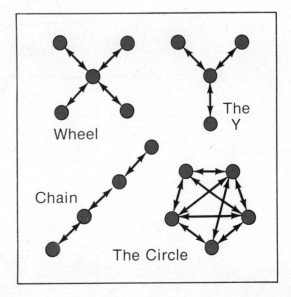

Informal Channels of Communication

Formal communication messages may deal with organizational objectives, operating procedures, policies regarding relationships between departments, and methods of carrying out basic company philosophy. At the management level, decisions may be hammered out orally and then written down for distribution throughout the company. But written formal communication is, of course, not the only type of communication. An ever-changing, complicated **grapevine** of informal, unofficial communication winds around the formal, official communication channel. Employees naturally stop by other offices to chat. They talk shop at social gatherings and visit informally on breaks and at lunch. They need to talk about their feelings and attitudes and to speculate about events and people. Moreover, people increase their feelings of security and acceptance through personal contact with others on the job.

Speech communication that pertains to unofficial messages about work situations can sometimes be distorted. Much of the information is incomplete. There is a tendency to jump to conclusions without verifying facts and sources. Misinformation can result in employee dissatisfaction.

Fortunately informal communication channels can serve as an effective force within a company if managers and workers use them wisely. Ideally each person will recognize that other people see things differently and that speech messages in different contexts may be misunderstood. Furthermore, determining the truth in a speech message before passing it on will help maintain healthy relationships between employees. In brief, formal and official channels of communication and informal channels of personal contact can complement each other within a company organization.

> *"A lively grapevine reflects the deep psychological need of people to talk about their jobs and their company as a central life interest."*
>
> Keith Davis

> *"Gossip runs faster over grapevines that are sour."*
>
> Anonymous

Barriers to Communication in Business

It would be a happier world in which to work if there were no communication problems—no injured feelings, no upset people. But the business world functions on the tasks which people do together as well as on the relationships they maintain with each other. Consequently barriers may occur because of too many levels in the organizational structure, inadequate avenues for vertical or horizontal communication, poor feedback systems, or crowded communication channels.

People communicate with each other most successfully when they know, like, and respect each other. Because the communication **climate** (the

FIGURE 2-12

The grapevine cluster. Not everyone gets the oral message sent by A, and those who do get the message may not receive the original version.

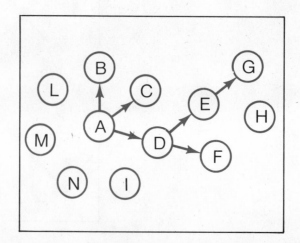

atmosphere) is work oriented rather than socially oriented, people may not feel comfortable with each other. You may not know that Joe Simpson's irritability on the job is due to his son's injury in a motorcycle accident or that Sue Hanley's lack of concentration is related to her concern for a fellow worker. Thus, barriers may occur because of a lack of formal or informal group contacts, incompatible needs and expectations, differences in group loyalties, or inequality in status roles.

The size and shape of the organization in which you work affect your communication with others. As you present yourself to your fellow employees on a daily basis, you should understand the structure of your organization and how people operate within the structure to accomplish the goals of the business. An organizational structure does not spring to life all at once. Structure is the outcome of many decisions that are made through the organizing process to balance the business tasks, human resources, and authority relationships. Organizational effectiveness is the capacity of an organization to survive, adapt, maintain itself, and grow in the face of changing conditions. This constant change can and will affect your communication.

CHAPTER SUMMARY

People are linked together in the way that they receive and process information from the empirical and symbolic worlds. As our senses take in information, we choose what we want to pay attention to. We select, sort, organize, and store mental images. We then relate this information to what we already know. This process is called thinking.

Each one of us is unique because of past physical, mental, and psychological experiences as well as varied cultural backgrounds. These are filters which serve to shape our thinking. From our thoughts come our feelings and actions. So, perception not only shapes our behavior but forms the basis for speech, influences listening, and determines our feedback to others.

In the huge and complex organization of modern business, communication problems can exist. Specialized tasks, various levels of authority and responsibility, and the expectations of business personnel create an environment in which communication barriers can occur. But business organizations provide a framework of channels that are designed to keep communication flowing. Presenting yourself effectively in a business environment means being aware of all the factors that affect your communication with your co-workers.

PERCEPTUAL PUZZLES* *(Group Discussion)*

Purpose: To discover how your perceptions differ from those of others.

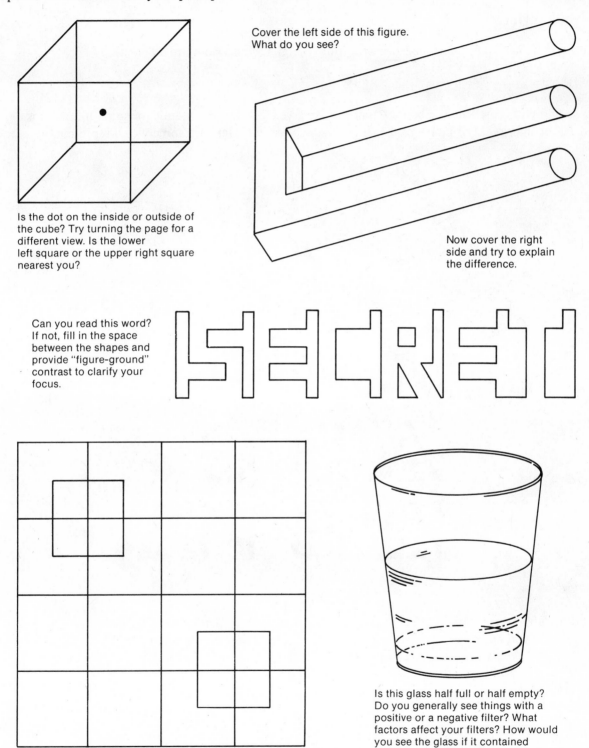

Is the dot on the inside or outside of the cube? Try turning the page for a different view. Is the lower left square or the upper right square nearest you?

Cover the left side of this figure. What do you see?

Now cover the right side and try to explain the difference.

Can you read this word? If not, fill in the space between the shapes and provide "figure-ground" contrast to clarify your focus.

How many squares can you count?

Is this glass half full or half empty? Do you generally see things with a positive or a negative filter? What factors affect your filters? How would you see the glass if it contained medicine? your favorite beverage?

* Answers to the activities on this and the following page are given on page 71.

How Would You Do It?

Plant 10 trees. Plant them in 5 rows with 4 trees in each row. Space all the trees in each row an equal distance apart. Draw a diagram indicating how you would plant the trees.

Can You Do This?

Take six matches of the same length. Form four triangles whose sides are all equal.

How Do You See a "Year"?

How would you represent an abstract concept like a year? (The word stands for something that is agreed upon rather than reality.) Draw your mental image of a year. Here are some visual representations.*

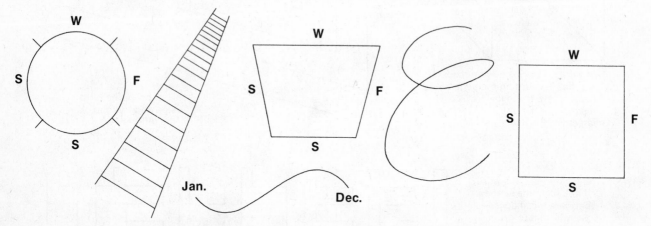

What Is the Middle Figure in Each Row?

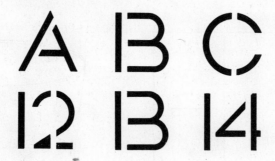

The above is an example of the effect of context—the surrounding factors that provide perceptual clues. The middle figure can be the letter *B* or the number *13* depending on the sequence that surrounds it.**

---

   * Randall P. Harrison, *Beyond Words: An Introduction to Nonverbal Communication,* © 1974, p. 86. Reprinted by permission of Prentice-Hall, Inc., Englewood Cliffs, NJ 07632.
   ** Gail E. Myers and Michele Tolela Myers, *The Dynamics of Human Communication* (New York: McGraw-Hill Book Co., 1980), p. 36. Reproduced with permission.

INFORMAL COMMUNICATION "THROUGH THE GRAPEVINE" *(Group Activity)*

Purpose: To show the way an informal message system works. To repeat a verbal message several times in order to note changes which may occur.

Briefing:

1. Five volunteers are needed. Four volunteers will leave the room and return when they are called in, one at a time.

2. The instructor will read a story slowly, clearly, and distinctly to the first volunteer and to the class members.

3. When the story is finished, one of the volunteers outside who has not heard the story will enter the room. The first volunteer will repeat the story as remembered.

4. The second volunteer will repeat the story to the next, and so on.

5. Class members will listen carefully, take notes in the spaces provided below, and identify at what point the story changed. A message may change in the following ways:

   a. Some information is omitted.
   b. Some details become more important.
   c. Some details are added.
   d. Some information is added to make sense.
   e. Some details are combined.
   f. Some words are changed to suit the speaker's vocabulary.

Debriefing:

1. Why was it impossible to repeat the message exactly as it was given?

2. Was there some information that remained consistent from person to person? Why?

3. What kinds of overall changes did you notice in the story as it was repeated?

4. How does this activity relate to informal communication in real life?

Use this space to make notes as you listen to each individual's story. Note when each message changed.

1. Information omitted

2. Details emphasized

3. Details added

4. Information added

5. Details combined

6. Vocabulary changes

7. Other changes

PERSONAL INVENTORY *(Individual Activity)*

Read the following statements, and score yourself honestly. You might ask a close friend to help you do this exercise.

Scoring: 1 point = Never   3 points = More often than not   5 points = Almost always

Write your score for each statement in the blank at the right of the statement.

1. I tend to qualify my statements by adding such phrases as, "It seems to me . . . ," "In my opinion . . . ," "To the best of my knowledge . . . ," or "I think. . . ." _____

2. I can admit I have made a mistake. _____

3. I am usually careful to check the accuracy of my perception before I make comments about a topic. _____

4. I generally verify my perception by making comparisons to previous experiences, repeating the experience to be sure, using several of my senses, or checking with other people. _____

5. I permit other people to express their viewpoints without getting angry, insisting that I am right, or ignoring them. _____

6. I try to view people as individuals who are unique and therefore different from myself rather than stereotyping them into rigid categories based on their behavior or appearance (for example, football players are not smart, fat people are usually happy, or blondes have more fun). _____

7. I am careful about using *closure* (filling in missing details or information) because I try to see or hear accurately rather than make my perception fit what I want to see or hear. _____

8. I listen to the opinions of others but withhold my personal judgment until I check other sources. _____

9. I ask questions to check my interpretation of what is said before I comment on the statements of other people. _____

10. I try to express myself in specific, descriptive terms that other people can check through observation, rather than making broad general statements. _____

11. I am willing to change my behavior when I perceive that my attitude or actions prevent me from getting along with others. _____

12. Before coming to a conclusion, I wait until I have enough information to justify my decision. _____

13. I try to use empathy—to step into the shoes of another person—before I discount her or his opinions. _____

14. I am willing to change my mind. _____

15. I listen to myself as I talk to see if my attitude is appropriate for the particular situation. _____

Total Score _____

STRUCTURE OF ORGANIZATION REPORT *(Oral Report)*

Even if you have never held a job, you are aware of organizations and the way they are structured. Think of your school, a department store, a social club, a hospital, etc. Select a business in which you know an employee or with which you are acquainted and draw an organization chart for that business. Label each box on the chart with the title of the position (not the name of the individual who fills the position). Identify the formal channels of communication and authority by linking each position to another. Provide a key to indicate the kind of relationships. If you are aware of informal channels of communication, show how these wind around the formal positions. In your report to the class, show how the structure of the organization affects oral communication.

Questions to Help in Planning:

1. How free do the people at the low levels feel about talking to people at high levels?

2. What is the direction of the information flow? What kinds of information go up? What kinds come down?

3. What would happen if an organizational level were neglected in the communication flow?

4. How is the communication that comes down accepted by people at the low levels?

5. How well do people at the middle and upper levels understand the problems of people at the low levels?

6. How accurate is upward communication?

7. What differences are there between vertical and horizontal communications in the organization you have chosen?

Examples of Communication in Organizations

Key: _____ Lines of Authority
— — — — — Lines of Oral and Written Communication

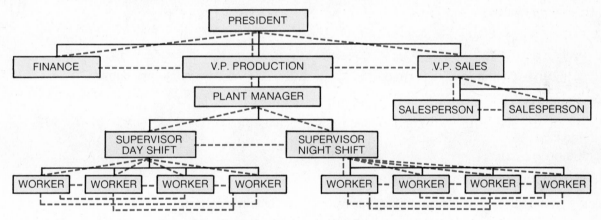

Vertical Organizational Structure

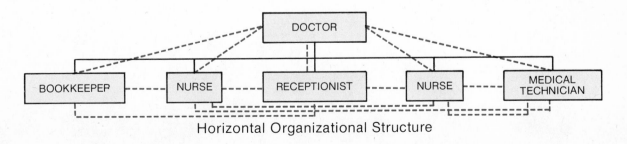

Horizontal Organizational Structure

SUGGESTED OUTLINE FOR ORAL REPORTS *(Student Reference)*

Introduction to the Thesis: Plan an introduction to your thesis that will do three things:

Get Attention   **A.**   Focus the attention on your report.
Involve Listeners   **B.**   Get your listeners involved by asking a question or using the word "you."
Establish Speaker **C.**   Tell how you know about the company you are reporting on.

Thesis: I will report on the organizational structure and the communication in _____ company.

Main Point **I.** _____ company is structured in this way. (Use a visual aid.)

Main Point **II.** _____ company uses oral communication in this way.

OR

Thesis: The horizontal organization of _____ company encourages effective oral communication.

Main Point **I.** This is the organizational structure.

Main Point **II.** This is the way oral communication flows through the company.

OR

Thesis: I will report on how the structure of _____ company affects communication in the company.

Main Point **I.** Communication is effective between lower levels and middle management.

Main Point **II.** Communication is less effective between upper management and lower levels.

Main Point **III.** Communication has improved through the reorganization of several departments.

OR

Thesis: I'd like to report on a department in _____ company and how communication is affected.

Main Point **I.** This is the way the department is structured.

Main Point **II.** This is the way communication is affected.

Conclusion

Summary **A.** Restate your thesis and main points.

Focus   **B.** Tell why you would like your listeners to remember this information.

Name _____ Class _____ Score _____

CRITIQUE SHEET FOR ORAL REPORTS *(Instructor's Evaluation)*

POSSIBLE POINTS: 70   (Each question: 10 points)

1. Was the visual aid neat, clear, and complete and was it handled well by the speaker? _____

2. Was the speaker's voice loud enough to hear easily and were pronunciation of words and articulation of sounds correct? _____

3. Did the speaker control nervous mannerisms, stand confidently, and maintain eye contact? _____

4. Was the information interestingly organized and clearly expressed? _____

5. Was the introduction effective and the conclusion well summarized and focused? _____

6. Was the report well prepared and obviously practiced? _____

7. Were the goals of the assignment met? _____

Total _____

Instructor's Comments:

SPEAKER'S NAME _____

Delivery Critique Form

Possible points: 50   (Each question: 10 points)

1. Was the opening clear and well planned, and did it make you want to listen?   _____

2. Was the eye contact strong and well distributed among the listeners?   _____

3. Were the speaker's movements—facial expressions and gestures—effective?   _____

4. Was the visual aid handled appropriately?   _____

5. Was the speech well organized and obviously practiced beforehand, and did the speaker have a strong desire to communicate?   _____

Total   _____

On the back, write a word of praise and a suggestion for improvement next time.

SPEAKER'S NAME _____

Delivery Critique Form

Possible points: 50   (Each question: 10 points)

1. Was the opening clear and well planned, and did it make you want to listen?   _____

2. Was the eye contact strong and well distributed among the listeners?   _____

3. Were the speaker's movements—facial expressions and gestures—effective?   _____

4. Was the visual aid handled appropriately?   _____

5. Was the speech well organized and obviously practiced beforehand, and did the speaker have a strong desire to communicate?   _____

Total   _____

On the back, write a word of praise and a suggestion for improvement next time.

SPEAKER'S NAME _____

Delivery Critique Form

Possible points: 50   (Each question: 10 points)

1. Was the opening clear and well planned, and did it make you want to listen?   _____

2. Was the eye contact strong and well distributed among the listeners?   _____

3. Were the speaker's movements—facial expressions and gestures—effective?   _____

4. Was the visual aid handled appropriately?   _____

5. Was the speech well organized and obviously practiced beforehand, and did the speaker have a strong desire to communicate?   _____

Total   _____

On the back, write a word of praise and a suggestion for improvement next time.

SPEAKER'S NAME _____

Delivery Critique Form

Possible points: 50   (Each question: 10 points)

1. Was the opening clear and well planned, and did it make you want to listen?   _____

2. Was the eye contact strong and well distributed among the listeners?   _____

3. Were the speaker's movements—facial expressions and gestures—effective?   _____

4. Was the visual aid handled appropriately?   _____

5. Was the speech well organized and obviously practiced beforehand, and did the speaker have a strong desire to communicate?   _____

Total   _____

On the back, write a word of praise and a suggestion for improvement next time.

SPEECH COMMUNICATION BARRIERS IN BUSINESS *(Group Discussion)*

Purpose: To identify specific barriers in business communication and to describe them in a real context. To explore available solutions. To apply textbook theory to business situations.

Briefing: Work in a group of five or six. Select one person to be the group observer.

To the observer: Sit outside the group circle and do not participate in the discussion. Read the information on page 64 and then complete a communication flow chart. At the end of the discussion, make a brief report of your observations to the group.

To the group: Read the following list of speech communication barriers aloud. Each person should check several problems which are familiar. Select several problems to discuss. Describe a real situation in which a similar problem occurred. Use fictitious names for the people involved. Identify the causes of the problem. What created the barriers? Suggest specific behaviors that the individuals could have used to solve the problem.

Communication Barriers:

_____ 1. Different language codes.

_____ 2. Lack of a common vocabulary.

_____ 3. Failure to word a question to get the information sought.

_____ 4. Conflicting orders being received.

_____ 5. Message relayed through too many people.

_____ 6. Lack of access to a person of higher rank.

_____ 7. Lack of listening or hearing.

_____ 8. Failure to decode verbal messages accurately.

_____ 9. Failure to hear a speaker as that person wants to be heard.

_____ 10. Inability to express thoughts or feelings in words.

_____ 11. Failure to pay attention to feedback.

_____ 12. Inability to be specific, concrete, and direct in verbal messages.

_____ 13. Personal biases shaping the encoding of messages.

_____ 14. Lack of organized ideas in providing information.

_____ 15. Lack of common goals within a group.

_____ 16. Failure to articulate group goals.

_____ 17. Withholding information, distorting information, or deliberately misinforming.

_____ 18. Responding positively, although not understanding or agreeing.

_____ 19. Failure to validate a perception or an assumption.

_____ 20. Jumping to a conclusion before having all the facts.

_____ 21. Not being informed or aware of particular job responsibilities.

_____ 22. Failure to meet the expectations of others.

OBSERVER REPORT *(Individual Report)*

Purpose: To observe the discussion between a group of classmates. To report on the participation between group members. To report only observations, not judgments.

Briefing: You have been chosen to listen carefully to the verbal participation during this discussion. Read the following directions and study the sample below.

1. On a separate sheet of paper, draw a circle to represent each group member.

2. Write each group member's name within a circle.

3. Start your flow chart after the discussion is well under way.

4. Each time someone speaks, draw an arrow from the person speaking to the person being spoken to, and keep a tally of the number of times each person talked.

5. Keep a record for only ten minutes. Indicate the total time of the observation.

6. When the discussion is finished, report the results of your observation to the group.

Example of a Communication Flow Chart:

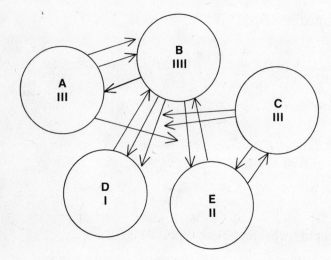

TIME: _____ 2:35 _____ to _____ 2:45 _____

REPORT:

A talked three times, twice to B, once to the whole group.

B talked four times, once to A, twice to D, once to E.

C talked three times, twice to the whole group, once to E.

D talked once to B.

E talked two times, once to B, once to C.

Debriefing: After the observer has reported to the group, use the following question for a discussion: "Which behavior style did each member seem to use?" (see p. 42).

WHO'S WHO IN YOUR CLASS? *(Group Activity)*

Purpose: To discover how you view your fellow class members and how they view you. To create an individual profile. To record personal feelings.

Briefing: It is important for members of the class to review each other's names for this activity. Sit in a large circle so that people can see each other.

You have been working with your classmates for some time. As your instructor slowly reads the questions below, *select the name of a class member* who best fits the category. Write that person's name and the category number on a separate sheet of paper to turn in *without your signature.*

1. To whom would you go for help with an urgent business problem?

2. Who has given you the best listening response?

3. Who would be a good supervisor?

4. Whom would you trust with a confidential business matter?

5. Whom would you like to help you organize an office party?

6. With whom would you like to attend the party?

7. Who would be a good instructor for a training session?

8. Who could deliver a clear verbal message to you on the telephone?

9. Whom would you consider a serious business competitor?

10. To whom would you lend your automobile?

Debriefing: After the papers are collected and turned in, several students may volunteer to chart the results for the class and give an oral report during the next class period.

As you listen to the report, make a profile of how your peers see you by recording below the number of votes that you received in each category.

1. Helper _____   6. Companion (or Date) _____

2. Listener _____   7. Instructor _____

3. Supervisor _____   8. Telephone Communicator _____

4. Confidant _____   9. Competitor _____

5. Organizer _____   10. Partner _____

In the space below, record your *feelings* about the way your classmates see you. Identify both positive and negative feelings.

BUSINESS COMMUNICATION PROBLEMS *(Group Discussion)*

Purpose: To select a business problem for discussion, to role play the conversations in the case, to analyze the communication barriers, and to recommend a way to prevent or solve the problem.

Briefing:

1. Work with a group of four or five people.

2. Select one of the following cases. Read the parts aloud.

3. Analyze the communication barriers that seem to appear in the problem.

4. Decide what could be done to prevent or correct the barriers. Make a report to the class.

Case 1: Going Over Their Heads

Joe Hobson and Annie Salveson are insurance agents for United Republic Insurance Company.

Joe: Annie, can you believe this? The office doesn't even have a record of my sales for last month.

Annie: Are you saying that they have been lost?

Joe: I don't know if they have been lost or if someone has misplaced them, but I'm going to raise some dust around here until they're found.

Annie: Talk to Mr. Amberson. As office manager, he is responsible for the records in our office.

Joe: I can't talk to him. He'll think I'm blaming him and he won't do a thing about it. I've had trouble with him before. I'm going to call the home office and see if the records were turned in.

Annie: Joe, you can't do that. Don't you remember when we took our agent's training? We had to sign a statement agreeing to communicate by following the chain of command.

Joe: Listen, Annie, I can't wait around while the office manager checks with the district manager and while Henderson asks the regional manager. If those records don't arrive in the home office, I'll lose my commission for this month. It was a big one, too. I'm calling the home office right now.

Case 2: A Problem of Image

Mrs. Benson is a vice-president of the Mervin County Bank; Linda Fernandez is a teller. She has been employed at the bank for three months.

Mrs. Benson: Linda, do you think you are dressed appropriately for work?

Linda: What are you talking about, Mrs. Benson? This is my favorite yellow sun dress.

Mrs. Benson: But is it appropriate for working in the teller's cage?

Linda: You aren't going to tell me what to wear, I hope.

Mrs. Benson: I'm afraid I'm going to make some suggestions, Linda. It's my job.

Linda: What do you want me to do—go home and change?

Mrs. Benson: I want you to think carefully about the bank's image, Linda. I don't expect to have to speak to you about this again.

Case 3: What Happened Here?

At Acme Systems Company, Mr. Cardella has appointed Al Briggs project coordinator for a $1 million contract. He will be designing processing systems for an electronics firm. The customer gave Acme a written list of ten specifications which the drawings had to meet. Al hired five drafters to design the 88 drawings needed for the 16 processing systems. Mr. Cardella received the drawings and then called Al into his office.

Mr. Cardella:	Al, I have a tough time understanding why these drawings are incorrect.
Al:	So do I, Mr. Cardella. I met with the drafters after I hired them and I outlined all the information that was pertinent to the drawings.
Mr. Cardella:	Did you give them the specifications?
Al:	Yes, I certainly did. They told me they understood the requirements for the job.
Mr. Cardella:	But these drawings have a completely different set of dimensions. They simply won't do.
Al:	I know that, Mr. Cardella. I've fired the drafters, and I'll get busy trying to find someone who can handle this correctly.
Mr. Cardella:	You'll do more than that, Al. The project is behind schedule, and you are responsible. You'll have to make a report to the company management this afternoon.

Case 4: On the Carpet

Carol Wu is the front-end manager at Harrison's #4 store. She supervises and evaluates all cashiers, sackers, head cashiers, cashier trainers, and concession personnel. Larry Hayes is a cashier trainer. He works in the area supervised by Carol. His job is to orient new personnel to store policies and to train them as cashiers. Carol called Larry into her office.

Carol:	Larry, I asked you if Jack, the new trainee, would be ready to start work on the cash registers by today. Jack now tells me that he isn't ready yet. Why not?
Larry:	Carol, I've been working with Jack all week. I've put him through the whole training program.
Carol:	I know that, Larry. But why isn't he ready to take over today? A week is time enough for you to train someone.
Larry:	Well, that kid is just too stupid to learn how to handle a cash register. I'm worn out from having to deal with him.
Carol:	I've never known anyone who couldn't be trained, Larry. I'm going to assign Jack to Amy for further training, and I'm going to ask the store manager to reprimand you. That's all.

Case 5: I'd Rather Do It Myself

A new department has been developed within the Maxim Company. Rachel Garner has been transferred from her old department in the company. She has been promoted to supervisor of the new department. She is responsible for determining the structure of the new department and developing job descriptions for each position. She reports to Mr. Starner.

Mr. Starner:	Rachel, I've called you in today because I am concerned with the amount of overtime you've been working. For the past two months, you've worked 15 to 20 hours over your regular hours. Are you having trouble setting up the new department?
Rachel:	Oh, no, Mr. Starner. Everything is going fine.
Mr. Starner:	But Rachel, several people have reported to me that you feel that the job requires at least three people to assist you in order to complete the job within the specified time frame.
Rachel:	Well, I don't know who told you that, but it isn't true.
Mr. Starner:	But Rachel, you've missed two assigned deadlines at this point.
Rachel:	I know, sir, but I turned in the reports within 24 hours of the deadline.
Mr. Starner:	Rachel, I really need to know what problems you are having and what we can do to help you.
Rachel:	Nothing, honestly, Mr. Starner. I'll work very hard to get the job completed.

CHECKLIST OF COMMUNICATION TERMS *(Quiz)*

Check your understanding of the terms presented in this chapter. Record the number of the term in the blank preceding its definition. Note there are more terms than definitions.

Definitions	**Terms**
a. ___8___ Filling in missing details to make sense of something.	1. reality
	2. symbols
b. ___5___ The ability to perceive from another person's viewpoint.	3. assumptions
	4. filters
c. ___12,1___ The environment around you that can be seen, heard, smelled, tasted, and touched.	5. empathy
	6. classification
	7. symbolic world
	8. closure
d. ___4___ (3,10,11,14) Factors that limit your view of the world and shape your thinking.	9. self-image
	10. values
e. ___9___ The way you perceive yourself.	11. attitudes
	12. empirical world
f. ___13___ Your ability to choose stimuli to which you will pay attention.	13. selective perception
	14. labels
	15. roles
g. ___11___ Your tendency to respond in positive, negative, or neutral ways to people and things.	16. climate
	17. abstracting
	18. perception
h. ___7___ Coded messages such as signs, language, maps, etc.	19. beliefs
	20. figure
i. ___3___ Guesses about people and events based on previous experience.	21. ground
	22. grapevine
	23. self-esteem
j. ___14___ The words you choose to describe what you perceive.	24. formal channels of communication

SOLUTIONS TO PERCEPTUAL PUZZLES *(Pages 53-54)*

CUBE AND DOT: There is no one correct answer. Some people see it one way; others see it another; still others can shift their perception and see it both ways.

THREE-PRONGED FIGURE: This is a clever drawing that looks very complicated. Put your finger over the circle in the middle on the right. Can you now see that the first and third circles could have been drawn larger and then there would be a normal two-pronged figure?

FIGURE-GROUND: If you shade in the space between the shapes, the word SECRET is revealed.

SQUARES: Answer: 40. You probably discovered that you needed to define the word "square" to communicate accurately.

1 large square
4 squares (9 blocks each)
9 squares (4 blocks each)
18 squares (16 single blocks plus 2 combinations of 4 small blocks)
8 squares (the smallest blocks)

$1 + 4 + 9 + 18 + 8 = 40$ squares, each with 4 equal sides and 4 equal angles.

GLASS OF LIQUID: The glass may be described as half full or half empty. The way you talk about it tells your listener something about you or about the contents of the glass.

TEN TREES: The ten trees can be planted as shown below. The word "row" may have created a barrier that prevented you from solving the problem.

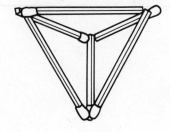

MATCHSTICK TRIANGLES: You may have assumed that the matches had to lie flat on the table. The solution is to form a triangle with three matches on the table. Then at each corner of the triangle, stand one match up and bring the three together to form a pyramid. You may have to hold the matches with your thumb.

VISUALIZING A "YEAR": These figures are only the way some people "saw" a year and drew it. Yours is probably just as interesting. If you liked doing this, try drawing your mental representation of "business" or "symbol."

LETTERS AND NUMBERS: Note that the center figure in each line is exactly the same. You depend upon the context of surrounding figures to decide whether the center figure is a "B" or a "13." We use the context to help us give meaning to symbols.

CHAPTER 3

Let's Talk About the Business of Broadening Your Listening Skills

Your listening skills are of primary importance in the communication process. If you do not receive oral messages accurately and sensitively, speaking to you is of little use and communication fails. If you do receive messages accurately, however, you can feed back appropriate responses and effective communication can take place. Your objectives for this chapter on listening and feedback are the following:

Chapter Objectives

1. Distinguish between hearing and listening.
2. Explain the three characteristics of skilled listening.
3. List at least ten specific skills used in listening for content.
4. Differentiate between Listening Rule One (Feed back the content) and Listening Rule Two (Feed back for intent).
5. List three explanations for the basis of feedback.

"Nobody ever listened himself out of a job."

Calvin Coolidge

Of all the speech communication skills you bring to your job, listening may well be one of the most important. And yet, has anyone ever suggested that you take a course in listening? Probably not. But how effective would any speech be if there was no one to listen? Both skills—listening and speaking—are needed in speech communication.

Most of your waking day is spent in communication. This communication time is divided into the following approximate percentages:

45 percent listening
30 percent speaking
16 percent reading
9 percent writing[1]

---

[1] Paul T. Rankin, "Measurement of the Ability to Understand the Spoken Language," unpublished doctoral dissertation, The University of Michigan, 1926.

According to these percentages, you listen more than you speak, read, or write. Since you spend so much of your communication time listening, it is an important communication skill to develop.

When you listen, you take in sensory messages and receive input. On the job, you listen to oral messages from many people such as the personnel manager, your supervisor, and your fellow employees. You have to listen well, decode messages accurately, and sort out and retain information. Well-developed listening skills help build successful relationships with people in the business environment.

Clearly, speaking and listening are different sides of the same coin. Communication is incomplete, ineffective, and intermittent without skills in both areas. Listening skills are so important that many businesses require listening tests as part of the hiring process.

Poor listening skills can result in costly problems:

1. Accidents that cause physical injury. ("I didn't hear anyone say that this is a hard-hat area.")
2. Production breakdowns that result in lost time and money. ("I didn't remember the supervisor saying to insert the plate from the left side.")
3. Lost sales and lost customers. ("Why did she get so angry? I didn't know that she already had a vacuum cleaner.")
4. Arguments and misunderstandings between workers. ("Why didn't you pay attention when I gave you that deadline?")
5. Discontent between workers and management. ("I kept telling the boss that we could have saved time if we had combined the two steps into one. But no one listens to those of us who do the job!")

"The biggest block to personal communication is man's inability to listen intelligently, understandingly, and skillfully to another person."

F. J. Roethlisberger

These problems are compounded by the fact that even when they are listening well, people do not remember everything they hear. Studies of listening have demonstrated that immediately after someone talks, the listeners remember only about half of what they heard. Within eight hours, they have forgotten perhaps a third to a half more. Our listening powers need help. Oral messages just don't stick with us. Let's see if we can find out why.

THE LISTENING PROCESS

Like a quarterback without a pass receiver, a speaker can't complete a speech transaction without a receiver. However, receiving an oral message is not the same as understanding and remembering it. Hearing sounds and listening to messages are related, but they are not exactly the same. Let's consider the hearing process first.

Hearing as a Physical Sense

"Nature has given to man one tongue, but two ears, that we may hear from others twice as much as we speak."

Epictetus

Hearing is a fascinating physical process that works this way: Sound waves outside your body are set in motion by such things as someone's voice, a barking dog, or an automobile horn. These sound waves strike your eardrum and cause it to vibrate. Behind the eardrum are three tiny bones—called the hammer, the anvil, and the stirrup because of their shape—that carry the vibrations through the middle ear to the oval window, the entrance to the inner ear. When the stirrup vibrates in the oval window, matching vibrations are set up in the thousands of tiny, hairlike cells that make up the membrane of the inner ear. These vibrations are transmitted as nerve impulses to the cerebral cortex of the brain through connections in the fibers of the auditory nerve. The cerebral cortex receives the vibrations exactly as they were set in motion on your eardrum. A simplified diagram of this process is shown in Figure 3-1.

Of course, hearing does not operate by itself. All the five senses work at the same time, giving you a blend of sensory images that make food appetizing or a rock concert exciting. Remember, also, that you do not hear all the sounds that exist. Your hearing is limited to a range of frequencies. People with normal hearing are sensitive to a barrage of sounds within a range of 20 to 10,000 cycles per second.

Your hearing is often affected by a change in the pressure against your eardrums. For example:

1. Loud sounds grab your attention because the increased pressure against your eardrums causes discomfort or the sound occurs unexpectedly.
2. Strange sounds catch your attention because they are unfamiliar.
3. Soft sounds make you focus your hearing. Note how easily you hear your own name when it is whispered.
4. Variety in sound levels causes a difference in pressure on your eardrums. You pay attention to these sounds because they are interesting. Speech sounds, which often have much variety in sound levels, are easy to distinguish.

This information clues us as to ways in which we can be more effective speakers. We can vary our voices as we speak to increase the possibility that listeners will pay attention to what we say.

"Sound knocks on your eardrums and you hear it; listening is what you do with what you hear."

Erma Kline

Listening and hearing, often regarded as the same process, are not the same. Hearing is necessary to the listening process, but listening refers to what we do with the nerve impulses in our brains. Listening refers to the focused perception of selected stimuli and the sorting, categorizing, labeling, and storing of these stimuli. This is the thinking process. There is a limit to the number of stimuli we can pay attention to at any one time. However, there is no limit to the number of stimuli constantly competing for our atten-

FIGURE 3-1   The ear makes it possible for you to hear.

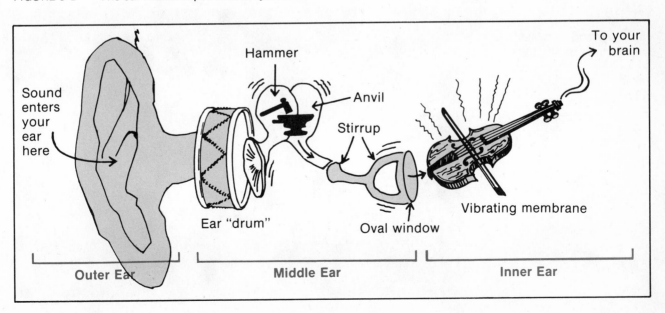

tion. If we could pay attention to all of them, a brain overload would result. So, in listening, we are constantly busy with the process of selecting only those stimuli to which we will pay attention.

Listening as a Skill

Listening involves more than just hearing sounds. It is an active process that involves decoding and interpreting the data received as sound. Therefore, communication is not complete unless the mental state of the receiver is changed by the sounds in some way.

Decoding Verbal Messages. In order to decode a verbal message, your body gears up to receive and process the information. Concentrated listening is characterized by a rapid heartbeat, faster circulation of the blood, and a slight rise in body temperature. Your eyes and ears absorb all the clues sent by the speaker, such as the words, the tone of voice, facial clues, and body movements. You mentally translate the words into mental images and thus make sense of the message. When you are deeply involved in listening, you are probably unconsciously running through this mental checklist of questions:

1. Why is the speaker giving me this information?
2. How does the speaker want me to respond?
3. How experienced in this subject and trustworthy is the speaker?
4. Is the speaker in a position to know the facts?
5. Is the speaker stating a personal opinion?
6. Is the speaker sincerely interested in relating information to me and to my interests?
7. Do I clearly understand the language?
8. Do I know which subjects or ideas the language symbols represent as used by the speaker?
9. Does the message describe what I already know?
10. Does the speaker's point of view have merit, even if it is different from my own way of thinking?
11. How do I really feel about what is being said?
12. Am I absorbing and remembering what the speaker intends to say?

PHOTO 3-1

Speakers add purposeful movements and gestures to help listeners focus their attention on the oral message.

As you pay attention to a message, you slide it through your personal experience system to make sense of it. As you listen, you actively take part in the communication process. Like most people, it is easy for you to listen to speakers who talk about subjects that interest you. But you need effective listening skills to concentrate on new information, on a complex subject you know little about, or on a message that does not concern you. Good listening is a developed skill.

Characteristics of Skilled Listening. Can you remember a time when someone really listened to you and heard you as you wanted to be heard? It is probably a warm memory because that person gave you undivided attention. You, in turn, responded to the person's concentration on your message. You received encouragement from the person's smiles, nods, etc., and you probably were fired to greater enthusiasm as you spoke. It is this quality of listening that inspires speakers because, in turn, skilled listening makes better speaking.

There are three major characteristics of skilled listening.

1. *A good listener participates willingly and actively in the communication process.*

Listening well requires physical energy. It takes a conscious effort to catch the message, flip it around, juggle it, take it apart, puzzle over it, and finally decide what sense it makes. A good listener is not a passive bystander who waits for something to happen. A good listener helps the communication process by (1) being poised and ready; (2) being open to ideas; (3) being physically and emotionally involved; (4) concentrating; and (5) responding with verbal or nonverbal feedback.

2. *A good listener uses the speaking-listening rate difference to advantage.*

People typically think faster than a speaker can talk. (The rate of speaking in ordinary conversation is about 125-150 words per minute.) The words rush out, tumble over each other, slow to a pause, proceed at a regular pace, and then stop. The speaker's voice hesitates and then more word sounds gush into the air. But you can listen to the message, decode and interpret it, and have time left over. It is estimated that human beings can think at a rate of 500-800 words per minute. Your active brain does not receive input as fast as it processes information. This gives you spare thinking time that can be put to constructive use.

When you talk directly with another person, it is easy to pay attention because the other person can watch your response. Thus, you can signal that you're listening carefully. But when you are a member of a large audience, it is easy for you to drift in and out, listen for a few seconds, and then think about something else. This is not good listening. You need to use, consciously and efficiently, the difference between the speaking rate and your listening rate. In order to use this time lag productively, process the information in this way:

a. Watch the speaker closely; think ahead of the speaker; anticipate the direction of the speech.
b. Focus on the ideas. Mentally select and list the important ideas discussed. Think in general terms and phrase a sentence that summarizes all the ideas. Compare this with the central idea that is being presented by the speaker.

c. Keep track of the supporting material. Look for examples, quotations, comparisons, stories, and visual aids to clarify ideas.

d. Relate the information to your own experience. "Yes, I remember when that happened." "I didn't know that." "Can I accept that idea?"

e. Identify your feelings. Ask yourself, "Why does that idea make me angry?" If you are irritated or annoyed as you listen, call a truce within yourself. Give the speaker a chance to develop the whole idea before labeling it as unimportant.

f. Check the basis of the ideas presented. "Where did that information come from?" "Are those current figures?" "How does the speaker know that?"

g. Analyze the quality of the ideas. "I wish the speaker would develop that statement more fully." "Presenting three alternatives is a good idea." "I've never heard it expressed that way before."

This kind of tuned-in, focused thinking helps you become actively involved in the speech encounter. It provides you with an efficient way of programming the speaker's talking rate and your own speedy mental process rate.

3. *A good listener is aware of the symptoms of poor listening.*

You often are aware when someone is not listening to you. But it is more difficult to recognize your own listening behavior. Beware of these poor listening behaviors when you are a member of the audience:

a. Criticizing the speaker. Placing blame on the speaker if you fail to listen or understand the ideas. "The speech was dull and full of vague statements." "Nothing was specific." "I can't listen effectively when the speaker paces back and forth."

b. Allowing yourself to be sidetracked. Refusing to get involved in the communication process by diverting yourself with activities such as doodling on your notebook cover, reading, solving a math problem, napping, or planning Saturday night's date.

c. Composing rebuttals. When the speaker says something you can't agree with, you may tune out the person for the next few minutes while you construct an opposing argument. Be careful of a "Yes, but . . ." attitude.

d. Protecting your feelings. Reacting emotionally to words or phrases that you don't like. Assuming the speaker is attacking you personally with language that upsets you.

e. Shaping what you hear. Listening for only the part of the speaker's message that fits your beliefs. Listening for details and omitting the whole picture. Deciding the message is not relevant to your needs by refusing to find any link between the speaker's message and your interests.

Unfortunately poor listening behavior also occurs in one-to-one situations as well as in small groups:

a. Listening to only a portion of a message and responding to just that portion.

b. Listening while checking your watch, gazing out the window, etc.

c. Listening in order to criticize the speaker or the speaker's point of view.

d. Changing the subject.

e. Saying what you want to discuss without referring to what the other person has said.

Although most people are guilty of poor listening behavior at some time, your goal is to become aware of and to develop good listening skills such as attention, comprehension, and retention.

Listening Barriers

The barriers that interfere with listening may be physical (something may be wrong with the hearing mechanism), but they are more likely to be psychological and result from attitudes, feelings, or lack of awareness. For example, these barriers could be:

Can't hear—"The p.a. system needs to be turned up."
Don't hear—"I do wish she wouldn't mumble."
Won't hear—"He never says anything important."
Can't understand—"I don't know any French."
Don't understand—"Why push this button before you begin?"
Won't understand—"I never did like math."

THE ROLE OF THE RECEIVER

Who says what to whom and with what results is a major concern to people in business and to communicators in general. In business, for example, if a product does not meet the needs of consumers, it will not sell. It is vital that businesspeople know the goals, attitudes, beliefs, and needs of the customers they serve. Thousands of dollars are spent on marketing research to learn about customers. Obviously, the customer who is the buyer of products and the receiver of advertising messages is tremendously important. Without the customer, there is no business. The same is true in communication. Without a receiver, there is no communication.

Importance of the Receiver

Receiving information and ideas accurately is as important as speaking in the communication process. If the speaker talks and the receiver chooses not to listen, communication fails. If the receiver elects not to pay attention, the message falls flat. If the receiver gets a message that is not intended, misunderstandings occur.

The receiver makes vital speech communication decisions such as:

1. Which messages to be exposed to. ("I would like to know more about the operation of our sales department, so I'll sit in on that meeting today.")
2. Which messages to pay attention to. ("That's a good point. I can use that information.")
3. Which messages to react or respond to. ("I'll finish that matter with a follow-up letter.")
4. How the message is to be interpreted. ("The supervisor didn't say we had to do it this way. It was only a suggestion.")
5. Whether the source of the message is trustworthy and believable. ("You were right the last time. I'll do it the way you suggest.")
6. Which messages directly benefit the listener. ("What can I personally use?")

Since receivers make conscious and unconscious decisions that affect the communication outcome, prepared speakers tailor their messages directly to their listeners. Careful audience analysis (gathering and thinking through the information you have about your receivers) will help you plan the speech message. Like a business that knows its customers, wise speakers know their listeners' interests and general background, and how they are programmed to respond.

You as a Receiver

Think about the things you bring to a speech situation that affect your listening. More than just your ears, you bring a number of experiences that shape your listening potential:

1. How you view yourself.
2. How you see the other person.
3. Your past experiences in similar situations.
4. What you expect to hear and how you expect it to affect you.
5. Your feelings about the present situation and the people involved.
6. Feelings carried over from previous, unrelated situations.

Clearly you do not listen as if you were an empty cup waiting to be filled. You are a living organism, responding to the sounds you hear and the symbolic messages you receive. You accept, reject, build on new information, dig deeper, fly off on new tangents, or perhaps remain unchanged as you listen. Ideally, listening is one way in which you can grow and develop.

Two Kinds of Receiver Skills

In some situations you listen for specific information or instructions. At other times, you listen to establish or maintain a relationship between yourself and someone else. These two kinds of receiver skills are (1) listening for content and (2) listening for intent. Both methods are called *active listening*.

"I learned to be a kind of sponge. I made it a point to get acquainted with people who knew more than I did and to listen to them thirstily. That's where I got the know-how I needed—through my ears."

Norman Vincent Peale

Listening for Content. Message content is the subject matter of the message. When you listen for content, you listen to understand, to remember, and to retain. You use a number of specific listening skills to determine meaning. These skills include listening to:

1. Determine the speaker's purpose and credibility.
2. Identify the central idea.
3. Separate the main points from supporting material.
4. Discover the organizational pattern.
5. Distinguish between fact and opinion.
6. Detect bias and prejudice.
7. Divide emotional argument from logical argument.
8. Recognize gimmicks and propaganda techniques.
9. Focus on facts such as names, places, and dates.
10. Note the fallacies (faulty reasoning) in the arguments.
11. Get the meanings of unfamiliar words from the context.
12. Recognize the same idea expressed in different words.

    Listening Rule One—Feed Back the Content. Before you respond to a speaker with your comments, rephrase or summarize what you think the speaker has said. This is called *paraphrasing*.

1. Repeat in your own words the message you heard the speaker say.
2. Start with, "If I understand correctly, you said . . ." or, "Your idea is . . ." or, "Do I understand you to mean . . . ?" or "In other words . . ." or, "Do I hear you saying . . . ?"

Permit the other person to acknowledge your summary or to clarify further if you have not interpreted the message as the speaker intended.

Using Listening Rule One assures the speaker that you are listening attentively, decoding accurately, and trying to verify your understanding. Do not merely echo the speaker's words, but grasp what the speaker means. You may find that paraphrasing for content slows the transaction somewhat, but it does increase the accuracy of communication.

The second kind of receiver skill is concerned with the person speaking rather than with the message spoken.

Listening for Intent. Some people believe that meaning is transferred like a gift: one person gives and another receives. You now know that this is not always true. A speaker does not literally get an idea across but can only express meaning in words. The listener must decide what the words mean and what the speaker intends them to mean. **Intent**, then, is the speaker's purpose for speaking. This purpose is often difficult for a listener to determine. Therefore, it is important to listen in a nonjudgmental way to the messages of others, particularly those people with whom you work.

Listening for intent is listening for the unspoken "why" in a speech message. This kind of listening has the same goal as listening for content: accurate understanding of speech communication. However, the quality of listening is different. It might be called listening with the third ear, listening at the second level, absorbing through the pores, or empathetic listening. However you describe it, this type of tuned-in listening gets beneath the words to the feelings. It seeks to learn the often unverbalized intent of the other person (that is, why the message makes sense to the speaker). It requires **empathy**, the ability to perceive from another person's point of view and to mentally and emotionally sense what the person is feeling.

Empathy makes a receiver sensitive to the vocal sounds and the physical clues sent by the speaker. Empathetic listening enables you to picture what it would be like to say what the speaker is saying in the way the speaker is saying it. Thus, empathetic listening allows you to sense how the speaker wishes to be heard. This kind of listening helps keep channels of communication open between you and the other person. It is important to listen both critically—for content—and empathetically—for intent. And it is ultimately necessary to understand when each kind of listening is appropriate.

"Great Spirit, grant that I may not criticize my neighbor until I have walked a mile in his moccasins."

Indian prayer

PHOTO 3-2

Paraphrasing helps the speaker determine whether the listener has interpreted the message correctly.

When listening for the speaker's intent, use these listening skills:

1. Accept the speaker as an individual who may be quite different from you.
2. Withhold your criticism or personal reactions.
3. Pay attention to what is *not* said, such as feelings, emotions, attitudes, etc.
4. Focus on the speaker's intonation as well as on the words themselves.
5. Create a climate in which the speaker is free to speak openly.

Listening Rule Two—Feed Back for Intent. Focus on the speaker's feelings that gave rise to that message. Let your eyes read facial clues and your ears pick up vocal clues that tell you what feelings lie beneath the words. You might comment:

"That makes you feel happy then?"
"You must be worried about them."
"You seem pretty upset about this mistake."
"You are really angry about what was said."
"These results seem to disturb you."
"I sense you are uncomfortable about this."

These comments invite the speaker to go below the surface and to express deeper feelings. They focus on the speaker's emotional state rather than on the listener's response. Thus, the speaker can continue to talk without stopping to think about the listener's reaction. By focusing on what the speaker is feeling, you make no judgments about the speech message but invite the speaker to explore more deeply.

You choose this kind of listening when the speaker's silent message may be more important than the words. For example, you may sense that the person is feeling strongly about his or her message, even though the words do not indicate strong feelings. Here you can allow the other person the opportunity to tell you why she or he is saying these words. Empathetic listening is not just silently paying attention with an occasional nod; it is the willingness to actively and silently take in the verbal and the vocal messages while concentrating on the nonverbal facial expression and movement. This requires total receptiveness.

Initially both listening rules require patience and practice. For example, it is difficult to listen and summarize what someone else has said when you are bursting to express your own ideas. Also, it is not easy to help someone get in touch with personal feelings. But it is worth the effort.

Listening as an Audience Member

As a member of an audience, how can you increase your listening effectiveness? These suggestions will help you to listen, retain, and remember what you hear as part of a large group.

1. **Prepare to listen well.** Sit where you can see and hear the speaker clearly. If necessary, adjust the room ventilation, close the door to shut out noises, or choose a different seat to avoid distractions. Then adopt a good listening position. If you slouch, you are more likely to be sluggish in response to the speaker. Be alert to catch the verbal message and be prepared to decode it as the speaker intends.
2. **Concentrate on the message.** Know what to listen for. Hunt for a generalized statement of the purpose of the speech. Fit the components of the speech together and mentally construct them into one central theme. The

details may be interesting, but they will seem irrelevant unless they support the ideas being proposed. Remember that the speaker needs your listening help to make sense of her or his words.

3. **React nonverbally.** Good listeners signal that the speaker has their attention. Keep your eyes on the speaker. If you fully support an idea, indicate encouragement through your facial expressions or by a nod. Respond actively. If necessary, play a role in relation to the speaker's role. For example, pretend that the speaker is your boss or your best friend and that you have a personal stake in the speaker's success.

BOSS (to employees at a meeting): "Now pay careful attention. I'll let you know at the end of the meeting who will write up the minutes."

4. **Retain and remember.** If you are not prepared to jot things down, you are likely to miss valuable information. Carry a small note pad and be prepared to take notes. Include the basic *who, what, when, where,* and *why* information. Since forgetting information usually takes place soon after a meeting or lecture, these notes will serve as a quick reference. Also, if you are required to be responsible and report the information, your notes can be rewritten as an orderly record soon after the meeting.

5. **Rephrase what you hear.** This is a good way to practice paraphrasing for content. Remember the main points and repeat them in your own words. Think with the speaker. Don't always expect to understand the importance of what you hear, but keep listening to see if you can figure it out. Ask for clarification if the speaker offers to answer questions. Above all, stay tuned in and allow the speaker to relate the entire message.

THE FEEDBACK CIRCUIT

Feedback is extremely important in business; the source wants to know whether the message has been received and accepted in the way it was intended. A company, for example, checks feedback by reviewing sales results. Pollsters check public reaction to television programs which, in turn, live or die on the basis of such feedback.

Feedback is clearly important to the business world and it certainly is vital to communication between people. Like the ON switch in an electrical circuit, feedback ensures a continuous flow of current. The speaker generates the power through a message, and the receiver's response completes the circuit. The participants are involved jointly in a message-response-message system that operates alternately, simultaneously, intermittently, or perhaps not at all.

Importance of Feedback

Feedback is important to the speaker and to the receiver. By receiving feedback, the speaker determines which adjustments must be made to the verbal message in order to communicate it. By reading feedback, the speaker decides to continue the message, repeat it, explain it further, or stop altogether. By giving feedback, the receiver influences the direction of the interaction. The receiver has many choices of feedback responses and may send a response that:

1. Answers a question
2. Asks for more information
3. Sparkles with friendliness
4. Disguises feelings
5. Changes the subject

FIGURE 3-2

Feedback completes the
communication circuit.

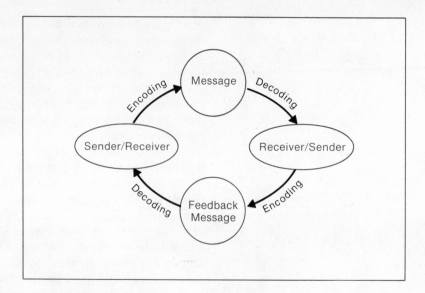

6. Indicates receptiveness
7. Criticizes the speaker
8. Invites the speaker to continue
9. Makes a judgment

Indeed, feedback to a spoken message may determine the direction of the conversation or whether the speaker continues at all. Thus, as a receiver of a message, you:

1. Listen
2. Decode
3. Respond in words or nonverbally

You also can choose to make one of several oral responses, such as positive statements, neutral statements, negative statements, questions, or no response at all—in itself a form of feedback.

As a receiver of an oral message, you decide to feed back a message to (1) keep the communication channels open; (2) further the interaction to a deeper level of intimacy and sharing; (3) change the direction of the conversation; or (4) snap the communication channels shut. Hence, the words you choose as a response tremendously affect the quality of the communication.

"When I speak I learn about my-self; when I listen I learn about others."

Stella Brisken

Feedback Situations

Circumstances frequently limit the amount of feedback available to the speaker. Consider these four kinds of situations in which different amounts of feedback are present:

1. **Zero feedback.** A speaker cannot always check for immediate feedback. Radio or television broadcasters, for example, do not know the direct response to their oral messages. Have you ever found yourself muttering a response to a television personality by agreeing or disagreeing with the person? With zero feedback, the speaker does not get the benefit of your comments.
2. **One-channel feedback.** In a public speaking situation, only the speaker talks. As a member of the audience, you listen and generally do not respond orally. But the speaker reads the feedback from the audience by watching

for nonverbal clues. The speaker looks at eyes, faces, and body positions—visual clues that indicate the interest and receptiveness of the listeners. Of course, these signals may be deceptive. A receiver may appear to be listening, but his or her mind may be elsewhere. When speaking to a large group, it is sometimes difficult to read the feedback clues accurately.

3. **Two-channel feedback.** Frequently in a public speaking situation, a question-and-answer period follows a speech. For example, your boss presents a new statement of company policy to a group of employees and opens the floor for questions. Employees then present oral feedback and ask questions about specific concerns. Perhaps you decide to respond. You will probably respond only to a portion of the message. Your question will direct the speaker's response to the area you want to discuss. Your feedback will control the direction of the communication. Although there is two-channel feedback in this communication, it is unlikely that you will feed back your total response to the speaker's message.

4. **Unlimited feedback.** With good friends and in informal situations, such as discussions or personal one-to-one meetings, there is a greater opportunity for unlimited feedback. Each person may respond to the other in terms of feelings, differences, sharing, or self-disclosure. Unlimited feedback is more likely to occur in conversations where people regard each other as equals and in which an ongoing relationship has been built upon trust.

Each of these situations is an encounter in which one person speaks to someone else or to a group of people. However, the opportunity to respond to the message is different. Thus, the amount and kind of feedback given and received varies. People generally feel they understand messages more clearly when two-way or unlimited feedback situations exist. And people certainly are more involved in the communication process when they have a chance to participate in the encounter.

BASIS OF FEEDBACK

The more we know about ourselves, you and I, the better we will understand why we respond as we do. This knowledge and understanding will help us to be better communicators with others. Let's look at some theories about ego states, life positions, and attitudes, and note how they affect our feedback to oral messages.

Ego States

Eric Berne, an American psychiatrist, developed a system of analyzing human interaction called **transactional analysis.** He observed that people consistently demonstrate three distinctly different patterns of behavior, or **ego states,** that are based on past feelings and experiences. Berne labeled these ego states that compose the total personality as the Parent, the Adult, and the Child. The **Parent** ego state is composed of behavior that is copied from parents or authority figures. The **Adult** ego state is the rational, coping part of the personality. The **Child** ego state is behavior that is preserved from childhood. Figure 3-3 summarizes these ego states.

It helps to think of each personality as a composite of three ego states in which only one ego state operates at a time. The Parent is that part of your personality which plays back the stored-up tapes of all the experiences of

FIGURE 3-3

The ego states: Parent, Adult, and Child.

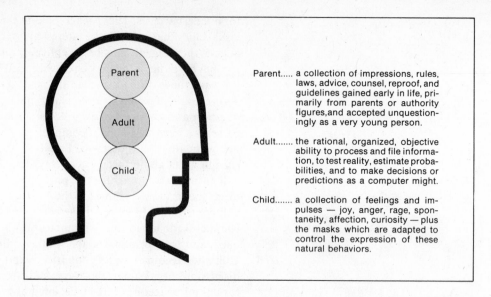

Parent..... a collection of impressions, rules, laws, advice, counsel, reproof, and guidelines gained early in life, primarily from parents or authority figures,and accepted unquestioningly as a very young person.

Adult....... the rational, organized, objective ability to process and file information, to test reality, estimate probabilities, and to make decisions or predictions as a computer might.

Child....... a collection of feelings and impulses — joy, anger, rage, spontaneity, affection, curiosity — plus the masks which are adapted to control the expression of these natural behaviors.

"The most important person to listen to is oneself, and our most important task is to develop an ear that can really hear what we are saying."

Sydney J. Harris

your early years. The Adult is that unemotional, intellectual ability which has learned to gather and process data and to cope logically. The Child emerges when you act spontaneously or naturally, just as you did as a child. Because the speech messages and nonverbal behavior of each ego state are observably different, an alert person can identify the particular ego state of another. By being aware of your words and actions, you can also recognize your own ego states.

These ego states relate to feedback because they provide the motivation for your intrapersonal (within yourself) and interpersonal (between yourself and others) responses. For example, if you are expected to give a speech to your class, these thoughts may run through your head:

Parent: "You never were good at public speaking. You are much better at athletics." Or, "Of course you can do it. You're just as good as they are."
Adult: "If it is expected, I'd better prepare the speech. If I don't have to be first, I can watch others and use their presentations as a model. Then I will handle the situation better."
Child: "I just can't get up there in front of all those people and talk."

Notice that these ego states provide different kinds of observable behavior. In the Parent ego state you may sound just like one of your parents. You may wrinkle your brow or purse your lips. In the Child ego state, you jump for joy at a winning score or burst into tears of rage. Rather than being childish in an unpleasant sense, this behavior is childlike in wonder and curiosity. This ego state contributes delightfully to the whole personality. The Adult ego state generally is oriented toward reality and toward testing what is observed. In this ego state, you consider reflectively, write down information, and weigh alternatives.

The verbal messages of the three ego states tend to be different. Different ego states may motivate the use of different words, as shown in Figure 3-4. The messages from your Parent ego state may be critical ("I told you that you should study more") or nurturing ("Let me show you how to do that"). Messages from your Adult ego state will be neutral ("Do I understand you to say the exchange rate is eight to one?"), or they may identify the difference between fact and inference ("It is my opinion that we should hold

FIGURE 3-4

Typical phrases you might use in each ego state. These will help you recognize from which state you or someone else may be reacting.

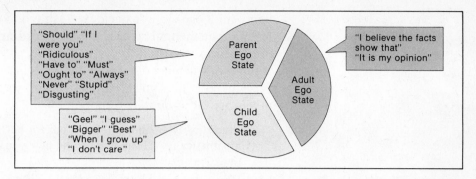

Source: Caroline Reynolds, *Dimensions in Personal Development* (Cincinnati: South-Western Publishing Co., 1977), p. 319.

a second meeting"). But messages from your Child ego state include "If only . . ." and "I wish . . ." statements. In brief, your different ego states motivate different responses or feedback:

Parent responses—Those critical or protective statements that reflect your judgments, values, or prejudices.

Adult responses—Those rational or intellectual observations that seek information, identify problems, clarify choices, reflect ideas, offer interpretations, report details, verify sources, and check understanding.

Child responses—Those responses that identify internal feelings or emotions.

Life Positions

A second way of analyzing feedback is to examine the basic position that you hold in regard to yourself and others. In his book *Scripts People Live*, Claude Steiner explains Eric Berne's belief that there are four basic life positions. These life positions are based on the feelings that people have about themselves and others. They are:

1. I'm OK, you're OK.
2. I'm OK, you're not OK.
3. I'm not OK, you're OK.
4. I'm not OK, you're not OK.

The first position is the central position. As people shift into the other three positions, they become increasingly disturbed and unhappy, unable to function in a satisfying way with others in social settings. Claude Steiner says:

The "I'm OK, you're OK" life position is the position people need to have in order to achieve their fullest potential. It is not intended to promote the notion that all of people's actions are acceptable. The existential position "I'm OK, you're OK" is a point of view about people apart from their actions and power, a point of view required in intimate, close relationships in order for emotional and social well-being to be possible. Berne implies that this attitude is not only a good point of view to hold but a true one as well.[2]

In other words, you can choose the "I'm OK, you're OK" position because you are born OK. If you move away from this position, you can use

---

[2] Claude Steiner, *Scripts People Live* (New York: Grove Press, 1974), p. 2.

your Adult ego state to decide to respond to others from the OK position. Rather than mentally repeat Parent recordings of earlier experiences which prejudice your attitudes, you can decide to perceive others as OK. In this case, then, you will not respond to others in critical or evaluative ways. This decision influences your feedback. If, for example, you decide that you and others are OK, you may respond:

Optimistically—"I hope it works out for both of us."
Empathetically—"I can understand how you feel, and I'll consider this when I make my decision."
Confidently—"All right. Let's try it your way."
Gracefully—"I guess I'm wrong."
Caringly—"I want to do whatever I can to help."

On the other hand, if you respond from position 2, 3, or 4, you may feed back:

Aggressively—"Why don't you be quiet before I get angry and hit you?"
Disparagingly—"Why can't you ever get anything right?"
Authoritatively—"I'm not asking you, I'm telling you."
Apathetically—"I really don't care what you do."
Dogmatically—"This is the way we have always done it, so don't you dare change it."
Loftily—"I really don't have time for chit-chat."
Critically—"Can't you do it any better than that?"
Defensively—"It's not my fault that this is incorrect. She checked my work."
Cynically—"She got the job because her father is the boss. I didn't have a chance."
Pessimistically—"I'll never get the sales account."
Reluctantly—"I'll do it *if* you think I should."

The important thing to remember about the I'm OK, you're OK position is that you make your decision rationally and then live by your decision in your relationships with others.

Attitudes—Competition and Cooperation

Your communication is more than a series of transactions or isolated feedback responses. It is a pattern of behavior that takes you through the good times as well as through the bad times. For example, you have learned ways of behaving when conflicts arise. Your attitude toward the other person is likely to be either *cooperative* or *competitive*. You may perceive a situation as a win/lose situation in which you compete to come out ahead of someone else. You may respond:

Defensively—to protect yourself.
Competitively—to get ahead of the other person.
Manipulatively—to maneuver the other person to act as you want the person to act.
Negatively—by withdrawing from the situation, rejecting the other person, or surrendering and playing the martyr role.
Aggressively—by striking out physically or verbally at the other person.

Cooperative attitudes are found in those who perceive encounters with others as win/win situations. These are the people to whom you are attracted. These magical people seem to have outgoing personalities, physical attractiveness, and charm. They care about what you think and feel, and they express this interest. One of the primary characteristics of these people is self-acceptance. They like themselves. They see their faults and virtues in a realistic way, and accept their humanness with all its imperfections. Because they accept themselves, they have the ability to accept others. They can laugh, enjoy, and respond openly with little anxiety about being undercut, criticized, or ridiculed. When you are with such people, your feedback is often open and free. It is difficult to resist the invitation to be spontaneous and cooperative when someone opens the communication door. It is also difficult to refuse a win/win (cooperative) invitation.

GIVING AND RECEIVING FEEDBACK

Not all the feedback you receive will be positive and helpful. But feedback is one of the ways you learn about yourself and the effects of your behavior. You learn from all the verbal and nonverbal feedback you receive.

Receiving Feedback

Feedback from other people will be of value to you only if you are aware of it and watching for it. The following suggestions will help you to be more open to the feedback you get.

1. Train your senses to observe accurately.
   a. Use your eyes to see nonverbal messages.
   b. Use your ears to hear vocal messages.
   c. Watch your own feedback and how it is received.

PHOTO 3-3

Cooperative attitudes can lead to free and open feedback.

2. Overcome external communication barriers.
  a. Limit the amount of information in your messages so that they can be understood clearly.
  b. Organize what you say so that others can follow your ideas.
  c. Select appropriate times for saying what you need to say.
3. Overcome internal barriers regarding the people you talk to.
  a. Build a climate of trust so that others feel comfortable about speaking honestly to you.
  b. Make it easy for others to tell you they do not understand.
  c. Take into account the gaps between you and others, such as differences in age, cultural or educational backgrounds, etc.
  d. Reduce defensiveness by not attacking others verbally, not showing superiority or snobbishness, or not sounding as if you know it all.
4. Be sure you are ready to accept feedback honestly before you ask others for criticism or evaluation.

Giving Positive Feedback

You are an alive, responsive human being who encounters situations that stir up angry feelings or frustrations every day. It is easy to feed back positive responses when you are cheerful, enthusiastic, or satisfied. But a skillful communicator uses the feedback tool consciously and carefully. In giving feedback, you can:

1. Avoid these inappropriate responses:
  a. Interrupting another speaker.
  b. Interjecting remarks that are not related to the message received.
  c. Responding by going off on a tangent.
  d. Pushing your personal judgment on someone else.
  e. Reacting angrily with an inconsistent remark.
  f. Ignoring the speaker.
2. Provide these appropriate responses:
  a. Practice checking for content by paraphrasing.
  b. Indicate your understanding by identifying the speaker's intent or feelings.
  c. Practice giving a clear indication of how much of the message you received:
    (1) Be honest about the depth of your understanding.
    (2) Be clear about your feelings at the time.
3. Provide appropriate nonverbal feedback:
  a. Use silence if you cannot find anything positive to feed back.
  b. Use touch (a friendly pat, a sympathetic hug) when you have no words to express your feelings.
  c. Check to be sure your nonverbal messages do not contradict the words you speak.

CHAPTER SUMMARY

Hearing is a physical means of receiving verbal sounds; listening is an active mental process that requires attention and comprehension; feedback is the response to a speaker's message. What you choose to listen to, understand, and interpret affects your response to the speaker. This feedback controls the way your communication proceeds.

A skillful listener focuses on the content of a message, identifies the speaker's purpose and major ideas, determines lines of reasoning, and understands the basis of the information. In interacting with another, the effective listener uses Listening Rule One (Feed back the content) to rephrase or summarize the message before responding, and Listening Rule Two (Feed back for intent) to determine why a speaker has expressed an idea. By withholding judgment and by empathizing with unexpressed feelings, the listener keeps communication flowing. As an audience member, a good listener comes prepared to concentrate and retain.

Feedback is important to the speaker as a means of determining how she or he is being received and also as a means of improving further messages. Feedback helps the receiver shape the direction of the communication. Although ego states, life positions, and attitudes determine many preset responses, these can be changed to improve feedback responses.

WORKSHOP ACTIVITIES

LISTENING EXERCISES *(Quiz)*

Briefing: Your instructor will read aloud nine selections of different types of material. Each exercise requires you to listen for different things. Answer the questions as your instructor rereads statements from each of the selections, or follow the directions given.

Listening for Information

Purpose: To listen for specific information. To evaluate listening and recall skills.

Listening Exercise #1: "Businessperson's Calendar." *Listen and follow directions.*

_____

Now listen as your teacher reads ten statements. Write "true" or "false" next to the number of the statement.

1. _____ 6. _____

2. _____ 7. _____

3. _____ 8. _____

4. _____ 9. _____

5. _____ 10. _____

Score _____

Listening Exercise #2: "Addressing Mail in the Eighties." *Listen for facts.*

1. _____   6. _____
2. _____   7. _____
3. _____   8. _____
4. _____   9. _____
5. _____   10. _____

Score _____

Listening Exercise #3: "Getting On and Off the Podium." *Listen for specific words and ideas.*

1. _____   6. _____
2. _____   7. _____
3. _____   8. _____
4. _____   9. _____
5. _____   10. _____

Score _____

Listening Exercise #4: "The Telephone Answering Service." *Listen to distinguish fact from opinion.* Listen as your teacher reads the selection aloud. Some statements will be repeated. Write "fact" or "opinion" after each statement is read.

1. _____   6. _____
2. _____   7. _____
3. _____   8. _____
4. _____   9. _____
5. _____   10. _____

Score _____

Listening for Content

Purpose: To increase skills in listening for specific content of oral messages.

Listening Exercise #5: "Dear Executive." *Listen to distinguish between fact and opinion.*

1. _____   6. _____
2. _____   7. _____
3. _____   8. _____
4. _____   9. _____
5. _____   10. _____

Score _____

Listening Exercise #6: "Modern Shipping." *Listen to determine the meaning of the following words from the context of the selection.* Write the meaning.

1. containerization _____
2. maritime _____
3. innovation _____
4. breakbulk _____
5. vessels _____

Score _____

Listening Exercise #7: "Sales Training Can Make the Difference." *Listen for general concepts and for specific details.*

1. _____
2. _____
3. _____
4. _____
5. _____

Score _____

Listening Exercise #8: "Time Theft—A Threat to Our Economy." *Listen to determine the main ideas.* Write the ideas in the order that the speaker stated them.

General Idea _____

_____

Main Idea I _____

_____

Main Idea II _____

_____

Main Idea III _____

_____

Main Idea IV _____

_____

Score _____

Listening Exercise #9: "Time Theft—A Threat to Our Economy." Listen to the same article again. This time *listen for supporting details.* Write the *thing* compared, contrasted, defined, explained, etc.

Comparison _____

Contrast _____

Definition _____

Example _____

Explanation _____

Score _____

Number of Correct Answers _____

PERSONAL LISTENING EVALUATION *(Individual Activity)*

Purpose: To evaluate personal listening habits.

Briefing: Follow the instructions below. Circle those items in which you need improvement.

List the reasons you tune out a speaker, such as boredom with the speaker, lack of interest in the subject, etc.

1.
2.
3.
4.
5.

List the ways you avoid listening, such as retreating into your own thoughts, interrupting, etc.

1.
2.
3.
4.
5.

Identify words, such as *cancer* or *examination*, that are negative stimulators for you.

1.
2.
3.
4.
5.

Identify words, such as *appreciate* and *thank you*, that are positive stimulators for you.

1.
2.
3.
4.
5.

Why is it important for you to listen to ideas that are contrary to your own beliefs?

_____

_____

_____

Explain below what the following phrases mean to you:

To listen with a rebellious ear. _____

_____

To listen with a deaf ear. _____

_____

With which individual in your life do you most need to improve your listening habits?

_____

A GIFT YOU MIGHT LIKE TO GIVE *(Individual Reference)*

Amanda is a 19-year-old student who works part-time to pay for her school expenses. In the middle of December last year, Amanda realized that she did not have enough money to buy Christmas presents for many of the people she loved. She already had purchased a present for her boyfriend. She had enough money for small remembrances for her mother and father, and a doll for her little sister. But she wished she had enough money to buy gifts for her favorite teacher, her best friend, her aunt, the neighbor who gave her a ride to class every day, and several good friends at her church.

Amanda was taking a course in speech communication at her university. One day she got an idea for gifts. She bought Christmas cards that were appropriate for each of her friends and wrote the following message on each.

```
Dear _____,

This card entitles you to three hours of
active listening from me anytime you need it
in the year to come.  I promise undivided,
concerned attention as you work out the problem,
and I will listen with encouragement and
patience.  Please feel free to call me at
991-4325 whenever you need me.

                    Affectionately,

                    Amanda Connelly
                    Amanda Connelly
```

CHECKLISTS FOR GIVING AND RECEIVING INSTRUCTIONS *(Individual and Group Activity)*

Briefing: Below is a list of suggestions for giving instructions. On page 100 is a list of suggestions for listening to instructions. Read each list. Check those behaviors in the first list that you believe speakers should perform. Check those behaviors in the second list that you believe a receiver should perform.

When giving instructions, speakers should:

1. _____ Ask if the receivers understand the language.

2. _____ Check to see if the receivers know specialized terms for things, processes, or personnel.

3. _____ Include personalized stories.

4. _____ Explain that the method presented is the only method that can be used.

5. _____ Speak loudly, clearly, and give instructions slowly.

6. _____ Establish a peer-to-peer relationship with the receivers, rather than an instructor-pupil relationship.

7. _____ Ask receivers to repeat instructions in order to check understanding.

8. _____ Use a step-by-step organization by breaking the ideas into easy stages.

9. _____ Use eye contact, facial expressions, and gestures to reinforce the verbal message.

10. _____ Have patience with questions from the receivers and take ample time to answer them.

11. _____ Explain the purpose or goal of the instructions.

12. _____ Identify from whose point of view the instructions are given when indicating "right" or "left."

13. _____ Include information about the desirability of the system presented.

14. _____ Provide visual explanations and accompany them with appropriate, purposeful movements and gestures when possible.

15. _____ Take a good position for communication by facing the receivers so that all can see.

16. _____ Require perfection in performing the instructions immediately.

17. _____ Assume that the receivers are interested and knowledgeable in the subject.

18. _____ Provide a favorable environment for listening by reducing noise and outside distractions.

19. _____ Expect and look for feedback from the receivers.

20. _____ Use shared experience to get understanding.

21. _____ Give the instructions only once, because it is the receivers' responsibility to understand them.

22. _____ Stand facing only one part of the group.

23. _____ Repeat the instructions several times in the same way to ensure understanding.

24. _____ Give only a few steps at a time.

25. _____ Assume that it is unnecessary to prepare to give instructions because of expert knowledge of the subject.

When receiving instructions, listeners should:

1. _____ Maintain eye contact with speakers.

2. _____ Keep an open mind and forget preconditioning (past experience) that might block receiving of the message.

3. _____ Find something else to think about if the information being presented is familiar.

4. _____ Avoid wasting time by asking the speaker questions.

5. _____ Concentrate on the speaker's verbal and nonverbal messages.

6. _____ Relate the information to previous or similar experiences.

7. _____ Verbally interject related personal experiences into the material being explained.

8. _____ Verify with other listeners what the speaker has said.

9. _____ Not take notes, because this prevents listeners from listening.

10. _____ Feed back honest responses. When confused, say so.

11. _____ Ask for clarification when terminology is not clear.

12. _____ Repeat what is said in their own words.

Debriefing: Join five other students for a group discussion on how each checked the speaker and receiver lists. You do not have to agree, but give the reasons for your choices. Ask one person to sit outside the group and observe the discussion. The observer will complete the form on page 101 and give an oral report on listening skills to the group at the end of the discussion.

OBSERVER REPORT OF GOOD LISTENING BEHAVIOR *(Oral Report)*

Write each group member's name:

1. _____
2. _____
3. _____
4. _____
5. _____

Watch for the following types of listening behavior. On the blank line following the behavior, write the number of the group member or members who exhibited the behavior. On line 7, write in other good listening behaviors and the numbers of the students who exhibited them.

1. Leaned forward to increase concentration: _____
2. Started to interrupt but then continued to listen: _____
3. Gave signals of attention, such as a nod, a smile, etc.: _____
4. Gave verbal signals, such as "Yes, I see," etc.: _____
5. Maintained eye contact with speaker: _____
6. Changed position to see the speaker better: _____
7. Other good listening behaviors: _____

_____
_____
_____
_____
_____

After the discussion has ended, move into the group and share your observations with them.

TAKE A MESSAGE *(Group Activity)*

Purpose: To increase awareness of listening skills. To practice techniques for improving listening in a situation where the speaker and the listener cannot see each other.

Briefing: When you are unable to see the speaker, receiving information accurately and completely and relaying information correctly may be difficult.

1. Work in groups of five or six. On a separate piece of paper, each group member will spend three to four minutes writing a business message which will include:

   a. The name of a company.
   b. The names of people in the company and their positions.
   c. Specific information, such as details, numbers, figures, etc. (Example: 36 boxes, January 6, 1983, $15.65 per order.)

2. One member of the group will be the sender; another member will be the receiver. A third member of the group will go to another part of the room in order to avoid hearing the message the first time it is given. (Other group members will observe this exercise the first time and will participate the next time.)

3. The sender will turn his or her back to the receiver and give the speech message. (The sender may pretend to be telephoning, speaking over a loudspeaker system, etc.) The sender should send a fairly complex, yet fair and realistic business message in order to test the receiver's skills.

4. The receiver should follow these suggestions as the message is being sent:

   a. Listen carefully.
   b. Take notes on key information.
   c. Ask questions.
   d. Request repetition of minute or difficult details.
   e. Check spelling.

5. The receiver will then repeat the spoken message to the supervisor (third group member). Other members of the group will verify the accuracy of the information.

6. Change roles and do the exercise several times.

Debriefing:

1. What prevented the accurate reception of the speech message?
2. What behavior is needed to ensure accuracy?
3. Identify some of your individual strengths and weaknesses in listening.

WHAT HAPPENED TO MY ORDER?* *(Group Activity)*

Purpose: To provide barriers to communication. To create a business situation in which a team must communicate five orders correctly from a salesperson through the home office by means of oral communication.

Briefing: Each team represents a company home office that receives and processes special orders from sales personnel in the field. Each team (company) competes with other teams by filling orders accurately and quickly through oral communication. The company that completes the orders accurately for the most months during the period of January through May will win.

Divide into teams of five players. Each team is composed of:

A. Incoming order clerk—gets the order and passes it on.

B. Process clerk—checks inventory and passes the order on.

C. Warehouse worker—fills order and passes it on.

D. Accounting clerk—credits account and passes order on.

E. Shipping clerk—writes orders in the spaces provided below and on page 104.

Decide who will fill each position. The positions (work stations) must be scattered around the room. Play the game quickly. Follow these instructions:

1. Team member *A* goes to the telephone reception center (an instructor or a designated student who is using the teacher's manual) and gets the order orally. *A* tells *B*, *B* tells *C*, *C* tells *D*, *D* tells *E*, and *E* writes the order on the appropriate order form below or on page 104.

2. As soon as *A* has given *B* the first order, *A* may go to the telephone reception center for the next order.

3. When all teams have completed the January order forms, the instructor will check them and credit the company that finishes first with the most accurate order form. If the first team to finish has not completed the orders accurately, the second team to finish may receive credit if its orders are correct.

4. For the March orders, you are to figure and total the amounts of the orders. On the April orders, a "distraction factor" (additional complication) will be added to the exercise. On the May orders, each team will be pressured additionally with three distraction factors.

January Orders:

1. _____

2. _____

3. _____

4. _____

5. _____

---

* Adapted by permission from the Learning Handbook, *Creating and Using Learning Games* by Craig Pearson and Joseph Marfuggi. © 1975 by Education Today Company, Inc., 530 University Avenue, Palo Alto, California 94301.

February Orders:

1. _____
2. _____
3. _____
4. _____
5. _____

March Orders:

1. _____
2. _____
3. _____
4. _____
5. _____

April Orders:

1. _____
2. _____
3. _____
4. _____
5. _____

May Orders:

1. _____
2. _____
3. _____
4. _____
5. _____

Debriefing:

1. What did you learn about listening from this activity?

2. Why is it important for people who work together to cooperate with each other?

3. What conclusions can you draw about communication in business from performing this activity?

LISTENING RULE ONE—FEED BACK THE CONTENT *(Group Activity)*

Purpose: To participate in a discussion process. To practice Listening Rule One.

Briefing: Work in groups of five or six people. Select one member of the group to serve as referee. Choose one of the following topics for discussion. Try to give personal examples that support or disprove your ideas about the topic. Express your feelings freely about the subject. Use Listening Rule One and feed back the content. *No member of the group may speak on the subject unless she or he has summarized what the person before has said to that speaker's satisfaction.* The referee will remind the group of Listening Rule One whenever necessary. Keep discussions to a minimum of ten minutes.

Topics for Discussion (choose one):

1. Give some methods of reaching a person who will not listen to what you say.

2. How can you encourage a person to speak freely about herself or himself?

3. What methods can you use to get someone at a higher level of authority than you, such as a boss, supervisor, or work leader, to listen to your ideas?

4. How do your attitudes and beliefs affect the accuracy of your listening?

5. Give examples of situations in which your personal bias interfered with the accuracy of your listening.

6. If someone criticizes you and you feel defensive, how do you respond without cutting off communication?

Debriefing:

1. How many times did your referee have to remind you of Listening Rule One?

2. How did you feel when someone accurately summarized or rephrased what you said?

3. What effects did Listening Rule One have on your group discussion?

LISTENING RULE TWO—FEED BACK FOR INTENT *(Group Activity)*

Purpose: To increase listening awareness. To discover clues that reveal the intent of the speaker. To determine if the feelings and attitudes of the listener affect reception of the message.

Briefing: Every speech message has two parts: content (the words actually spoken) and intent (the feelings or implications conveyed by the tone of voice). Work together in groups of four or five. Take turns role playing the people who are giving the six messages on the following page. When it is your turn, say the words in a way that will convey one of the four "intents" listed below the message and see if the other members can identify the "meaning" you intended. Discuss any misunderstandings that occur.

1. Boss (to employee): "You're late." (content)

   Which intent?

   a. "You have not arrived on time."
   b. "You're late again."
   c. "This has never happened before."
   d. "I'm surprised at you."

2. Manager (to worker): "I'm sorry, but I can't see you now." (content)

   Which intent?

   a. "Can't you see what a busy person I am?"
   b. "I really do wish I had time to talk to you."
   c. "Don't bother me. I don't want to discuss it."
   d. "Sorry—that's the way it is."

3. Worker (to fellow worker): "Your presentation was great." (content)

   Which intent?

   a. "I wish I could do as well as you do."
   b. "It really wasn't all that good, but I don't want to say so."
   c. ". . . but not as good as mine was."
   d. "I'm surprised that you did so well."

4. Department Head (to employees): "The contest is open to all employees." (content)

   Which intent?

   a. ". . . and each of you had better submit an entry."
   b. "I really don't care whether any of you enter or not."
   c. "I want a winner from this department."
   d. "What a waste of time."

5. Worker (to fellow worker): "Are you through with that report?" (content)

   Which intent?

   a. "Gee, but you're slow."
   b. "You sure are not doing your share of the work."
   c. "I just wanted to know."
   d. "They really are overworking you in this office."

6. Supervisor (to new salesperson): "You finally made a sale." (content)

   Which intent?

   a. "Good for you. You worked hard for it."
   b. "See, wasn't that easy?"
   c. "It sure took you long enough."
   d. "I was right. You should have been handling the customers that way all along."

Debriefing:

1. Give specific examples of the types of misunderstandings that occurred in your group. Why do you feel these misunderstandings occurred?

2. Does the way you listen have any bearing on your responses? Why?

3. A popular phrase in speech communication is: "Words don't mean—people mean." How does this phrase relate to this activity?

PRACTICE IN "FEED BACK THE CONTENT" *(Individual Activity)*

Purpose: To gain practice in the skill of restating the ideas of another person's message in your own words.

Briefing:

1. Focus on accurate decoding of the speaker's message.

2. Write the paraphrase as though you were feeding back a response that assures the speaker you understand the message.

3. Begin your feedback messages with such phrases as: "Are you saying . . . ?" "I hear you saying . . ." "Do I understand correctly that . . . ?" "Did I understand you to say . . . ?"

4. Remember that the purpose of this type of feedback is to show the speaker what you understood the message to mean. The speaker can then correct his or her message or tell you that you heard and interpreted correctly.

Example

Diana: "Don't wait on that bank customer. It will take 15 minutes and you won't get off for lunch."

Juanita: "Are you saying that the customer is slow?"

Diana: "No, I am saying that he always has ten transactions that he wants done." (Message explained)

Message One: "The company where I work has given a co-worker more seniority than people who have worked longer on the job because that co-worker is a minority group member."

Your Feedback:

Message Two: "The U.S. silver dollar has been shrinking in value for years—and it may soon shrink in size as well."

Your Feedback:

Message Three: "I heard a drug manufacturer say at a meeting recently that more than 10 million sleeping pills are taken by Americans each night and that the year's sale of aspirin has exceeded 11 million pounds. I'm sure the figure has increased since then."

Your Feedback:

PRACTICE IN "FEED BACK FOR INTENT" *(Individual Activity)*

Purpose: To gain practice in the skill of identifying the speaker's feelings that lie behind the verbal message.

Briefing:

1. Focus on the feelings or the reasons why the message was said.
2. Write as if you were responding to the speaker's nonverbal communication as well as listening to the words.
3. Begin with "I hear you saying . . ." "I sense that you are . . ." or "That makes you feel. . . ."
4. Read the messages aloud as if they were spoken.

Message One (clasping hands and rubbing them): "I wish I could understand your brother. He is so hard to reason with and he won't meet anyone halfway."

Your Response:

Message Two (while nervously pacing around the room and repeatedly looking out the window): "Oh, he'll be here any minute. He's very dependable."

Your Response:

Message Three (after handing you a sheaf of papers and looking at her watch): "Here. Take care of these for me, will you?"

Your Response:

Message Four (in a high, forced tone, while avoiding eye contact with you): "Of course there's nothing wrong."

Your Response:

PARTNERS IN IMPROVEMENT *(Pairs and Group Activity)*

Purpose: To work in pairs and to feed back constructive criticism about the use of sending and receiving skills. To work with a group in a problem-solving activity.

Briefing: This activity requires you and your partner to observe each other as you participate in a task-oriented project with a group. It also gives you the opportunity to feed back your observations privately to your partner. Follow the steps listed below.

1. Select a classmate as a partner. Identify yourselves as student #1 and student #2.

2. For the first part of the exercise, student #1 will be the group participant and student #2 will be the observer. For the second part of the exercise this will be reversed.

3. Student #1 is to read "Color Mates" below and write down the answer.

4. Student #2 is to read the Partner Observer Report on page 110.

5. Then all of the #1 students will gather in groups of five students each.

6. Each #2 student will sit outside her or his partner's group in order to observe the partner.

7. Each group of #1 students is to arrive at a single solution to the problem. When this is completed, the group may submit its answer to the instructor. (Answers are in the teacher's manual.)

8. Each pair of partners then will sit together for a private consultation. The #2 partner will explain to the #1 partner the results compiled on the Partner Observer Report and will give #1 the page to keep for a record.

9. Reverse the process using the second problem below, "Busy as Bees."

Problem for Student #1: Color Mates

A cabbie picked up three young couples and took them to a discotheque. One girl was dressed in red, one in green, and one in blue. The boys wore outfits of the same three colors. When all three couples were dancing, the boy in red danced close to the girl in green and said: "Isn't it funny, Mable? Not one of us is dancing with a partner dressed in the same color." What color is the partner of the girl in red wearing?

Individual Answer _____   Group Answer _____

Problem for Student #2: Busy as Bees

Four college girls who share an apartment are listening to an album of music while one of them does her nails, one does her hair, one puts on makeup, and one is reading. 1. Myra isn't doing her nails and isn't reading. 2. Maud is not putting on makeup and is not doing her nails. 3. If Myra is not putting on makeup, Mona is not doing her nails. 4. Mary is not reading and she is not doing her nails. 5. Mona is not reading and she is not doing her nails. What is each girl doing?

Myra _____   Maud_____   Mary _____   Mona_____

Source: From *Aha! Insight* by Martin Gardner. W. H. Freeman and Company. Copyright © 1978.

PARTNER OBSERVER REPORT *(Report to Partner)*

Observer's Name _____ Partner's Name _____

Briefing: Carefully observe your partner during her or his participation in the group discussion. Be prepared to discuss privately the results of your observation with your partner by providing feedback in a tactful, helpful, and constructive manner. Use the questions below as a guide. Make notes on this sheet, tear it out, and give it to your partner.

General Skills:

1. How many times did your partner talk during a particular portion of the discussion? Keep a record for at least ten minutes. Indicate whether your partner spoke at the beginning, middle, or end of the discussion.

   Number of Times Your Partner Spoke: _____

   _____

   When: _____

   _____

2. What specific nonverbal behavior, such as movements, gestures, facial expressions, and tone of voice, did you observe that seemed helpful? List these behaviors.

Receiver Skills: Identify specific receiver skills that were demonstrated by your partner during the discussion. Did your partner:

1. *Listen well* by maintaining eye contact with the speaker, leaning forward, nodding, etc.?

2. *Decode accurately* by feeding back the content of the speaker's message (the words and ideas) before responding?

3. *Decode empathetically* by feeding back the speaker's message for intent (feelings and motives) before responding?

4. *Ask questions* by requesting more information, further details, definitions of words, and examples, or by inviting the speaker to share more deeply?

5. *Give specific, positive feedback?*

BUSINESS COMMUNICATION PROBLEMS *(Group Discussion)*

Purpose: To use the problem-solving method to discuss business communication problems.

Briefing: Work in groups of five or six. Choose one student to be the observer and fill out the Observer Report on page 113. Select one of the following cases to discuss.

1. One person in the group will read the case narrative aloud. Others will volunteer to take the speaking parts that follow each narrative.

2. Identify and discuss the communication barriers in the case.

3. Examine any external factors in the case (outside of verbal communication) that may have contributed to the problem.

4. Role play again. Let each employee in the case describe how he or she would like things to be.

5. List the solutions that are available to each. What action can each person take? What choices does each person have?

6. Each group should make a recommendation about a solution to the case. Who should do what? How should it be done? What obstacles need to be overcome?

Case 1: Too Busy for Feedback

Ruthie worked as the concession cashier for the Gemini Drive-In Theater in Dallas. According to her job description, Ruthie's work entailed ringing up food prices and tax and collecting money from customers for their purchases. Every hour she was to check her register to determine how much money had been collected within the hour. Then she was to write the amount on a piece of paper and submit it to the manager, Mr. Vinson, at the end of the work night.

On Monday night, there were 50 people inside the snack bar, which was designed to hold only 30 people. Ruthie did not take hourly readings. Rather, she filled the customers' orders for cold drinks, popcorn, hot dogs, etc. At the end of the night shift, the manager asked Ruthie for her hourly readings. Ruthie replied that she did not have them. When she said good night and left for home, the manager did not respond. The following evening when Ruthie arrived for work, the manager fired her for not doing her job.

Ruthie:	Oh, Mother, I'm so mad I don't know what to do. I've been fired, and Mr. Vinson didn't tell me until I reported for work tonight. That's really a raw deal. He could have said something to me about it last night before I left work. We had a really big crowd in the concession stand, and I just couldn't count the money in the register when people were standing in line waiting for popcorn and soft drinks. I can't do everything at once. I didn't tell him how much money was collected every hour. He should have stressed that counting the money was more important than collecting it—if that's the way he feels. I'm really angry—because he fired me with no notice and because his demands are too high. Why doesn't he count the money himself if it is so important? He just plays manager and lets me do all the work. It's just not fair.
Mr. Vinson:	When I hired Ruthie, I made it perfectly clear that she was to take an accurate count of the money in the register every hour. She knew it was a part of the job. She's just too people-oriented and she doesn't like handling money accurately. I was right to fire her. I can't have someone who doesn't do her job right. I'll have to find someone who can handle the job description.

Case 2: All Wrong

Inventory is one way that a business gets feedback on the quantity of stock or supplies on hand. At the Liberty House Department Store, all employees are required to participate in the annual inventory. John Cooper, a sales clerk, was assigned to the toy department.

All new employees were called to a meeting where the mechanics of taking inventory were explained by Ms. Delgado, a manager. John had been hired since the previous inventory and was considered a new employee. His supervisor, Mr. Seleg, told him to attend the meeting. But John told his supervisor that he was familiar with inventory procedure and did not attend the meeting.

Hours after the store-wide inventory was completed, John was called into Ms. Delgado's office and informed that his area was incorrectly inventoried. John had inventoried the entire toy department on only a few inventory forms. The company, however, required that each shelf have its own inventory sheet. John and his supervisor were required to stay overtime and do the entire department inventory again with no compensation.

Mr. Seleg: Well, that John certainly has caused a problem by his stubbornness and "know-it-all" attitude. I told him to attend the inventory meeting. It was a direct order. But he disobeyed me and then, by doing the toy inventory all wrong, made me look bad to Ms. Delgado. Now I have to stay late and miss the basketball game. Darned kid, it's all his fault for not obeying orders.

John: How was I to know they had changed the inventory forms since last year? I had checked with the other salespeople and they told me how it was done last year and I'm perfectly familiar with the method. Now they want each shelf inventoried on a separate sheet. That's a bunch of extra work and not at all necessary. Now Old Seleg is going to hold it over me because he had to stay late. Sometimes you just can't win.

Case 3: Feedback Is Essential to Business

The Landsdown Furniture Company has three departments: Administrative, Merchandising, and Advertising. Mr. Jay is the Merchandising Manager. Mrs. Moore, the buyer of case goods, works directly for Mr. Jay. Mr. Perry is the Advertising Manager.

Every Monday morning, Mr. Jay and Mr. Perry meet to discuss future sales and promotions for the company. On Monday morning, October 24, Mrs. Moore informed Mr. Jay that she had purchased some bedroom sets and wanted to promote them for a sale on November 15. Mr. Jay and Mr. Perry met and discussed these new items and planned a campaign for the promotion of the bedroom sets. The merchandise was to be in the warehouse by November 10, thereby giving the stock clerks time to display the furniture in the store's showroom.

According to company procedure, the ads were released for the bedroom set sale on Friday, November 14. Mrs. Moore checked with Receiving on Friday afternoon, November 14, to determine why the merchandise was not as yet displayed. She was told by the stock clerks that it had not yet arrived. Mrs. Moore telephoned the manufacturer in Salem, North Carolina. She was told that there had been a delay in production and that the Landsdown Furniture Company would not be receiving the merchandise for another two weeks. By this time, it was 4:00 p.m. and too late to cancel the ads that were to appear in the next morning's newspaper.

Mrs. Moore: I'm simply furious and I don't know whether I'm angrier at the manufacturer for not notifying me that the bedroom order would be delayed, or at Jay and Perry for not verifying the arrival of the merchandise before they released the ad. I know that I'm getting the blame for the foul-up, but they could have called Receiving before they released the ad. They've done that before. Well, I know that Mr. Jay is going to call me in for a reprimand interview and I'm just not going to take the blame.

Mr. Jay: That woman has caused us a great deal of embarrassment. It's her responsibility to be sure the goods have been shipped before she tells us to plan the promotion. I'm going to call her in for a strong reprimand. She won't get by with this sloppy behavior again. It makes my department look terrible when an ad appears in the paper and we don't have the merchandise.

Mr. Perry: Boy, is my face going to be red tomorrow when those ads come out and we don't have the bedroom sets on the floor. Those merchandising people are making us look like fools. I could have pulled the ads if they had notified me sooner that they hadn't received the furniture. Jay just is not in control of his department if he lets Moore get away with this.

Observer Report

Briefing: Keep a record of the signs of good listening behavior that you observed during the discussion. Write the name of each person who:

1. Summarized what a previous speaker said before commenting.

_____

2. Looked directly at the speaker.

_____

3. Gave verbal signals, such as "I see," "Go on," etc.

_____

4. Asked questions about what the speaker said.

_____

5. Leaned forward to increase concentration.

_____

6. Referred to a previous speaker.

_____

7. Reflected to the speaker what the listener was feeling.

_____

8. Gave nonverbal signals of attentive interest.

_____

9. Gave positive reinforcement by smiling, nodding, touching, etc.

_____

10. Pulled his or her chair closer to the speaker or group.

_____

11. Started to interrupt, but then continued to listen.

_____

12. Asked another person to speak louder.

_____

SAMPLE DEMONSTRATION SPEECH OUTLINE *(Individual Reference)*

Materials needed: Seven flags—red, yellow, green, checkered, black, blue, white

Introduction to the Thesis

Attention Step   **A.** (Wave checkered flag) Almost everyone who has been to the races knows what this flag means!

Involve Audience   **B.** How many have been to car races? How many have seen car races on TV?

Establish Self   **C.** Being a racing fan myself, I thought you'd like to know how the officials communicate with race drivers on the track.

Thesis: I'm going to describe and explain the use of these seven flags in racing.

Development of the Thesis (Body of speech)

Transition (I'm going to talk about two groups of flags; the first have general meanings for all race car drivers.)

Main Point   **I.** Let me explain the red, yellow, and green flags that apply to all drivers on the course.

     A. The green flag means the track is clear.
       1. Show flag—waved to signal start of race.
       2. Explain—drivers use it to "Go!"
     B. The next often-used flag is the yellow flag.
       1. Show flag—wave it to signal "Caution."
       2. Explain—car stalled, trash on track, warning, can be a frightening time.
     C. The red flag signals "Danger."
       1. Show flag—wave it to signal "Stop immediately!"
       2. Explain types of dangers.
       3. Describe—"heart-stopping experience."
       4. Example—first use (other than rain) at Indy 500 in 1969.

Transition (Now that I've explained the general uses of flags . . .)

Main Point   **II.** Let me discuss flags used to signal individual drivers.

     A. The blue flag with the orange stripe is the passing flag.
       1. Show flag—waved to signal "Slow driver."
       2. Explain—signals driver to proceed with care, new car on track not going as fast.
       3. Example—1983 Indy 500 race.
     B. The black flag warns a driver about his own behavior.
       1. Show flag—unfurled and waved; furled and pointed.
       2. Example—1963 Indy 500 race.
     C. The white flag indicates "There is only one more lap."
       1. Show flag—wave it.
       2. Describe—the flag drivers want to be first to see.
     D. The checkered flag is shaken at the winner.
       1. Example—1977 Indy 500.

Transition (Let me summarize for you.)

Conclusion

Summary   **A.** Officials communicate with drivers by means of flags; red, yellow, and green apply to all drivers; blue, black, white, and checkered signal to individual drivers.

Focus   **B.** Now that you know what the flags mean, you'll understand what's going on!

DEMONSTRATION SPEECH OUTLINE *(Individual Outline)*

Purpose: To present an informative speech in which you tell the class something they do not know. Time: 4-5 minutes.

Briefing: Select a topic to demonstrate, for example, a product (new phone system, pocket knife with 13 functions, etc.) or a process (how to balance a checkbook, how to fold letters for different-size envelopes, etc.). Draft your speech on scratch paper; prepare the outline below to turn in; practice speech orally using 3″ x 5″ cards; bring your materials to class on the day you speak.

Introduction to the Thesis

Attention Step   **A.**

Involve Audience   **B.**

Establish Self   **C.**

Thesis:

Development of the Thesis (Body of speech)

Transition (   )

Main Point   **I.**

Transition (   )

Main Point   **II.**

Transition (   )

Main Point **III.**

Transition (Let me summarize what I have told you.)

Conclusion

Summary **A.**

Focus   **B.**

CRITIQUE SHEET FOR DEMONSTRATION SPEECH *(Instructor's Evaluation)*

Briefing: Tear out this page and hand it to your teacher before you speak.

POSSIBLE POINTS: 100   (Each question: 10 points)

1.   Was the introduction to the thesis carefully planned to get attention, involve the audience, and establish the speaker's credentials?   _____

2.   Were the visual materials well planned so that the entire audience could see clearly?   _____

3.   Was the thesis clearly stated?   _____

4.   Were the main points clear enough so that the audience could write them down or remember them?   _____

5.   Was the speaker's voice loud enough to be heard easily and were the pronunciation of words and the articulation of sounds correct?   _____

6.   Did the speaker control nervous mannerisms, stand confidently, and maintain eye contact with all members of the audience?   _____

7.   Did the speaker seem enthusiastic, well prepared, and confident in the presentation?   _____

8.   Did the presentation meet the time requirement?   _____

9.   Did the conclusion summarize the thesis and main points and focus on the desired audience response?   _____

10.   Was the goal "to tell the audience something they did not know" fulfilled?   _____

Total   _____

Instructor's Comments:

CHECKLIST OF COMMUNICATION TERMS *(Quiz)*

Check your understanding of the communication terms used in this chapter. Write the number of the term in the blank preceding its definition. Note there are more terms than definitions.

	Definitions		**Terms**
a. _____	The ability to perceive from another person's view and to sense what that person is feeling.	**1.**	middle ear
		2.	content
b. _____	This feedback behavior is impulsive, natural, and spontaneous, and springs from one ego state.	**3.**	Listening Rule Two
		4.	empathy
		5.	Child ego state
		6.	intent
c. _____	A situation in which a speaker has no way of knowing how his or her message is being received.	**7.**	Listening Rule One
		8.	one-channel feedback
		9.	Adult ego state
d. _____	The feedback you use when you summarize or rephrase someone's message to explain what you heard.	**10.**	two-channel feedback
		11.	life positions
		12.	zero feedback
e. _____	The speaker's unspoken "why" or feelings about the message given.	**13.**	hearing
		14.	active listening
		15.	unlimited feedback
f. _____	The behavior patterns that Eric Berne labeled the Parent, the Adult, and the Child.	**16.**	Parent ego state
		17.	paraphrasing
		18.	ego states
g. _____	One of these is "I'm OK, you're not OK."	**19.**	inner ear
h. _____	The part of the ear that contains the hammer, anvil, and stirrup.		
i. _____	You use this when you feed back, "You seem pretty upset."		
j. _____	This is the ego state that says, "How disgusting!"		

CHAPTER 4

Let's Talk About the Business of Brushing Up Your Language Skills

The words you choose to speak (language) and the instrument with which you deliver the words (your voice) are two powerful tools of oral communication. This chapter will discuss how meaning is conveyed with language; the next chapter deals with the speaking voice. After you have read and discussed this chapter and have participated in the workshop activities, you should be able to do the following:

Chapter Objectives

1. Explain how language is used in thinking and speaking.
2. Compare the use of language to mapping a territory.
3. Differentiate between concrete and abstract levels of language.
4. Give specific examples of reporting, inferential, and judgmental language.
5. Name ways in which language can obstruct clear meaning.

"Perhaps of all the creations of human kind, language is the most astonishing."

Lytton Strachey.

You have inherited a vast body of word symbols that make up the message-producing system of spoken language. You select words to share your feelings, to express thoughts, to illuminate ideas, and to initiate action. You create oral messages that provide information, influence behavior, evaluate events, and frame your own unique way of looking at the world.

Through language, you turn your firsthand experiences into mental pictures that you react to and ponder. This thinking process uses language to blend the outer world with your personal inner world. You, therefore, create meaning through language, and you recreate meaning for others as you use language in speaking.

Words are powerful. For example, the sounds of language flow into patterns that can crackle with information:

"All new employees in Department H will report to the training session in Room 480 at 11:30 a.m."

Or create a message of inspiration:

"That's one small step for a man, one giant leap for mankind."

Ideally, language is a highly functional tool; it is a message-producing system that serves communicators well when used skillfully. When spoken, language is the flexible, ever-changing primary means of communication. Our language is rich in contributions from other languages, alive with new terminology that reflects a changing society, and as diverse as the people who speak it.

Using language well is vitally important because your listeners rarely separate you from what you say. The way you use spoken language, together with the image you present, conditions your listener to accept or reject your oral messages. Thus, as an effective businessperson, you need to understand the power of spoken words. You may be a storehouse of information, but this will be of little use if you cannot share this information through language. You will use language in business to define responsibilities, share ideas, make decisions, and manage the efforts of others. It is essential to focus on the vivid, precise, and accurate expression of ideas. Your efforts pay off as your listeners understand your oral messages more clearly.

In this chapter we will discuss language using these terms:

Abstracting—selecting details of mental images to put into language at concrete, specific levels or at higher general levels.

Referent—the object or event to which a term refers.

Denotative meanings—the meanings found in dictionaries which are agreed upon and widely used.

Connotative meanings—personalized, associated meanings added to symbols from experience.

Reporting language—statements of observation that give details of "who," "when," where."

Judgmental language—personalized statements including inferences, opinions, values.

LANGUAGE AS A TOOL FOR THINKING

Language is an astonishing invention that is a product of the human brain. People invented language in order to create, symbolize, and shape meaning. Language was needed as a tool for thinking. Human beings required an instrument to help make sense of the experience of living. Language is so important that it is almost a sixth sense!

Creating Meaning

In Chapter 2, you learned that perception functions because you are sensitive to sights, sounds, smells, and happenings that surround you. You react by forming mental images of your experiences. Language enables you to transform these experiences into symbols. Language makes it possible for you to reflect on an experience after it happens and to predict, on the basis of past experience, what might happen in the future. Thus, language helps create **meaning**, which is the importance of events and the relationship of one thing to another.

For example, you may see someone eating a thick, creamy mixture in a cone. Let's say you have never tasted this particular concoction. You don't know the name of it, but it resembles a pleasant experience you remember as ice cream. You mentally predict that this treat will be equally delectable, and you order by pointing to it. The salesperson says the name of this commercial product is Tasty Whip. So, through experience, you have a new name and meaning for the thick, creamy mixture. You perceived the experience through your senses. You supplied the label or name of the product by attaching a language symbol to your perception of the experience.

Symbolizing Meaning

The process through which you turn your perceptions into language is called **abstracting**. It is a creative, personal mental form of shorthand. For example, a simple pen stroke in shorthand represents an alphabet sound or a common phrase. A few strokes stand for a whole idea. When **abstracting**, you use language to transform personal experience into symbols.

Abstracting Details. The verb *abstract* means "to take from" or "to select." From your study of perception, you know that you select or abstract a part of what goes on around you through selective perception. In order to think about what you select, you use language to *describe, label, classify, interpret*, and *generalize*. In order to speak, you abstract details of your perception to report or interpret. In other words, you describe, specifically, the things you observe, or you think less specifically by leaving out details. You also can think very generally and abstractly. The steps in the abstracting process may be described like this:

Step One: *Happening.*
No language required. The real world is moving, growing, changing, multiplying, vegetating, dividing, and adapting all around us.

Step Two: *Perceiving.*
No language required. The individual abstracts through selective perception a portion of all that is going on:
a. Using the senses to focus on some things and to filter out others.
b. Extending the senses by using instruments such as magnifying glasses, binoculars, microscopes, telescopes, and amplifiers.

Step Three: *Describing.*
Using language to abstract details of the object in order to think about it—details such as size, shape, sound, height, and function. Words are necessary to identify characteristics of objects.

Step Four: *Classifying.*
Language required to compare this item or experience to similar items or experiences and categorize or label. This involves combining past experience with present observations.

Step Five: *Interpreting.*
Language required to make a conclusion through inference, judgment, or assumption about the results of the perception.

Step Six: *Generalizing.*
Language required to think in broad terms, leaving out specific details and covering a wide area and different kinds of relationships.

Step Seven: *Further generalizing.*
Language required to think at an even higher level of abstraction, which is more panoramic and less related to the specific item that was observed in the perceiving step.

Through abstracting, language makes it possible to think about things in new ways. For example, you can think about intangible things (those that cannot be touched). You can mentally create new relationships between things. But because language is symbolic and represents things in the real world, it either specifically or more generally stands in place of reality. Thus, you can use language on a number of levels of abstraction—at a low level in which the words are very close to what can be observed, or at a high level in which the words are more general and less related to what is observed. This is how your perception of reality is turned into the symbolic world of language. Figures 4-1 and 4-2 provide examples of the process of abstracting.

Language makes it possible to move further and further away from the details that are perceived. Each higher level is more abstract, omitting specific details and covering wider mental territory.

Recognizing Levels. How general will language permit you to be in the abstraction process? You can go to as high a level and as far from reality as you care to go. Sometimes, you think at a level that seems to have little relevance to the real world at all. But you can think up and down in levels of abstraction very quickly—from very descriptive and specific to more general and back again. Try it. Which of these columns of words are arranged from specific (low level) to general (high level)? Read from top to bottom.

1	2	3	4
pencil	animal	houses	transportation
instrument	pet	town	vehicle
tool	dog	county	truck
equipment	Fido	state	pickup

The first and third groups are arranged from specific to general. The second and fourth groups are arranged from general to specific.

How does abstraction (the levels of language) affect your speech communication? If your listener is not thinking at the same abstraction level, your verbal message may not make sense. The more descriptive (specific) your statements, the lower the level of abstraction, or the more closely the words fit what you perceive. For example, if you say, "Get those reports out immediately," your listener may have difficulty understanding the message. Which reports? How soon is "immediately"? A lower level of abstraction says, "Type and mail the purchasing reports before noon today, please."

Must you always speak so specifically? Of course not. You must find the appropriate level of language that you and your listener share. To illustrate, you want your doctor to explain your physical ailments in words that you can understand, rather than in medical terminology. When speaking to another doctor, however, your doctor will use a language which both doctors share. You can choose the level of language at which you speak and thus communicate more effectively.

Shaping Meaning

How do you know the shape of the earth? Can you distinguish between a gulf and an ocean by looking at the water? What is it like on the moon? Each person has an immense body of acquired information. How did you acquire it? From firsthand experience in the empirical world? Or from the symbolic world of pictures and language—speaking, hearing, reading, and writing? Much of your knowledge comes from the symbolic world. Hence, language influences your thinking. Specifically, language shapes meaning through filtering, distorting, and limiting the way you think and speak.

FIGURE 4-1   Language makes it possible to think and talk about things and events at different levels of abstraction—from concrete and descriptive levels close to the perceived object (reporting language) to general and abstract levels (inferences and judgments) that are less specifically related to particular objects. In our use of language we move up and down the levels of abstraction in line with our receiver's level of understanding.

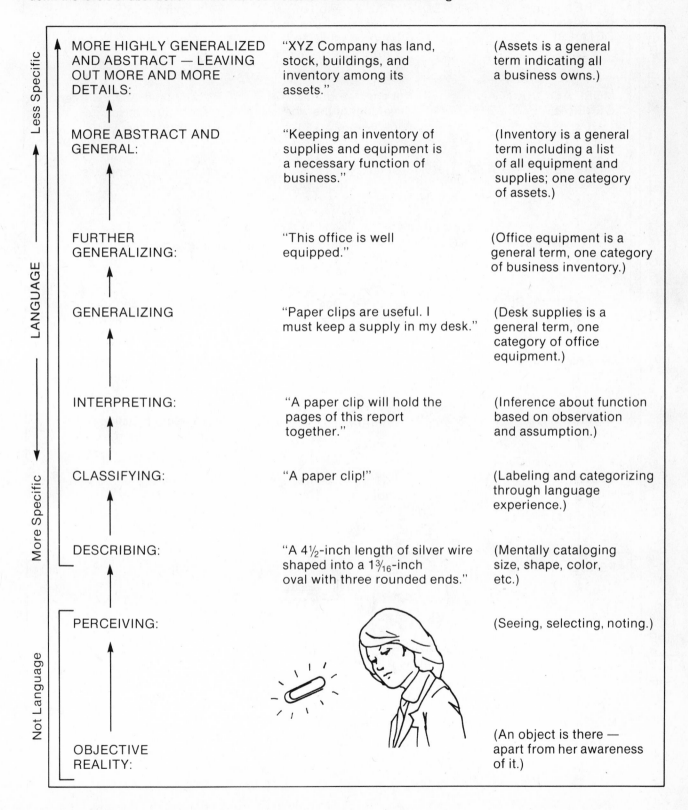

MORE HIGHLY GENERALIZED AND ABSTRACT — LEAVING OUT MORE AND MORE DETAILS:	"XYZ Company has land, stock, buildings, and inventory among its assets."	(Assets is a general term indicating all a business owns.)
MORE ABSTRACT AND GENERAL:	"Keeping an inventory of supplies and equipment is a necessary function of business."	(Inventory is a general term including a list of all equipment and supplies; one category of assets.)
FURTHER GENERALIZING:	"This office is well equipped."	(Office equipment is a general term, one category of business inventory.)
GENERALIZING	"Paper clips are useful. I must keep a supply in my desk."	(Desk supplies is a general term, one category of office equipment.)
INTERPRETING:	"A paper clip will hold the pages of this report together."	(Inference about function based on observation and assumption.)
CLASSIFYING:	"A paper clip!"	(Labeling and categorizing through language experience.)
DESCRIBING:	"A 4½-inch length of silver wire shaped into a 1³⁄₁₆-inch oval with three rounded ends."	(Mentally cataloging size, shape, color, etc.)
PERCEIVING:		(Seeing, selecting, noting.)
OBJECTIVE REALITY:		(An object is there — apart from her awareness of it.)

Less Specific / More Specific / Not Language

LANGUAGE

FIGURE 4-2   Another example of the use of language in abstracting.

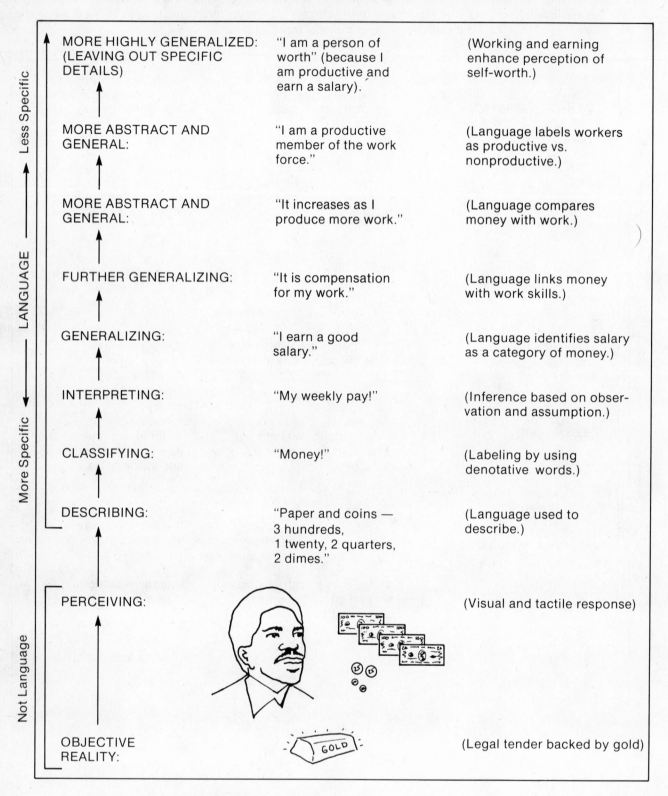

MORE HIGHLY GENERALIZED: (LEAVING OUT SPECIFIC DETAILS)	"I am a person of worth" (because I am productive and earn a salary).	(Working and earning enhance perception of self-worth.)
MORE ABSTRACT AND GENERAL:	"I am a productive member of the work force."	(Language labels workers as productive vs. nonproductive.)
MORE ABSTRACT AND GENERAL:	"It increases as I produce more work."	(Language compares money with work.)
FURTHER GENERALIZING:	"It is compensation for my work."	(Language links money with work skills.)
GENERALIZING:	"I earn a good salary."	(Language identifies salary as a category of money.)
INTERPRETING:	"My weekly pay!"	(Inference based on observation and assumption.)
CLASSIFYING:	"Money!"	(Labeling by using denotative words.)
DESCRIBING:	"Paper and coins — 3 hundreds, 1 twenty, 2 quarters, 2 dimes."	(Language used to describe.)
PERCEIVING:		(Visual and tactile response)
OBJECTIVE REALITY:		(Legal tender backed by gold)

Less Specific / More Specific — LANGUAGE — Not Language

Filtering Awareness. Language focuses your awareness. For example, when the French word *detente* (relaxing of international tension) came into frequent use, you probably became conscious of a new government policy. Thus, language guided your observation.

1. Language invites people to perceive things for which words are familiar and to ignore things when the words are unknown.

For example, a small, L-shaped metal implement may not appear to be a tool until someone calls it an Allen wrench. Then you note that its end is hexagonal to fit a particular type of screw. Or if you don't know the word *slalom*, this downhill race in skiing might escape your attention.

2. Language enables people to lump things together in categories and label them as if they were all the same. This is called **stereotyping.**

People may categorize each other by nationality (German, Mexican, Irish, Korean, etc.), by occupation (teacher, doctor, plumber, engineer, etc.), by religious beliefs (Baptist, Unitarian, Catholic, atheist, etc.), or by skin color (black, white, yellow, etc.). It may be hard to think of Deborah Mosier as a person whose job is airplane piloting. Language makes it easier to think, "Deborah is a pilot." Thus, Deborah and what she does for a living are regarded as the same. So, language is a classifying device that frequently forces people to overlook important differences between individuals in the same category.

3. Language protects people from unpleasant, undiplomatic, or uncomfortable subjects by providing substitute words called **euphemisms.**

Because subjects such as death, physical appearance, sex, and menial work are personal and emotional in content, people often cannot talk directly about them. When someone dear to you dies, it is easier to say, "Ann passed away." In order to be more socially acceptable, people speak of being terminated rather than fired, pleasingly plump rather than fat. These examples color perception by using words which sound more positive than the specific description. So, words can filter perception in the empirical world.

Distorting Reality. The assumptions you make are shaped by the language you use. You may say, "The sun rose" and assume you have described what happened. Actually you are aware that the rotation of the earth caused the appearance of the sun rising. The conventional phrase "The sun rose" tells more about what you saw than what actually happened. Language may distort what you mean in other ways:

1. Transitive verbs indicate an action (someone doing something to someone else) even though the doing is actually an interaction (people responding to each other). For example: "Akira *taught* the students." (This assumes that the students learned without doing anything themselves.) "Sue *managed* the office staff." (What did the office staff do?) "Joe *sold* a car to the customer." (Did the customer have nothing to do with the purchase?)

2. The verb *is* conveys the impression that reality exists as it is described. Actually, you can only describe what you perceive to be reality. For example, you may say, "The wall *is* green." At the moment and under the existing conditions, you are identifying your ability to distinguish light reflections and to categorize them according to the color spectrum (a human classifi-

cation). It might be more accurate to say, "The wall appears to be green right now." Is this clumsy and unnecessary wording? Perhaps. But be careful of the verb *is*. In the bright morning sun, the same wall may appear yellow; and at dusk it *is* gray. What color *is* the wall at night when the lights are out?

Limiting Choices. To review, language can filter or distort meaning. In addition, it limits thinking because of the lack of precise words to describe existing conditions. It is often easier to describe the empirical world (perceived with the senses) than the symbolic world (representing the empirical world). To illustrate, you can mix real paint in varying amounts and describe the colors:

Light Gray   Dark Gray

White————————————Gray————————————Black

Or you can order your steak cooked exactly as you like it:

Rare—red, cool center
Medium rare—red, warm center
Medium—pink, hot center
Medium well—broiled throughout
Well done—charred outside, broiled throughout inside

It is difficult to talk about intangible qualities (those not perceived through the senses) when describing people. What are the degrees of honesty, for example? How much of someone else's property must be taken before the person taking the goods is dishonest? Language limits the choices here to *either* honest or dishonest. A person is either happy or unhappy, good or bad, generous or stingy, for an issue or against it. Because of language, things and qualities seem to be divided into opposites. But the world you experience has more choices than language offers. Fortunately you can recognize the limits of language and refuse to permit language to cut your thinking short.

LANGUAGE IN SPEAKING

Just as Morse code is a system of communication in which dots and dashes stand for alphabet letters, spoken language is a communication system in which oral sounds represent meaning. But spoken language, with its potential for sharing infinite shades of meaning through vocal tones, is far more complex than communicating words through dots and dashes.

Recreating Meaning

"Language is the dress of thought; every time you talk your mind is on parade."

Samuel Johnson

Just as you can think in abstract language, so you can share what you think through speaking language. You recreate in oral language the ideas in your mind. Specifically, you think (perceive, abstract, and symbolize) and then you talk (translate these created images into language sounds carried by air waves). These recreated ideas expressed in speech can be heard and decoded by a listener who understands the same language and shares the same meaning.

Using Common Referents. How does a common language system develop? Actually it can only work when people agree to symbolize a certain thing by using a particular word to refer to that thing. When you talk, for example, you use language sounds that represent to you certain referents. A **referent** is the object or event to which a term or symbol refers. The word creates a similar mental image in the mind of your listener, if the listener has the same referent for the word. So, if both of you are thinking of the same thing, you understand each other. Because each of you has unique experiences, you must have a basis for the same referents. Thus, the experiences you have shared make it possible for you to communicate.

Sharing Common Terms. Even when you and someone else have had the same experiences, you may call things by different words. Since words are symbols for things, it is important to share the same terms in order to understand each other. For example, when you point to a tall object that is rooted in the ground, you are likely to say, "That is a tree." The word *tree* represents the object to you but may not represent the object to someone else.

People are so accustomed to speaking their language they often forget that the symbol is not the object itself but the word agreed upon to represent the object. Of course, when the referent is not tangible (capable of being touched or sensed), it may be difficult to identify. For example, words stand for a variety of referents:

> **Objects**—concrete or empirical things which can be tasted, touched, seen, or heard, such as a dog, table, or pencil.
> **Processes**—a systematic series of steps taken toward some end, such as working, writing, or just being.
> **Concepts**—abstract ideas existing in the mind or in the behavior of human beings, such as democracy, beauty, philosophy, etc.

The important thing to remember is that there is no essential link between the word and the thing that you use it to represent. The word becomes useful only when you and others agree to permit the symbol to represent the thing. Try it with your classmates. If everyone agrees to call the chairs in your classroom by a symbol that you make up, the symbol then will represent the objects on which you sit. These *koleits* or *gotays* (or whatever language sounds you choose to represent these objects) will map out a particu-

FIGURE 4-3

People communicate when they share common language and experiences.

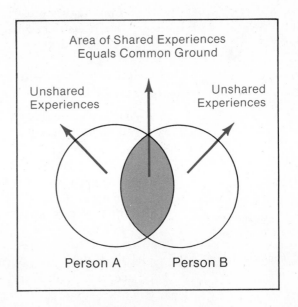

Area of Shared Experiences
Equals Common Ground

Unshared Experiences

Unshared Experiences

Person A   Person B

FIGURE 4-4

Real objects are represented by language symbols. This object has been labeled "tree" in the English language.

French—"arbre"
Spanish—"árbol"

Italian—"àlbero"
German—"baum"

lar mental territory if you agree to it. Of course, a stranger will not understand you. But you can explain that during your class time, in your particular room, and with this certain group of people, you have agreed on a new word to represent the chairs. A language symbol derives its power to represent an object when people agree to use it. But the word chosen does not change the object. A chair obviously retains its own unique characteristics whatever it is called.

Mapping Common Territory. If you are to share your mental images with another person, you select familiar symbols and use them to point out referents that are understood. You also construct a symbolic picture of your mental image. For example, words are like maps (symbolic representations of actual places). Road maps, city maps, or aeronautical charts provide valuable information if they are accurate. You can learn from maps what a territory looks like and determine your location.

A map, then, is a human representation of a particular geographic territory. To create a map, it is important to:

1. Observe the territory to be represented.
2. Select the characteristics or unique details of the area.
3. Mentally picture the area.
4. Transfer the mental picture into graphic symbols by:
   a. Using a common reference point such as north, south, east, or west.
   b. Identifying details in accurate relationships to each other such as plotting to scale, etc.
   c. Choosing a key to identify symbols such as using the color blue to represent rivers and lakes, or black lines crossed with short bars to stand for railroad tracks, etc.

In similar fashion, your oral messages map out the mental territories you have created.

1. You carefully observe the things you receive through sensory perception.
2. You choose details that are characteristic of the area to be symbolized.
3. You transfer your mental picture into oral language by:
   a. Using terms that are common to speaker and listener;
   b. Supplying enough detail so that the referent is clearly identifiable (and moving to a more descriptive abstraction level if necessary);
   c. Providing a common frame of reference (mutual experience) so that the listener can visualize the territory which is symbolically represented.

Remember that the map is never the territory. If your oral message is to be decoded accurately, however, the word picture must accurately represent what you have in mind.

"Watch your speech. A person's command of the language is most important. Next to kissing, it's the most exciting form of communication mankind has evolved."

Oren Arnold

Obstructing Meaning

If you map your mental picture accurately and use symbols that are agreed upon, there should be few communication problems. After all, you can check the meaning of a word symbol in a dictionary.

A dictionary provides words and their denotative meanings. **Denotative meanings** are specific meanings generally agreed upon by speakers of the language. A dictionary also records the uses of words in a particular context, such as science, medicine, or philosophy. But the denotative meanings provided by dictionaries are fairly abstract meanings agreed upon by people in the past. Spoken language is constantly changing. New symbols are developed. New ways to use old symbols appear. Therefore, no dictionary can accurately predict how a symbol will be used in the future. A dictionary has to be frequently updated to reflect the changing patterns of the language. Our language develops and changes to reflect new ways of thinking.

Where do word symbols come from? They are:

Inherited—words have been passed on, gathered, and recorded in dictionaries.

Borrowed—taken from other languages and assimilated through use when there is no native symbol quite as appropriate. Examples are *status quo* (Latin), *R.S.V.P.* and *café* (French), and *kindergarten* (German).

Invented—made up by specific groups of people, such as musical groups, ethnic groups, the military, the business community, etc. Examples are *rock, hijacking, disc jockey, bivouac, disco, G.I., shrink, laser,* and *FORTRAN.*

> *"Language is not an abstract construction of the learned, or of dictionary makers, but is something arising out of the work, needs, ties, joys, affections, tastes of long generations of humanity, and has its bases broad and low, close to the ground."*
>
> *Walt Whitman*

Hindering with Connotations. One of the reasons for problems in communication is that you play an active part in flavoring the meaning of your word symbols. You learn a symbol through your experience with it. For example, *home* is a word denoting the house, apartment, or other shelter that is the residence of a person, family, or household. But *home* to you is a word that represents your own personal collection of sounds, smells, feelings, and possessions. In other words, you add your own experience to word symbols. These are called **connotative meanings**. They are associations that you relate as a secondary meaning to the denotative or explicit meaning of a word. And these feelings are unique to you. For example, based on personal experience, the following words may be emotionally laden or trigger unpleasant meanings:

test	taxes	surgery	quota
shots	cancer	AIDS	terminated

You, of course, may have your own personal list. But words connote (suggest or call up) individual experience, and these experiences differ. To illustrate, *beach* denotes an expanse of sand or pebbles along the edge of a body of water. Your mental image of a beach may include "a warm, white strip of soft sand beside a refreshing blue ocean" or "a cold, fishy wet place with hard-to-get-rid-of particles," depending on your previous experiences on a beach.

So, for each person, these word symbols take on individualized, connotative meanings. It is this personal experience which may be difficult to share with others. If another person's experience is different, how can you communicate through speech? You can remember that THE MEANINGS OF WORDS ARE INSIDE PEOPLE!

FIGURE 4-5   Maps are graphic representations of territory. Words are verbal representations of mental territory. To be useful, maps and words must be precisely related to their referents.

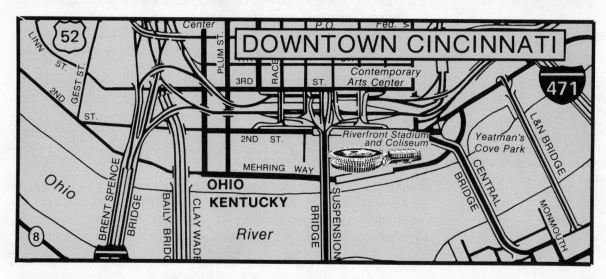

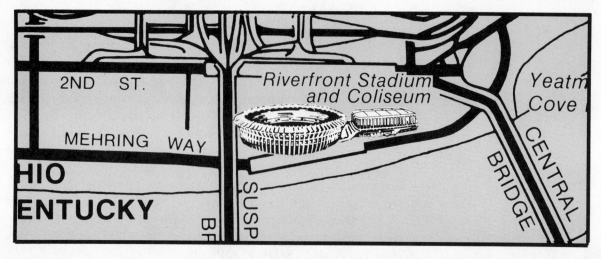

Chapter 4   Brushing Up Your Language Skills

Blocking with Jargon. If meaning is inside people, then specialized terms may be further obstructions to communication. In business, for example, an employee must learn the **specialized language** of the firm for which she or he works. And each type of business has its own jargon—words unique to that business. From a small gas station to a large manufacturing plant, each industry has terms that describe:

products	problems
procedures or processes	types of tools
personnel positions	equipment

Think of computer language, banking terms, the language of advertising, newspapers, and merchandising. Each company has a specialized language which may seem like a private code to a new employee. Thus, to learn the business is to understand and use the terminology by which employees communicate. If you were to work as a certified public accountant, these terms would be essential to communication:

credit	variances	payoff
debit	slack	repairs
liabilities	principal	revenue
discounting	liquidity	subsidiary
dividends	annuity	parent

And if you were to work for a large grocery store, you would learn specialized meanings for:

number three	go backs	OT
graveyard shift	call in	rack
sweep the lot	facing	close

Employees who work together develop a language that is specialized in the context of the business. Moving into a new department might necessitate learning a new set of terms. Language used by employees on a production line, for example, is different from the language used in the front office. Learning the language of the business is part of talking business.

On a new job, you will learn the names for various forms to be completed, the accepted expressions describing a piece of work, and the appropriate titles for various positions held by people in your business. Once you learn the language of the business, you will communicate more comfortably with your fellow employees.

> "The brick may not care in the least whether it is called a brick, or structural material; but the brick layer may behave differently if he is called laborer or artisan or construction engineer."
>
> John Condon, Jr.

LANGUAGE AS A MESSAGE-PRODUCING SYSTEM

This chapter has been exploring the way we think and speak with language symbols. Language is truly an amazing tool. Yet probably the most astonishing feature of language is the means by which it conveys messages.

Reporting Language

Some statements are called "statements of observation." They are expressed in **reporting language**, in which the information can be measured or observed by the listener as well as the speaker. If the listener accepts the accuracy of a thermometer, a yardstick, or a document on file, the listener can verify the statement in the empirical world. For example, note the difference between the following:

> **Statement of Observation**—"The cash receipts for today are $395.68."
>
> and
>
> **Statement of Inference**—"We didn't do much business today."

The first statement reports results that can be verified by counting; the second statement offers an opinion.

So, reporting language is low in abstraction, is precise in details (it often includes who, what, when, where, why, and how information), and omits personal opinions and judgments. Statements of observation can be verified or checked by another person. Does the following sound like reporting language to you?

> The light yellow four-door 1982 Buick Skylark, with license plate MPV 497, is parked directly in front of the west entrance of the Administration Building and has its lights on.

> *"I believe the best method of communication remains language—which means for us the English language—straightforward, concrete, specific."*
>
> *Edwin Newman*

Judgmental Language

The language that includes evaluations, opinions, feelings, and judgments is more abstract than reporting language. It is probably the language of most messages because such statements are made anytime, by anyone, and deal with more than what is observed. Thus, **judgmental language** is the result of mixing observation with experience and arriving at assumptions, inferences, and personal evaluations.

> **Assumptions**—those generally held beliefs or guesses that what was true in the past will hold true in the present or future. Example: "My dog has always greeted me at the door, and (I take for granted that) he will meet me today."
>
> **Inferences**—conclusions about the unknown that are based on what has been observed in the past and what is assumed in the present. Example: "I infer that the writer of this letter is angry because he lists three complaints about our product and has taken the trouble to write us about them."
>
> **Slanting**—statements which select for mention only those details that support a particular point of view. Example: "My friend could not possibly have caused this accident because she has never before had an accident."
>
> **Evaluating**—judging the worth of a particular thing based upon a personal value system. Example: "I think it's a good letter because it says just what I think myself."

Judgmental language is so much a part of the message-producing system that people are often unaware of how frequently they use it.

In improving your use of the language tool, you can:

1. *Be alert to the statements you make. Listen to yourself.*
   a. Check your assumptions before you proceed. Try not to accept symbolic information without sufficient data. Be wary of believing that each situation is exactly the same as you have experienced before.
   b. Separate statements of inference from statements of observation. Be cautious about the difference between what you know (and can verify) and what you *think* you know. In other words, if your statement goes beyond what you can observe, recognize that you may be inferring or drawing shaky conclusions.

c. Identify your bias or slanted point of view by providing a reason for your statement which clarifies why you are speaking as you are.
   d. In stating your opinion, recognize that you are evaluating on a personal basis which may not be the same as another person's. Add qualifiers (comments indicating personal evaluation) to statements such as these:
   "This typewriter is the worst one in the whole office." (In my opinion)
   "This is a great place to work." (As I see it)
   "What an outrageous way to behave!" (In my judgment)
2. *Be aware of how your messages sound to your listener.*
   a. Locate areas of common ground in subject matter and language.
   b. When explaining or giving directions, keep at a low level of abstraction and include specific information that tells who, what, when, where, why, and how.
   c. Choose words carefully. Clarify your referent (the object or idea that you are discussing). Recognize that you and your listener may see the same thing differently.

Our emphasis so far has been on the way language creates, symbolizes, and shapes meaning. Language, then, is the "what" of the verbal message. But when you speak the language, you give the words special meanings through your voice. The vocal message that accompanies the words is important, too. It provides the "why" of the spoken words. Chapter 5 will deal with speaking—the oral delivery of language.

CHAPTER SUMMARY

"If language is not correct, then what is said is not what is meant; if what is said is not meant, then what ought to be done remains undone; if this remains undone, morals and arts will deteriorate; if morals and arts deteriorate, justice will go astray; if justice goes astray, the people will stand about in helpless confusion. Hence there must be no arbitrariness in what is said. This matters above everything."

Confucius

This chapter has covered how language is used in thinking and speaking. Through language symbols, we create meaning for ourselves as we think. We recreate meaning for others as we use language in speaking. Words are concrete and specific as well as general and abstract. We move up and down these levels of language as we communicate by speaking generally or by becoming more specific when it is necessary to be more clear. But we must be wary of the pitfalls of obstructing communication by using language to distort reality or limit choices, or by selecting language that is not shared by our listeners. In business, it is important to learn the specific terms used to describe processes, personnel, products, or equipment. Each business has a specialized language of its own. Language is helpful to our communication when we are aware of the differences between reporting and judgmental language.

WORKSHOP ACTIVITIES

BUSINESS LABELS *(Pairs)*

Purpose: To examine a specific way of abstracting in business.

Briefing: Choose a partner and do this activity together. Business organizations use specialized terms for people who do a particular kind of work. Sometimes the term describes the work at a low level of abstraction (very specifically) and sometimes at a high level (more generally). Compare the two labels in each group below. Put a check before the term that is lower in abstraction or more concrete.

	Example: _____ wordsmith	___✓___ résumé writer
1.	_____ bus driver	_____ intercity transportation specialist
2.	_____ garbage collector	_____ sanitation engineer
3.	_____ oral surgeon	_____ dentist
4.	_____ data systems specialist	_____ programmer
5.	_____ bank clerk	_____ security teller
6.	_____ regulatory inspector	_____ customs inspector
7.	_____ funeral director	_____ embalmer
8.	_____ personnel director	_____ job analyst
9.	_____ buyer	_____ merchandise manager
10.	_____ commercial artist	_____ layout artist
11.	_____ architect	_____ landscape architect
12.	_____ engineer	_____ civil engineer
13.	_____ environmental scientist	_____ meteorologist
14.	_____ shop worker	_____ machinist
15.	_____ cook	_____ chef
16.	_____ ironworker	_____ welder
17.	_____ floor covering mechanic	_____ carpet installer
18.	_____ model	_____ photographic model
19.	_____ carpenter	_____ construction worker
20.	_____ custodian	_____ janitor

Debriefing: Discuss your decisions in class and clarify your differences. Why do you suppose a higher level of abstraction might be selected to describe a particular position? See the quotation on p. 131 by John Condon, Jr. How do these titles illustrate "euphemisms"?

SYMBOL VS. THING *(Individual Activity)*

Purpose: To distinguish between symbols and their referents.

Briefing: Sometimes it is difficult to separate a symbol from the thing it represents. Each of the following items exist in the real world (each can be touched, smelled, heard, tasted, or seen) or stands for something else (a symbol). Check your understanding of which are *symbols*, which are *real* (known through the senses), and which can be both. Put a check in the correct column.

1. Ohio road map   symbolic _____   real _____   both _____

2. automobile   symbolic _____   real _____   both _____

3. a letter from a friend   symbolic _____   real _____   both _____

4. advertisement   symbolic _____   real _____   both _____

5. cup of coffee   symbolic _____   real _____   both _____

6. midnight   symbolic _____   real _____   both _____

7. a name   symbolic _____   real _____   both _____

8. a tree   symbolic _____   real _____   both _____

9. a state line   symbolic _____   real _____   both _____

10. dollar bill   symbolic _____   real _____   both _____

11. telephone   symbolic _____   real _____   both _____

12. the metric system   symbolic _____   real _____   both _____

Debriefing: Check your answers for this activity with those found in the teacher's manual. What have you learned from this activity?

Name _____   Class _____   Score _____

INFERENCES = *O* + *A* *(Individual Activity)*

Purpose: To examine the basis for statements of inference.

Briefing: Study the definitions and examples below. Then read the three sets of statements at the bottom and label them as indicated in the instructions.

DEFINITIONS:

Statement of *observation*—a statement based on what is seen, heard, smelled, tasted, or touched. It is likely to be fairly accurate. An observation can be verified by comparing it with the observations of other people.

Statement of *assumption*—a generally accepted belief that something true in the past is still true now.

Statement of *inference*—a statement that includes more than an observation. Inferences generally blend observations with assumptions. Statements of inference may or may not be true.

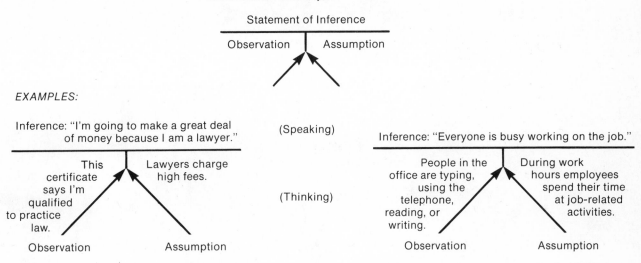

Observation + Assumption = Inference

Identify the statements below by writing *I* (inference), *O* (observation), or *A* (assumption) in the blank before each one.

_____ There goes a boy running down the hall.
_____ He must be late for class.
_____ People don't run in a classroom building unless they're late.

_____ I'll ship this package by express mail.
_____ I've got a package to mail.
_____ Express mail has always gotten my packages to their destination on time.

_____ When the sun shines, the weather is usually good.
_____ The sun is shining and it's warm out.
_____ It's going to be a good day for a picnic.

UNCRITICAL INFERENCE TEST* *(Quiz)*

Purpose: To demonstrate inference-observation confusion.

Briefing: Read the following little story. Assume that all the information presented in it is definitely accurate and true. Read it carefully because it has ambiguous parts designed to lead you astray. No need to memorize it, though. You can refer back to it whenever you wish.

Next read the statements about the story and check each to indicate whether you consider it true, false, or "?". "T" means that the statement is *definitely true* on the basis of the information presented in the story. "F" means that it is *definitely false*. "?" means that it may be either true or false and that you cannot be certain which on the basis of the information presented in the story. If any part of a statement is doubtful, mark it "?". *Answer each statement in turn, and do not go back to change any answer later and don't reread any statements after you have answered them. This will distort your score.*

To start with, here is a sample story with the correct answers circled:

Sample Story

You arrive home late one evening and see that the lights are on in your living room. There is only one car parked in front of your house. The words "Harold R. Jones, M. D." are spelled in small gold letters across one of the car's doors.

STATEMENTS ABOUT SAMPLE STORY

1. The car parked in front of your house has lettering on one of its doors.   **(T)**   F   ?
    (This is a "definitely true" statement because it is directly corroborated by the story.)

2. Someone in your family is sick.   T   F   **(?)**
    (This could be true and then again it might not be. Perhaps Dr. Jones is paying a social call at your home or perhaps he has gone to the house next door or across the street.)

3. No car is parked in front of your house.   T   **(F)**   ?
    (A "definitely false" statement because the story directly contradicts it.)

4. The car parked in front of your house belongs to a man named Johnson.   T   F   **(?)**
    (May seem very likely false, but can you be sure? Perhaps the car has just been sold.)

So much for the sample. It should warn you of some of the kinds of traps to look for. Now begin the actual test. Remember, mark each statement *in order*—don't skip around or change answers later.

---

* With permission of William V. Haney, *Communication and Interpersonal Skills*, 5th ed. (Homewood, IL: Richard D. Irwin, Inc., 1986), pp. 213, 214, 222.

Test Story

A businessman had just turned off the lights in the store when a man appeared and demanded money. The owner opened a cash register. The contents of the cash register were scooped up, and the man sped away. A member of the police force was notified promptly.

STATEMENTS ABOUT TEST STORY

1. A man appeared after the owner had turned off his store lights.   T   F   ?

2. The robber was a man.   T   F   ?

3. The man who appeared did not demand money.   T   F   ?

4. The man who opened the cash register was the owner.   T   F   ?

5. The store owner scooped up the contents of the cash register and ran away.   T   F   ?

6. Someone opened a cash register.   T   F   ?

7. After the man who demanded money scooped up the contents of the cash register, he ran away.   T   F   ?

8. While the cash register contained money, the story does not say how much.   T   F   ?

9. The robber demanded money of the owner.   T   F   ?

10. A businessman had just turned off the lights when a man appeared in the store.   T   F   ?

11. It was broad daylight when the man appeared.   T   F   ?

12. The man who appeared opened the cash register.   T   F   ?

13. No one demanded money.   T   F   ?

14. The story concerns a series of events in which only three persons are referred to: the owner of the store, a man who demanded money, and a member of the police force.   T   F   ?

15. The following events occurred: someone demanded money, a cash register was opened, its contents were scooped up, and a man dashed out of the store.   T   F   ?

Debriefing: Your instructor will read the correct answers from the teacher's manual. Score your correct answers. Discuss these questions orally. What mental images did you add to the words in the story? What conclusions can be drawn from this test?

BUSINESS JARGON *(Group Activity)*

Purpose: To find meanings for new terms. To communicate with others by using a new vocabulary. To solve a problem as a group by overcoming a language barrier.

Briefing: Pretend you work for a company whose business terminology is new to you. In order to do a certain task, you must find out the meaning of the new terms, get information to solve the problem, and share the information you have with the members of your group.

Task: You will be divided into groups. Your group is to prepare an important shipment that must go out immediately. Seven packages, labeled *A* through *G*, are to be put into one or the other of two crates. Your group is to decide which packages will go into each crate. Your company uses the terms *rabo, zoffer, minik*, and *wamboo* for measuring length.

You will be given cards containing information that relates to the group task. You may share this information orally, but you must keep the cards in your hands throughout the exercise.

Your Group Answer:

Crate I will have packages _____

Crate II will have packages _____

Debriefing: Be prepared to defend your solution orally and to graph it on the board.

Use this space for figuring:

ON THE JOB *(Group Activity)*

Purpose: To discuss ways to improve speaking exchanges.

Briefing: Read the following statements. Rate their importance by assigning them a number from 1 (*most* important) to 10 (*least* important) and writing this number in the column headed "Individual."

   Join other students. Compare your ranking for the three most important. Discuss these. Try to arrive at some agreement. Place the agreed-upon rankings in the "Group" column. One of you should serve as the group observer and fill out the report on page 146.

Individual   Group

_____ _____   **A.** Give credit to the work of others. Everyone builds on work done by other people.

_____ _____   **B.** Ask questions. It is better to ask than to make mistakes.

_____ _____   **C.** Move slowly. You may have ideas about how to improve the job immediately, but other people may be fearful of quick changes.

_____ _____   **D.** Get an agreement on priorities. What you think should be done first may not be important to others.

_____ _____   **E.** Cooperate with others in your work group. Barging ahead on your own without consultation may cause difficulties.

_____ _____   **F.** Do your homework. Get as much information as possible before you present your ideas.

_____ _____   **G.** Listen to the comments you make about others. Do you sound as if they are enemies or work partners?

_____ _____   **H.** Watch the use of emotionally laden words. Your choice of language may create hard feelings.

_____ _____   **I.** Identify your particular role in the organization. Adjust your speech messages and behavior to fit the role.

_____ _____   **J.** Adapt your speech messages to the situation. Recognize that speech messages deal with content (subject matter) and with process (maintaining healthy relationships with others).

Debriefing: Each group may have one member present the group's decision of the three most important choices to the class. The reasons for the selection should be part of the report.

OBSERVER'S REPORT *(Oral Report to a Group)*

Purpose: To look, listen, and report the results of the activity on page 145. To help group members recognize their verbal and nonverbal behavior as they work with others.

Briefing: Sit outside the group circle. Observe two kinds of behavior:

1. **Participation and interaction.** Fill out a flow chart on a separate sheet of paper for ten minutes of the discussion period. Correctly mark the time. Keep track of who speaks, to whom, and how many times. (See page 64 for an example of a communication flow chart.)

2. **Listening.** Some kinds of listening behavior create a good group climate (atmosphere). Identify by name any classmate whose behavior fits any of the descriptions below.

At the end of the discussion, report the results of your observation to your group. Try not to judge or make inferences. Merely state what you saw and heard.

A.   Write each group member's name:

1. _____

2. _____

3. _____

4. _____

5. _____

B.   Communication Flow Chart indicating participation and interaction. (Use separate sheet.)

C.   Listening: Write the name of the student who exhibited these good listening behaviors:

1. Leaned forward to increase concentration _____

_____

2. Started to interrupt; stopped; continued to listen _____

_____

3. Gave signals of attention—a nod, a smile, etc. _____

_____

4. Gave verbal signals—"Yes, I see," etc. _____

_____

5. Maintained eye contact with speakers _____

_____

6. Called other speakers by name_____

_____

Be prepared to move into the group and share your observations after they have finished their discussion.

SPEAKING ASSIGNMENT—ORAL REPORT ON A BUSINESS LANGUAGE

Purpose: To give a report on a business language.

Briefing: Each business develops a language of its own to establish communication regarding:

products problems
procedures or processes tools or equipment
personnel positions

If you have ever held a job with a particular company (airline, real estate, insurance, public relations, broadcasting, car rental, food service, office, hospital, bottling company, security, clothing manufacturer, dentist, etc.), you probably are familiar with its specialized language. Plan a five-minute presentation for your class that identifies some of the language used in a particular business. Outline your ideas on a separate sheet of paper. Use the outline form below.

Introduction: Identify the business. Explain your source of information and how you acquired the information.

Body of the Report: Organize the terms under categories such as the ones listed above. Explain each term in simple, understandable language to an audience that is unfamiliar with the business. Show some of the objects you are discussing or use a chart that lists the terms you plan to discuss.

Conclusion: Use a simple summary that restates what you have said.

Sample Report Outline

Introduction: I have worked at the Baskin-Robbins 31 Flavors Ice Cream Store for two years. We use some terms that are general business terms and some that are unique to the ice cream business.

Thesis: I would like to explain three types of business terminology.

Development of the Thesis (Body of report):

Main Point **I.** These are terms that define the jobs and responsibilities of the personnel:

trainee senior sales staff owner/manager
sales staff staff leader district manager

Main Point **II.** These are management terms used in the operation of the business:

customer count payroll payroll average
flash gross profit daily sales average

Main Point **III.** These are terms used to identify equipment in the ice cream store:

dipping cabinet walk-in taste spoon
tub flavor board collars
dipping well party case hot signs
scooper four hole fountain
spade

Conclusion: I hope you have learned some of the three types of business terminology used at Baskin-Robbins.

CRITIQUE SHEET FOR ORAL REPORTS *(Instructor's Evaluation)*

Briefing: If you are instructed to do so, tear out this sheet and turn it in to your instructor before you speak.

POSSIBLE POINTS: 100   (Each question: 10 points)

1. Did the speaker begin with a strong opening statement that caught attention and set the audience up to listen?   _____

2. Was information about the business provided so that the specialized language was understandable to this audience?   _____

3. Was the thesis statement clear?   _____

4. Was the information of the report broken into an understandable organizational pattern?   _____

5. Was the speaker's voice loud enough to be easily heard?   _____

6. Did the speaker handle his/her body to minimize distracting mannerisms?   _____

7. Was good eye contact maintained with all members of the audience?   _____

8. Did the speaker end the report with a strong summary or comment?   _____

9. Did the speaker maintain a strong sense of communication with the audience?   _____

10. Did the report meet the five-minute time limit?   _____

Total _____

Instructor's Comments:

SPEAKER'S NAME_____

Delivery Critique Form

Possible points: 50   (Each question: 10)

1. Did the opening identify the business and explain how the speaker learned the terms? _____

2. Was the thesis statement clear? _____

3. Were the specialized terms well explained? _____

4. Did the manner in which the speaker handled voice and body add to the presentation? _____

5. Did the report meet the time limit? _____

                                    Total _____

                    On the back, write a word
                    of praise and a suggestion
                    for improvement next time.

SPEAKER'S NAME_____

Delivery Critique Form

Possible points: 50   (Each question: 10)

1. Did the opening identify the business and explain how the speaker learned the terms? _____

2. Was the thesis statement clear? _____

3. Were the specialized terms well explained? _____

4. Did the manner in which the speaker handled voice and body add to the presentation? _____

5. Did the report meet the time limit? _____

                                    Total _____

                    On the back, write a word
                    of praise and a suggestion
                    for improvement next time.

SPEAKER'S NAME_____

Delivery Critique Form

Possible points: 50   (Each question: 10)

1. Did the opening identify the business and explain how the speaker learned the terms? _____

2. Was the thesis statement clear? _____

3. Were the specialized terms well explained? _____

4. Did the manner in which the speaker handled voice and body add to the presentation? _____

5. Did the report meet the time limit? _____

                                    Total _____

                    On the back, write a word
                    of praise and a suggestion
                    for improvement next time.

SPEAKER'S NAME_____

Delivery Critique Form

Possible points: 50   (Each question: 10)

1. Did the opening identify the business and explain how the speaker learned the terms? _____

2. Was the thesis statement clear? _____

3. Were the specialized terms well explained? _____

4. Did the manner in which the speaker handled voice and body add to the presentation? _____

5. Did the report meet the time limit? _____

                                    Total _____

                    On the back, write a word
                    of praise and a suggestion
                    for improvement next time.

CHECKLIST OF COMMUNICATION TERMS *(Quiz)*

Check your understanding of the terms presented in this chapter by putting the number of the correct term in the blank before its definition. Note that there are more terms than definitions.

Definitions

a. _____ A mental image of a thing or event being referred to.

b. _____ Specific meanings of words agreed upon by speakers of a language.

c. _____ A conclusion about the unknown based on an observation and an assumption.

d. _____ The term often applied to the specialized language of a particular business.

e. _____ A process of using language at different levels of detail, ranging from specific to general.

f. _____ A substitute word that sounds less harsh or offensive than the original term.

g. _____ Lumping people together into one category on the basis of a single characteristic.

h. _____ Using statements which support only one view of a situation.

i. _____ The associated meanings added to the primary meaning of a word.

j. _____ Language that includes opinions, generalized statements, inferences, and/or judgments.

Terms

1. meaning
2. abstracting
3. reporting language
4. denotative meanings
5. referent
6. judgmental language
7. stereotyping
8. inference
9. connotative meanings
10. euphemism
11. describing
12. labeling
13. classifying
14. interpreting
15. generalizing
16. distorting
17. processes
18. concepts
19. specialized language
20. jargon
21. slanting
22. objects

CHAPTER 5

Let's Talk About the Business of Polishing Your Speaking Skills

This chapter deals with your speaking voice and how it conveys the language you speak. It might be said that language provides the words while your voice is the music that makes the words meaningful. Included in the workshop activities are a number of suggestions for improving your voice. After you have read and discussed this chapter and practiced the suggestions in the workshop activities, you should be able to do the following:

Chapter Objectives

1. Describe the four steps in creating speech sounds.
2. Define the five characteristics of the speaking voice.
3. Create changes to make your voice more interesting.
4. Increase your vocabulary and polish your pronunciation skills.
5. Improve your articulation skills.

"There is no index of character so sure as the voice."

Benjamin Disraeli

The sound of your voice identifies you. It is a part of your image—the picture created as people hear you. Your speaking voice is an instrument that reflects your health, feelings, moods, and attitudes. Your voice adds positive messages, such as warmth, friendliness, and sincerity, to your speaking exchanges. When your vocal tones are vibrant, clear, and full, your words carry power and impact. Your speaking voice—words plus vocal tones—is a dynamic tool for talking business.

Because you operate your speaking mechanism with little conscious effort and have been doing it for a long time, you may not realize how you sound to others. But you are probably well aware of how the voices of others affect you. For example, a voice that is thin or whiny, nasal or twangy, weak or high-pitched, rough or harsh may call so much attention to itself that the speaker's message is lost. You may even tune the speaker out.

If you are to exchange oral messages with others, your speaking voice should be an asset. Because you are recreating meaning for someone (painting a word picture of your mental image), you must carefully select your language. Your voice must clearly express the subtle tones that convey to your listener precisely what you mean. The sounds of the words must be clearly understood. Your voice is a tool that helps your words trigger meaning in your listener's mind. The sounds you produce are the basis for a speaking exchange.

SPEAKING—A HUMAN SKILL

The speaking tool consists of the voice and the articulated sounds of oral language. A good speaking voice should be capable of reflecting the speaker's intent (purpose) and reinforcing the spoken message. Actually it is a flexible instrument that can be finely tuned, adapted to the situation, and responsive to the speaker's purpose. For example, you can soften the volume, lower the pitch, and slow the rate of words. When you speak, you transmit a message in words. But the **delivery**—the manner in which the words are spoken—often makes the message come alive for the listener. Because the delivery is so important, you must know something about the production of speech sounds.

Four Steps in Creating Speech

A product you manufacture and market each day is your speaking voice. You have the equipment and the know-how to use it. The processes that function together to produce the human voice are:

1. The **brain**, which acts as a magnificent computer, scans the available store of symbols, and rapidly triggers the nerve fibers to set muscles into action.
2. The **nervous system**, which activates the appropriate muscles so that compacted air is forced up from the lungs to set tiny vocal cords vibrating in the voice box.
3. The **vibrations** (vocal sounds), which are enriched and enlarged as they resonate in the areas of the throat, nose, and mouth, and create a voice that is uniquely yours.
4. The **organs of articulation**, which are located primarily in the mouth. They shape the voice into the individual sounds of oral language.

Human speech is a complicated physical and mental process. Speaking combines thinking with incredibly fine coordination of various parts of the body. It is only because of our superior human nervous system that messages are encoded almost automatically into understandable language symbols. It is an amazing production job. Let's look more closely at the effect on the product—speech.

The Breathing Process. A good speaking voice is characterized by strong, full tones. Specifically, compressed air is expelled from the lungs through contraction and relaxation of the diaphragm and the abdominal and rib muscles. But breathing for speech is different from normal breathing. In relaxed, ordinary breathing, each breathing cycle of inhalation and exhalation of air is approximately equal. For example, watch a person who is sleeping. The chest and abdomen rise and fall in a steady in-and-out rhythm.

However, in breathing for speech, this rhythm changes because you need a long, controlled exhalation of air to furnish the power for your voice. You inhale quickly; while speaking, you exhale slowly. Thus, the compressed air expelled from the lungs is forced up the windpipe to provide the energy to vibrate the vocal cords.

While referring to Figure 5-1, review the following components of the human breathing mechanism:

Voice box—called the larynx, this tiny structure contains the vocal cords.
Windpipe—the air passage from the throat to the lungs. This tube permits air to be inhaled and exhaled to and from the lungs.
Bronchial tubes—air tubes from the windpipe to the spongy air-holding lungs.
Lungs—a mass of tiny air sacs that hold air and are expanded or contracted through muscular pressure.
Diaphragm—the primary source of vocal power, this large, dome-shaped muscle below the lungs increases air capacity in the chest by a downward contraction and exerts pressure on the lungs for exhalation of air.
Abdominal and rib muscles—other muscles that work with the diaphragm in contracting to cause pressure on the lungs to expel compressed air.

It is perfectly possible to speak with little awareness of the breathing process. However, to improve the speaking voice, it is important to control the dynamic stream of air that provides the power. If you lack control, your voice tones will sound breathy or shallow.

FIGURE 5-1   The human breathing mechanism provides the controlled exhalation of air for the voice.

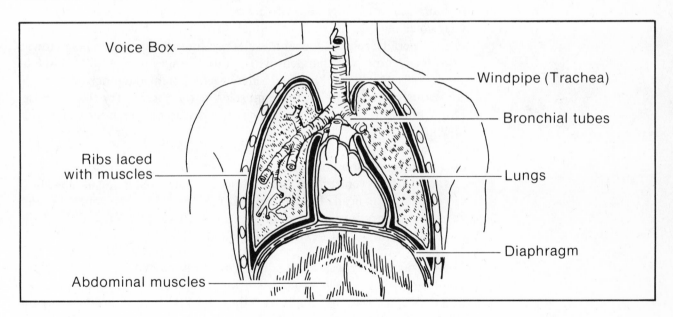

"Nervousness can be defined as when you feel in a hurry—all over—but you can't get started."

Anonymous

This natural breathing process works with little difficulty for most people until they speak before a group in public. Suddenly they may become aware of the irregularity in their breathing cycle. The effect feels like butterflies fluttering just under the rib cage. Because muscles are involved in the breathing cycle (inhaling and exhaling), they become tense when a person feels the pressure of public performance. Do you recall the feelings of tight jaw muscles, uncomfortable sensations in the pit of the stomach, clammy hands, etc.? This discomfort is frequently called stage fright.

One way to reduce the symptoms of stage fright is to control consciously the breathing function. To reestablish a regular rate of breathing for speaking, take a few deep breaths as you walk to the speaker's stand. Pause a moment, breathe normally, look up, smile, and begin to speak.

Pay attention also to the power of the pause—fleeting bits of silence blended in with the words. This silence recaptures the attention of the audience and gives you the chance to regulate your breathing once again. These frequent and varied periods of silence can be as much a part of communication as words. Fast talkers often avoid the pause and give the impression of nervousness. Good communicators blend speech with nonspeech to give the impression of poise and control.

The Vocalizing Process. The second process in the production of the voice is the creation of sound. At the upper end of the windpipe and behind the base of the tongue is the larynx, or voice box. The **larynx** contains the vocal cords that vibrate to produce voice sounds when air passes from the lungs up the windpipe. You can feel your larynx if you lightly touch your Adam's apple and say your name several times aloud. There is a tiny flutter against your fingertips. Now try swallowing and feel this flexible structure move up and forward. During the act of swallowing, two tiny cords are drawn together across the air passage to prevent foreign objects from entering the lungs. During the act of speaking, air passing up the windpipe builds up pressure and blows the cords apart. It is the rapid, periodic movement of these tissues as they stretch across the air passage that creates vocal sound.

Your normal pitch is determined generally by the length and thickness of your vocal cords. But failure to achieve the basic pitch level that is best for your voice may result from emotional disturbances, habit, or nervous tension. Generally, relaxed throat muscles produce lower, more relaxed tones. Conversely, note what happens when you are angry or tense. The pitch of your voice may rise and the quality may become tight and pinched. You can consciously work to relax these muscles of the throat. Try this exercise. Drop your head. Think of it as heavy—heavier. Imagine it is the weight of a bowling ball! Now roll your head over and lay it on your shoulder. Keep your shoulder at normal level. Continue by rolling your head back, then over to the other shoulder, then down toward your chest. Reverse the process and do this several times. Now produce a rich, relaxed sound of "ah-h-h-h" as you roll your head. Remember that tension affects the sound of your voice. So, to produce clear and relaxed speech sounds, work to keep the muscles of your throat flexible and relaxed.

The Resonating Process. The sound you produce by the vibration of the vocal cords would be weak and thin if you did not have **resonating areas** (see Figure 5-2) to strengthen and enrich the sound. The sound produced by the vibration of guitar strings **resonates** or resounds in the body of the guitar, where the sound becomes louder and richer in quality. The three main resonating areas for the voice work in much the same way as a guitar body. These areas, which provide **resonance** (intensification and enrichment) for the vibrations of the vocal cords, are the:

Pharynx—the open area at the back of the throat above the larynx.
Nasal cavities—open areas above the roof of the mouth.
Oral cavity—the mouth.

FIGURE 5-2

The resonating areas of the
voice.

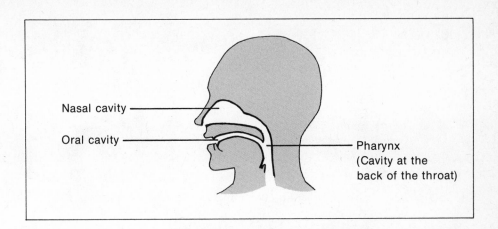

Note the effect on the sound of your voice when you block one of these
resonating areas. If you clamp your jaw shut tight, lock your teeth together,
and say your name aloud, your voice will resonate very little in the mouth.
Thus, the sound of your voice is flat and unpleasant. What happens if you
hold your nose and speak? Note the nasal quality of your voice. This is
because the sound is "trapped" and cannot be emitted through the nose.
Now try holding the sound at the back of your throat and creating a growl-
ing vocal quality as you speak. The way you use the resonating cavities helps
to create the way you sound. An open, balanced use of the three areas produces a vocal sound that is most desirable—pure, rich, and clear.

Try listening to your voice on a tape recorder. Do you like the way you
sound? Does the resonance seem balanced and rich? Or does it sound thin
and flat? If it sounds unpleasant, do these exercises. Try the neck roll over
and over until you relax the throat and jaw area. Work for a loose, lower jaw
as you sound a rich full "ah-h-h-h" again. Now try holding the sound of
"m-m-m-m-m" as you push the sound up to fill your head. Touch your
cheeks and forehead to feel the vibration. Do the same with the final sound
of "sing-ng-ng." With practice you can improve the quality of your voice.

The Articulating Process. To this point, we have only discussed vocal
sound—only the voice! But speech is more than voice. It includes the individual sounds of language that are produced primarily in the mouth.

Articulating means the shaping of the approximately 46 vowel, consonant, and diphthong (vowel blends) sounds of standard American English. Through intricate adjustments of organs located in the mouth, voice
sounds are changed into intelligible sounds. These are the primary organs of
articulation (see Figure 5-3):

Lips	Hard palate (hard roof of the mouth)
Tongue	Soft palate (soft, back roof of the mouth)
Jaw	
Teeth	

The sounds of speech are created when these **articulators** change the shape
of the oral cavity for vowel sounds and modify the breath stream being
expelled for consonant sounds. For example, some consonant sounds are
exploded (make a "p" sound); some are created by friction (make an "s" or
"th" sound); and some are tiny breath stops (make a "t" sound). The position
of the tongue and shape of the mouth determine the difference in vowel

FIGURE 5-3

The organs of articulation are located in the mouth.

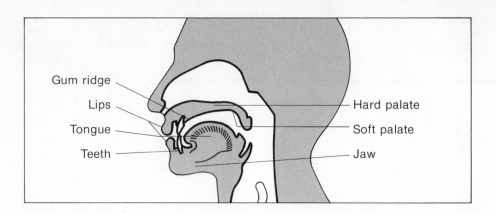

Gum ridge
Lips
Tongue
Teeth
Hard palate
Soft palate
Jaw

sounds. So you, with lightning-quick adjustments, string the sounds together into distinctive patterns called speech.

Of course, the language sounds people speak sometimes are not understood. Mumbling or indistinct speech may result from carelessness, sluggishness, or imitation of another person. Many people are unaware of the need for care and precision in the rapid shifts from one sound to another. Articulation errors result.

Errors in pronunciation can also cause your speech to be misunderstood. **Pronunciation** is the accepted sound of a word. **Articulation** is how well you use the tongue, lips, etc., to clearly and precisely produce the intended sound. So, if you think the word *library* should sound like "liberry," you will mispronounce the word even though you use your articulators perfectly in producing the sounds "li-ber-ry." What if you know the accepted sound but say "liberry" instead? Perhaps you were speaking hurriedly and did not move your lips and tongue enough to produce the right sounds. In this case, you are articulating poorly.

The following may be either articulation or pronunciation errors:

Addition of vowel sounds—"ath-a-lete"
Omission of vowel sounds—"nacherly" for "naturally"
Substitution of vowel sounds—"git" for "get," "crick" for "creek"
Addition of consonant sounds—"sta-stis-tics"
Omission of consonant sounds—"gover-ment" for "government."
Nasalizing nonnasal sounds—"kãow" for "cow," "tãuwn" for "town"
Substitution of consonant sounds—"Babtist" for "Baptist," "assessory" for "ac(k)cessory"
Reversing sounds—"hunderd" for "hundred"
Slurring sounds—"doncha" for "don't you," "whajado?" for "what did you do?" and "gunna" for "going to."

In any situation, you want to be understood when you speak. Since speaking is one of the most complex activities you undertake, use your speech tool carefully. Your relaxed jaw; flexible, active tongue; controlled breathing; and rich, full tones will improve your speaking.

Five Unique Vocal Characteristics

The speech messages you deliver in words are accompanied by **vocal messages.** The manner in which the words are spoken often makes the message clear and understandable. The vocal tones that accompany words may affect the reception of the message by the listener. For example, because your voice is an audible representation of your physical and emotional state, the vocal tones may reinforce positively the words you speak. Or the tone may send a conflicting, negative message. Think of how these words would sound if spoken in tired, unenthusiastic tones:

"Yes, indeed. I'll be glad to do it."

Would you believe the words or the vocal message sent by the voice? In contrast, the same words (which indicate gladness) spoken in a vibrant, clear, enthusiastic manner will be enhanced by the sound of the voice. The sound of the voice—the music behind the words—frequently conveys meaning.

Voices reflect what is going on inside people more accurately than people sometimes know. Voices may indicate doubt, hesitancy, regret, confidence, self-assurance, sympathy—a whole host of inner feelings that the words alone do not convey. Try this yourself by saying aloud, "I really don't know," in different ways. See how many different messages you can transmit vocally using the same set of words.

Five vocal characteristics that accompany the verbal message are pitch, rate, volume or intensity, quality, and enunciation. All these affect the words you say.

1. **Pitch**—the highness or lowness of the sound of the voice.

People tend to respond favorably to relaxed, controlled, well-pitched (neither too high nor too low) voices. The pitch of your voice, you remember, is determined by the length and thickness of your vocal cords. Also, the tension or stress you feel affects your pitch. It will be higher when you feel tense, so relaxation is often the key to lower pitch. But voices that are pleasing to listen to do not remain at one pitch. They rise and fall in varied patterns of pitch. In normal conversation, your voice uses a multitude of different inflection patterns, rising and falling in different ways. It is delightful to listen to. However, in reading aloud or speaking from a manuscript, you may have noticed that speakers' voices tend to flatten out and become monotonous in pitch. The secret for improvement here is to make reading aloud sound like conversation. The speaker can create the music behind the words (vocal variety in pitch) if she or he works for a conversationally communicative presentation. Reading orally should sound like talk.

2. **Rate**—the speed and timing with which the words and sounds are spoken.

Each person has a normal rate of speaking which is adjusted to various situations. Some people think and speak slowly. Others use a rapid overall rate. But the timing of spoken words must be consistent with the message delivered and with the listeners for whom the message is designed. Remember, words are not encoded one by one. Rather, speech is spoken in phrases—groups of sounds—separated by pauses of different lengths. Some phrases spill out rapidly, others move crisply. Some sounds are drawn out and the whole group of sounds is delivered slowly. This variety is easy to listen to, and variation in rate and timing helps the speaker express meaning.

FIGURE 5-4   Variations in vocal tones make a voice interesting to listen to.

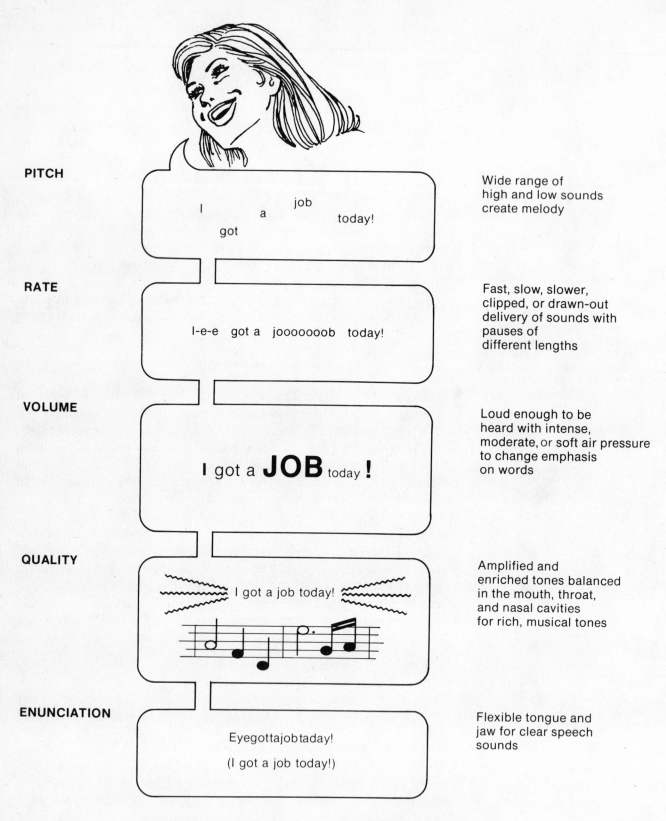

PITCH — Wide range of high and low sounds create melody

RATE — Fast, slow, slower, clipped, or drawn-out delivery of sounds with pauses of different lengths

VOLUME — Loud enough to be heard with intense, moderate, or soft air pressure to change emphasis on words

QUALITY — Amplified and enriched tones balanced in the mouth, throat, and nasal cavities for rich, musical tones

ENUNCIATION — Flexible tongue and jaw for clear speech sounds

You do this beautifully in ordinary conversation. Thus, you can carry this over to public speaking situations.

If you are to speak before a group, your sense of timing will require practice. Hence, experienced speakers "talk" their speeches aloud in private. Thus, they can prepare for an audience by working on use of effective pauses, phrasing ideas carefully, focusing on important ideas, and tossing off unimportant words (*a, the, of,* etc.) to achieve variety in rate. You, too, can benefit from this kind of practice. It will make your ideas seem spontaneous and direct when you speak to your listeners.

3. **Volume or intensity**—the loudness and softness with which words are spoken.

It is most annoying to be unable to hear a speaker, whether from the public platform or across a table. An effective voice should be as loud as the occasion demands. But all phrases are not delivered with the same intensity because they would tend to sound the same. Some words or ideas are spoken with greater force or intensity; some with less. This contrast keeps the listener's attention.

The problem of adequate loudness deserves some mention. Because you can be sure you are using appropriate volume only by checking the feedback from your listeners, you should watch the people to whom you are speaking by maintaining eye contact. You will be able to tell from their nonverbal clues, such as facial expressions and head tilt, whether you are being heard. When speaking to a larger group, direct your voice to those

PHOTO 5-1

The contrast in the speaker's intensity keeps the listener's attention.

seated farthest away. But again, variety in volume is most desirable. Dropping to a quieter tone, building to an intense climax, or emphasizing important ideas by saying them louder or pausing before or after them creates listener interest.

4. **Quality**—those characteristics of a voice which make it unique to the individual.

Can you answer a telephone and identify a friend by voice alone? Can you even identify the mood of your friend by the sound of the voice? The same is true for you. Your physical condition, your vocal mechanism, your feelings and emotions, and the way your voice resonates give you a unique vocal quality. If you are careful to use your resonators (throat, nose, and mouth) openly and let your tones be relaxed and pleasing, your voice will add positive dividends to your speech.

5. **Enunciation**—the clarity with which the sounds of language are produced.

The final vocal characteristic to discuss is related to the organs of articulation and the care with which you use them. There are many reasons why a speaker may develop poor habits of enunciation:

1. As a child, the speaker may have imitated an adult who did not speak distinctly but who served as a role model for the child.
2. The speaker may have learned English as a second language and has difficulty reproducing some English sounds clearly.
3. The speaker may have a physical limitation in some organ of articulation.
4. Cultural influences may have caused some sounds to be omitted or poorly formed.
5. The speaker may be careless, lack interest, or have little training in speaking.

Whatever the reasons for slurred or faulty enunciation, it is difficult to decode such verbal messages. Consonants that supply crispness and punch are lost. Vowels that add richness and melody are distorted. But this problem can be overcome. It requires practice of speech exercises that are designed to focus on problem areas. It also requires a relaxed jaw, a flexible tongue, and a desire to produce clear, distinct speech.

Vocabulary Building

In addition to developing an interesting speaking voice, you will want to expand your speaking vocabulary and increase the accuracy of pronunciation. If you are like most people, your reading vocabulary is larger than your speaking vocabulary. That is, you recognize words and their meanings from the context of the printed page, but you may hesitate to say the words. You may be unsure of the accepted sounds or the emphasized syllables.

The problem stems from the fact that we use a 26-letter alphabet in writing but our spoken language includes more than 40 sounds that are spelled in a variety of ways. Hence, it is not always easy to know which sounds to use. Also, words are divided into syllables. In every word, one syllable is stressed more strongly than the others. So, unless you have heard the word spoken frequently, you may hesitate to use it in speaking.

There are two ways to enlarge your speaking vocabulary. First, listen carefully to the speech of others. Good speakers choose interesting, vivid, and precise words. You can add these words to your vocabulary by listening to the way they are used and pronounced by others.

Second, increase your speaking vocabulary by checking the pronunciation in a dictionary. When you look up words to verify spelling, also check acceptable pronunciation. The diacritical markings over the letters, particularly the vowel sounds, indicate the preferred pronunciation. Each dictionary has a key word to clearly indicate the sound of each letter. Words are also divided into syllables with the syllable receiving the strongest emphasis marked. Check your pronunciation of these frequently mispronounced words: *harass, athlete, accessory, affluent, formidable.*

THE SPEAKING EXCHANGE

Business talk revolves around business subject matter. It also flows between people. At either end of a verbal business message is a person who is functioning in two roles—as an employee and as an individual. That person brings specialized skills and knowledge to the job each day plus personal beliefs, attitudes, and values. It is the vocal delivery of the verbal message that reflects the attitudes and feelings of speakers. In dealing with people about job-related matters, it is vital to pay attention to the people on the other end. The way something is said determines whether the message is understood and accepted—and many times whether the job gets done. The way people speak to you has much to do with whether you tackle the job with enthusiasm or reluctance.

CHAPTER SUMMARY

In delivering the words we speak, we add a vocal message to the verbal message. Our voices provide additional meaning to the words. A good speaker understands the four steps in creating speech sounds: breathing control for a solid foundation; relaxed throat for clear tones; balanced use of the resonating chambers for maximum amplification; and precise articulation of the sounds of speech. We can create more interesting voices by concentrating on the unique vocal characteristics of pitch, rate, volume or intensity, quality, and enunciation. In order to improve speech communication skills, you can increase vocabulary and pronunciation accuracy by listening to good speakers and by using a dictionary.

Finally, the two-way speech communication flow between people is divided into two areas—the words used to talk about the job, and the way words are delivered by the voice to maintain good working relationships.

WORKSHOP ACTIVITIES

VOICE ANALYSIS *(Individual and Group Activity)*

Purpose: To record and listen to your voice. To respond to the questions as you listen and analyze the sound of your voice.

Briefing: Tape-record two examples of your voice—once talking, once reading. For the first recording, explain which of the workshop activities you have most enjoyed. Then prepare to read orally one of the ceremonial speeches on pages 173-174 of this book for the second recording. Several students might help you fill out this page by listening to your voice with you.

1. Is this a voice I could listen to comfortably for any length of time?

   yes _____   no _____   maybe _____

2. Would I describe the voice as pleasant?   yes _____   no _____   somewhat _____

   interesting?   yes _____   no _____   somewhat _____

   expressive?   yes _____   no _____   somewhat _____

3. Was the pitch of the voice what I expected to hear?

   higher _____   lower _____   about right _____

4. Were the inflection patterns pleasing, varied, and melodic?

   yes _____   no _____   moderately _____

5. Did I hear particular inflection patterns repeated over and over?

   yes _____   no _____

6. Were there variations in loudness—some soft, some more intense?

   yes _____   no _____   occasionally _____

7. Were there changes in rate and interesting pauses?   yes _____   no _____

8. Did I hear words that were not pronounced clearly and distinctly? Which words?

9. Would I describe the energy level of the voice as:

   tired _____   enthusiastic _____

   monotonous _____   lively _____

   put-on _____   bored _____

   hesitant _____   engaging _____

   uninterested _____

10. Were there differences between the speaking tape and the reading tape? If so, list these differences.

11. On a separate sheet of paper, make a list of vocal qualities that need improvement.

VOICE IMPROVEMENT EXERCISES *(Individual Activity)*

Purpose: To perform easy activities that will increase vocal effectiveness.

1. Put your hands at the bottom of your rib cage, squeeze tightly, and say loudly, "boomlay, boomlay, boomlay, boom!" You should feel strong, vigorous action of the diaphragm. If not, keep trying until you do.

2. Hold a lighted candle four inches from your lips and say, "Peter Piper picked a peck of pickled peppers." If the flame goes out, you are exhaling more air than necessary. You are likely to get popping sounds on a public address system. Practice with the candle until the flame remains steady as you speak.

3. Try speaking in a whisper to a friend across the room. When you can be clearly heard, ask your friend to move farther away. Keep working on projecting a whisper until you can be heard in the next room.

4. Relax your throat and jaw by slumping forward in your chair. Let your head drop, your jaw sag, and your arms flop loosely. As you circle your head gently, yawn several times. Stretch your jaw wide. With relaxation and rich resonance say, "shock," "taught," "oyster," "proud," "beware," "squaw," "gong."

5. Stretch and yawn. Open your mouth as if to yawn again, but instead, repeat "ha, how, ho" several times. Keep the throat open as if you were going to yawn.

6. Imagine that you are going to call a meeting to order. Keep a relaxed throat and a round full tone as you say, "The meeting will come to order." Pretend that you are now speaking to a group of 50 people. Speak louder, but do not change the relaxed throat. Push from the diaphragm. Now pretend that you are speaking to a very large group of 300 people. Do not raise the pitch—just the volume level.

7. Work for a low and comfortable pitch by repeating, "alone, alon-n-n-n-ne, al-l-l-l al-l-l-l-l alo-o-o-on-n-n-n-ne."

8. Hold your nose and say the word "meaning." It should sound muffled because "m," "n," and "ng" are resonated in the nasal cavity but not emitted through the nose. Now say "meaning" in your normal voice and prolong the nasal sounds. Feel the vibration in your nose and cheekbones as you add richness with these sounds: "m-m-me-e-e-n-n-n-ing-ng-ng."

9. Work for a full tone with these words:

   "Mine eyes have seen the glory
      of the coming of the Lord;
   He is trampling out the vintage
      where the grapes of wrath are stored."

10. Hum the sound of "m-m-m-m-m." Feel the vibration. Hum the sound of "n-n-n-n-n." Say the word "sing-ng-ng-ng-ng-ng."

SPEECH ANALYSIS *(Individual and Group Activity)*

Purpose: To listen carefully to your articulation of speech sounds.

Briefing: If you recorded your voice, listen to the tape again. This time listen for the sounds of speech that you might improve. Several students may help you listen and make suggestions. Listen for the following:

1. Did you slur or omit words or sounds? If so, list them.

2. Did you precisely articulate the sounds in which the breath is stopped (p, b, t, d, k, g)? Say the sound—not the name of the letter—to isolate it.

3. Did you clearly pronounce (with no hissing) the sounds in which the breath is partially stopped (f, v, th, s, sh, z, zh)? Say the sound—not the name of the letter—to isolate it.

4. Is there a clear difference between "w" and "wh," "l" and "r"?

5. Are "m," "n," and "ng" well resonated in the nasal cavities and sounded through the nose?

6. Are the common words given their appropriate *un*stressed enunciation (a = uh, the = thuh, and = un/nd, of = ov, was = wuhz, etc.)?

7. Is the primary emphasis or stress on the nouns and verbs that convey meaning?

SPEECH IMPROVEMENT EXERCISES *(Individual and Group Activity)*

Purpose: To increase the energetic use of the tongue, lips, and teeth. To work for a relaxed jaw. To practice vocal variety and clear articulation.

1. A flexible tongue will aid your articulation.

   a. Tongue Stretch. Open your mouth and stretch your tongue out until you touch the tip of your nose. (You probably can't reach it—but try.) Pull the tongue in. Again extend the tongue and try to touch your chin. Repeat these exercises rapidly ten times.

   b. Tongue Sweep. Open your mouth and form a large circle with your lips. With the tip of your tongue, sweep around the rim of your mouth in one direction while you silently count to 20. Try to keep a steady pace but increase the rate. Now reverse and do it in the opposite direction.

2. Repeat the alphabet ten times using the jaw, lips, and tongue very energetically. Overdo the articulation.

3. Clench your teeth, lock your jaw, and use just your tongue and lips to say,

   "He thrust three thousand thistles through the thick of his thumb."

   Repeat it more rapidly and vigorously. Now release your jaw and articulate clearly.

4. With wide-open jaw movements say, "ah, ee, oo, aw." Repeat ten times.

5. With firm lip movements say, "boo, bee, bah, baw, moo, mee, mah, maw."

6. Say this in one breath and sustain the sounds: "For the moon never beams without bringing me dreams of the beautiful Annabel Lee." Repeat until you can be as strong at the end of the sentence as the beginning.

7. Build this sentence in intensity so that the climax comes after "burst." Be sure you do not punch the word "burst," but build up the intensity gradually.

   "The notes of the deep laboring organ burst / upon the ear."

8. Try these tongue twisters until you can repeat each five times clearly:

   "She sells seashells by the sea shore."
   "The big black bug bled black blood."
   "Which witch wore white?" (Make the "wh" and "w" sounds different.)

9. Crisp up your consonants:

   "To sit in solemn silence in a dull, dark dock,
   In a pestilential prison, with a life-long lock,
   Awaiting the sensation of a short, sharp shock,
   From a cheap and chippy chopper on a big black block."

   Gilbert and Sullivan

PRACTICE EXERCISES ON SPEECH SOUNDS* *(Individual Activity)*

Purpose: To gain practice in pronouncing and distinguishing the various sounds of the English language.

Briefing: Read the following exercise aloud to increase clarity of articulation and enunciation. Note that the same sound may be spelled in a variety of ways. Each underlined sound is pronounced the same as the other words in the group. The exercise contains the sounds of American English.

Vowels

1. be, beet, beat, people, key, piece, perceive, ski, quay, amoeba
2. it, pretty, been, women, business, build, syllable
3. ah, on, are, palm, heart, knowledge, sergeant, honest
4. at, plaid, salve, laugh
5. earn, urn, her, sir, colonel, worst, courage, myrrh
6. about, occur, problem, upon
7. love, does (verb), flood, much, tongue, us
8. to, too, two, student, knew, lieu, queue, true, you
9. look, woman, would, worsted, full
10. all, awl, broad, talk, vault, taught, office, ought
11. egg, head, debt, many, aesthetic, said, weather, heifer, leopard, bury, guess

Diphthongs (two vowel sounds blended together)

1. our, hour, doubt, brow, kraut
2. oh, owe, so, sew, coat, roe, row, dough, beau, yeoman, soul, brooch, apropos (when slighted or unstressed, this sound assumes the characteristics of a vowel)
3. I, aye, eye, tie, buy, by, high, aisle, isle, guide, height
4. able, main, say, mesa, grey, steak, they, neigh, gauge, bouquet (when slighted or unstressed, this sound assumes the characteristics of a vowel)
5. boy, coin
6. air, e'er, care, there, their, wear
7. ear, peer, pier, here

Consonants

1. pay, happy, shepherd, hiccough
2. best, ribbon, cupboard
3. tip, letter, thyme, asked
4. desk, add
5. kiss, cool, occur, echo, clock, khaki
6. give, rigging, ghetto
7. five, safe, cuff, soften, diphthong, laugh
8. vote, of, flivver
9. think
10. this, breathe
11. see, success, science, psychology
12. zest, buzz, as, because, xylophone
13. shop, passion, sugar, conscience, addition, appreciate, chic
14. pleasure, azure, regime, prestige
15. chat, catch, righteous
16. joke, manager, wage
17. wear, quiet, choir
18. where
19. may, limb, name, comment, hymn
20. now, funny, gnat, know, mnemonic, pneumatic
21. think, sing
22. like, will
23. right, arrive, rhythm, write
24. you, million, hallelujah (also combined with vowel in use)
25. hello, who

---

* Morris Philip Wolf and Shirley Kuiper, *Effective Communication in Business*, 8th ed. (Cincinnati: South-Western Publishing Co., 1984), pp. 130-131.

VOCABULARY BUILDING* *(Individual Activity)*

Purpose: To look up the correct pronunciation in a dictionary. To articulate each word in an effective oral manner.

1. administrator
2. affiliation
3. analyze
4. annual inventory
5. apropos
6. assessment
7. associates
8. business etiquette
9. businesses
10. bill of lading
11. client
12. clientele
13. commercial
14. commissions
15. consensus
16. consultant
17. coordinator
18. counseling
19. data processing
20. deducted
21. defective
22. dictating
23. division
24. employee
25. employer
26. entrepreneur
27. executive
28. fiscal
29. incorporated
30. initiator
31. innovation
32. inventories
33. itemized
34. marital status
35. merchandise
36. occupational
37. opportunity
38. option
39. participants
40. percentage
41. personnel
42. prerequisite
43. prospective buyer
44. receptionist
45. referral
46. strategy
47. supervisor
48. transaction
49. transportation tariff
50. vocational

---

* Compiled by Dr. Ray Spitzenberger, Wharton Community College, Wharton, Texas.

CONNECTED SPEECH SOUNDS *(Pair Activity)*

Briefing: When we speak to each other in comfortable, informal situations, we omit sounds, substitute sounds, blend sounds together, and speak a whole idea as a speech phrase rather than a complete sentence. When two people speak the same speech patterns, they probably understand each other. Would you understand this conversation? How does it differ from formal speech? Read the following conversation with a partner.

Two Fishermen Meet (Read across)

JOE: "Hiyamac"	MAC: "Lobuddy"
JOE: "Binearlong?"	MAC: "Coplours"
JOE: "Catchanenny?"	MAC: "Goddafew"
JOE: "Kindarthey?"	MAC: "Basenpicrl"
JOE: "Ennysizetoom?"	MAC: "Cuplpouns"
JOE: "Wachauzin"	MAC: "Wumsenminers"
JOE: "Wachadrinkin?"	MAC: "Kobeer"
JOE: "Igoddago"	MAC: "Tubad"
JOE: "Seeyaroun"	MAC: "Yeatakideezy"
JOE: "Guluck"	MAC: "Slong"

SPEAKING STYLES *(Individual Activity)*

Briefing: What you say can make a strong impact on your listeners, but the way you speak is equally important. Your speaking style often reveals strong, sometimes negative feelings you would rather disguise. Yet listeners pick up clues to these feelings from a speaker's manner. Can you recognize some of your mannerisms? Check the ones of which you are aware. Watch for others.

1. _____ When you are uncomfortable, do you tend to speed up the rate of your speech and come on a bit strong?

2. _____ When you are nervous or fearful, do you find your voice goes up in pitch because your vocal cords get tense?

3. _____ When you are depressed, tired, or sad, does your voice tend to trail off?

4. _____ When you are excited about your subject, do you speak loudly to get people's attention or to dominate the conversation?

5. _____ When you lack confidence in what you are saying, do you tend to talk too softly so that your listeners must strain to hear you?

6. _____ Can you feel your throat muscles get tight when you are angry and are trying to conceal it?

7. _____ Do you reveal your lack of communication confidence by overusing such cliché phrases as, "Right?", "I guess", or "Don't you know?"

8. _____ Do you show that you are unsure about what you are saying by punctuating your conversation with frequent "uh" or "ah" sounds?

9. _____ Do you often try to hide your feelings by giggling or making jokes?

10. _____ When you feel a strong need for acceptance, do you find yourself boasting or stretching the truth?

11. _____ Do you ever seek reassurance by saying something negative about yourself?

12. _____ When you don't agree with someone, do you hedge by saying, "I agree with you, but . . ."?

13. _____ When you are worried, do you use such phrases as, "Well, I guess it will turn out all right"?

14. _____ Do you find yourself agreeing with someone who seems very positive about a topic, even though you may have some doubts?

15. _____ Do you tend to talk too much when you are trying to reassure yourself?

SAMPLE CEREMONIAL SPEECHES FOR SPECIAL OCCASIONS *(Individual Reference)*

Purpose: To practice reading orally. To role play the presentation of a speech on a particular occasion. To use the following as models for the speaking assignment on page 175.

Briefing: The following examples are called *courtesy* or *ceremonial* speeches, because they are designed to suit a particular audience on a special occasion. Speeches of this type are carefully planned, clearly and originally worded, and practiced well so that the delivery seems spontaneous and sincere.

Read each of the following speeches aloud. You may use them as recording samples for voice and speech analyses. Stand as you read each one and imagine that you are speaking to the particular audience for whom they are written.

Speech of Presentation (Based on an Analogy)

The audience: Management and salespersons of Anderson Distributing Company and their spouses. About 120 persons are present.
The setting: The banquet hall of the LeClaire Hotel.
The occasion: An annual dinner at which the top salesperson of the year is announced. The president of Anderson Distributing Company makes this presentation.

Receiving the distinction of salesperson of the year is somewhat like winning the Boston Marathon. In running the marathon, everyone starts together. They run steadily. Facing obstacles, they push on, their spirit undaunted. And, if they haven't quit along the way, they cross the finish line. The winner is the one who comes in first. But really, all of the runners who finish can consider themselves winners.

I consider all of the salespersons gathered here tonight as "winners" because you didn't fall by the wayside. However, the award must go to the one who ran hardest, making the most sales; the one who ran the steadiest by always being available to the customer; the one who ran with determination even when the sale was difficult to make. That winner, who has displayed leadership, stability, and determination, is our top salesperson for 1987. Please congratulate with me . . . Carol Siefker.

Speech of Acceptance (Based on a Personal Story)

The audience: Five members of management and their spouses, 27 salespeople and their spouses.
The setting: A dinner at the Maple Bluff Country Club. The members of management and their spouses are seated on a raised platform facing the room. The salespeople and their spouses are seated at round tables on the main floor.
The occasion: The annual awards ceremony, dinner, a few brief speeches, climaxed by the announcement of Salesperson of the Year. The announcement has just been made and the honoree, Phil Swegler, is accepting his award.

If you have ever watched a cat the first time it hunts for a bird, you know that only one bird can be caught at a time. If the cat tries to catch two or three at once, it won't even get a feather.

Tonight in accepting this award for Salesperson of the Year, I have to thank my cat for letting me observe him. He taught me to take care of one customer at a time, close the deal, and then go out for bigger game.

Now that all of you know my secret, I hope you all will join me in selling your way to a fortune! Or at least to this gratifying award—Salesperson of the Year! Thank you.

Response to a Welcome (Based on a Quotation)

The audience: Twelve male members of the board of directors of a public relations firm. One female member newly elected.

The setting: A luncheon meeting in the executive suite. All are seated at a long table.

The occasion: A regular board meeting will follow the luncheon. The president of the board has just announced the election of Patricia Lopez as a new member and has made a brief speech of welcome. This is Ms. Lopez's response.

You have often heard the saying, "Behind every great man stands a woman." But for too long this quotation stereotyped women as a support group eagerly pushing a particular husband ahead. Today, freer life-styles accept women as partners with equal intelligence and ability. We are even encouraged to compete in the marketplace.

Women have come a long way, but only with the help of their comrades—men. You have accepted us into your world of business and have given us the chance to prove our worth.

Working with you in this top-ranking public relations firm has been a challenge, to say the least. As the first woman on the board of directors, I can only say, "Thank you for your trust."

Though many would point out the disadvantages of being the lone woman here, I am sure it will not hinder our work. I promise to give the board added insight into what 53 percent of America's population is thinking. And, in closing, I would add a slight twist to the age-old saying: no longer behind, but "Next to every great man will stand a woman."

Speech of Farewell (Based on a Phrase)

The audience: Employees of Hallman and Associates. There are about thirty men and women present.

The setting: A banquet room at the Marriott Hotel, 7:30, Friday evening.

The occasion: A farewell dinner honoring Tom Atherton, who is leaving the company to start his own business. The president of Hallman and Associates makes this presentation.

Study it, learn it, live it! That phrase is why Hallman and Associates is Number One in our field, and I know everyone in this room understands that Tom Atherton is the person who instigated the "Study it, learn it, live it" policy here at Hallman's.

We owe Tom much more than dinner and a gift. We owe him our deepest gratitude for showing us—and teaching us—the importance of product knowledge and the art of knowing your competitor.

Even though Tom is moving on, his methods and his successful policies will remain with us. I know everyone in this room wishes Tom the best of luck in his new business. We are happy for you, Tom, and we'll miss you!

SPEAKING ASSIGNMENT—COURTESY SPEECH *(Individual Oral Presentation)*

Purpose: To write a short analysis of an audience and a special occasion. To design and deliver a brief, appropriate courtesy speech.

Briefing: On the job you may be asked to speak on behalf of other employees: to express appreciation, welcome, gratitude, or goodwill. Speeches of this sort are:

1. Brief in length.
2. Carefully planned and practiced.
3. Designed to suit the occasion and the honoree.
4. Built around a story, quotation, proverb, or analogy.
5. Planned to be original, memorable, and dynamic.
6. Delivered with minimal notes.

Assignment: Select a particular audience and occasion. Analyze these to discover the purpose for a courtesy speech. Build the speech around an interest-getting device, such as an apt quotation. Make it brief but sincere. Practice it orally many times. Use only a note card with a few phrases as reminders. Deliver it to your class as if they were the audience you planned. The critique sheet for evaluation is on page 176.

Suggested Types of Courtesy or Ceremonial Speeches:

A. *Speech of Introduction:* This speech, designed to create audience interest in the main speaker, may provide biographical details about the speaker if these are unknown to the audience. If the speaker is known, the speech seeks to link the speaker and/or the speaker's subject with the needs of the audience. Focus on the speaker or subject.

B. *Speech of Presentation:* These words accompany a gift, a prize, or a trophy, and express appreciation or congratulations. Explain the significance of the award, the qualifications of the honoree, or the reasons it is being presented. Capture the feelings of the occasion and make the speech memorable for the recipient.

C. *Speech of Acceptance or Response:* When a gift or award is presented, a gracious response is appropriate. Acknowledge the object being accepted and what it represents, comment on its usefulness and why it is being awarded, and express sincere gratitude for the honor. Share credit with others, relate personal involvement with the group, and share personal feelings of appreciation.

D. *Speech of Welcome or Farewell:* A speech of welcome is designed to generate goodwill, to link the visitors to the group by noting common bonds, and to help the audience feel honored by the presence of the people being welcomed. A speech of farewell is extended to a person who is being transferred or is retiring. There are mixed feelings to be expressed. Look back to common experiences shared by all, and look forward to future meetings or new challenges. Wish the honoree success.

CRITIQUE SHEET—COURTESY SPEECH *(Instructor's Evaluation)*

Briefing: Tear out this page and hand it to your instructor before you speak.

SUBJECT OF SPEECH: _____

POSSIBLE POINTS: 50 (Each question: 5 points)

The Verbal Message (30 points):

1. Did the speaker identify the audience, setting, and occasion prior to the speech? _____

2. Did the speaker present adequate information, such as who the speaker is, why the award is given, etc.? _____

3. Did the speaker effectively represent the spirit of the audience and occasion? _____

4. Did the speaker include one of the requirements (quotation, analogy, story)? _____

5. Did the length of the speech suit the occasion? _____

6. Was the conclusion effective (i.e., did it lead to a climax, create anticipation, etc.)? _____

The Nonverbal Message (10 points):

7. Was the speaker enthusiastic, poised, and communicative? _____

8. Was the speaker's voice loud enough and interesting to listen to? _____

Effectiveness of Communication (10 points):

9. Did the speaker maintain interest? _____

10. Did the speaker fulfill the purpose of the assignment? _____

Total _____

Instructor's Comments

Words of Praise:

Suggestions for Improvement:

CHECKLIST OF COMMUNICATION TERMS *(Quiz)*

Check your understanding of the terms presented in this chapter by putting the number of the correct term in the blank before its definition. Note there are more terms than definitions.

<table>
<tr><td colspan="2">Definitions</td><td>Terms</td></tr>
<tr><td>a. _____</td><td>Open areas above the roof of the mouth that serve as resonators.</td><td>1. delivery
2. brain
3. nervous system</td></tr>
<tr><td>b. _____</td><td>Shaping the sounds of vowels and consonants by the tongue, lips, jaw, teeth, and palates.</td><td>4. vibrations
5. organs of articulation
6. windpipe</td></tr>
<tr><td>c. _____</td><td>Major muscle that increases lung capacity and provides controlled air pressure for rich vocal sound.</td><td>7. bronchial tubes
8. diaphragm
9. abdominal and rib muscles</td></tr>
<tr><td>d. _____</td><td>The speed and timing with which words and sounds are spoken.</td><td>10. larynx
11. vocal cords
12. resonating areas</td></tr>
<tr><td>e. _____</td><td>The highness or lowness of the sound of the voice.</td><td>13. resonates
14. resonance</td></tr>
<tr><td>f. _____</td><td>Two tiny membranes which draw together across the windpipe and are set into vibration by air being exhaled.</td><td>15. pharynx
16. nasal cavities
17. oral cavity</td></tr>
<tr><td>g. _____</td><td>The manner in which words are spoken.</td><td>18. pronunciation
19. articulation
20. vocal messages</td></tr>
<tr><td>h. _____</td><td>Lips, tongue, teeth, jaw, hard and soft palate.</td><td>21. pitch
22. rate
23. volume or intensity</td></tr>
<tr><td>i. _____</td><td>Those characteristics of a voice which make it unique to an individual.</td><td>24. quality
25. enunciation</td></tr>
<tr><td>j. _____</td><td>The accepted sounds and stress of a word indicated in a dictionary.</td><td></td></tr>
</table>

CHAPTER 6

Let's Talk About the Business of Integrating Your Nonverbal Skills

This chapter covers a series of behaviors and environmental factors known collectively as nonverbal communication. Although presented separately from verbal communication, these behaviors are an integral part of the way you send and receive messages. You will learn how verbal and nonverbal communication fit together and are integrated into the whole human communication system. After reading the chapter and participating in the activities, you should be able to do the following:

Chapter Objectives

1. Define and give examples of nonverbal communication channels.
2. Identify the relationship between verbal and nonverbal communication.
3. Describe the effects of place, setting, space, time, and occasion on business transactions.
4. Explain the importance of nonverbal communication in talking business.

A smiling recruiter for a large company steps to the office door, calls the next job applicant's name, and surveys the people seated in the waiting room. Each person is a prospective employee and is waiting to be interviewed. One young woman sits by herself. She has short hair and wears no makeup, and her white-collared navy blue dress covers her knees. Her fingers clasp and unclasp the purse she holds in her lap as she returns the recruiter's gaze without smiling. Across the room sits a college-age man in a brown three-piece suit. His vest has rolled up on his stomach, his left ankle rests on his right knee. His hair is straight and falls below his white shirt collar. Next to him lounges a man in matching sports shirt and slacks, white socks, and loafers. His legs are thrust out in front of him. The man is talking to a woman dressed in a rose pantsuit. Her heavy gold hoop earrings flash as she tosses her long hair and returns the recruiter's smile.

Company recruiters face a variety of candidates as they interview prospective employees for positions in the company. They already know the qualifications required for the job openings; their task is to match people to positions, learning as much as they can about each applicant. Three types of communication provide this information: reading a résumé, talking to each applicant privately, and observing each one individually. On the basis of this interview, the recruiter makes hiring decisions.

Suppose you are waiting to be interviewed. How will a recruiter evaluate you? The actual encounter starts even before you are called in to the interviewing room. The recruiter has already gained an impression of you from your application form and your résumé. All the information you put down is carefully absorbed, and the way you wrote it is also noted. The recruiter checks the care you took in writing or typing your résumé, looking to see if you included all pertinent data and if your spelling is accurate. These details give an indication of your ability to handle language. Now the recruiter is ready to interview you in person. The mental picture of you that the recruiter has gained from reviewing your written materials will be strengthened or refocused by what you say and how you look. When your name is called, you rise and walk to the door of the inner office. The recruiter stands in the open doorway and watches carefully as you approach, noting in a quick glance whether you move confidently with a sense of poise and balance, or get up self-consciously, awkwardly rearranging your clothes. The recruiter is looking at you as if you were already on the job, trying to visualize you in the position you have applied for and assessing whether you will make a good impression in that job. If you are a woman, the recruiter's eyes quickly take in the height of your heels, the length of your skirt, the way your accessories combine to make an attractive appearance. If you are a man, the recruiter scrutinizes the cut of your suit, your choice of shirt and tie, the shine of your shoes.

Even the handshake you give tells the recruiter something about you. Do you take the recruiter's hand firmly and respond cordially, meeting the recruiter's gaze? When you are invited into the office and pass close to the recruiter, more details are noticed—the cleanliness of your hair, the closeness of your shave if you are a man, the amount of makeup you are wearing if you are a woman. The recruiter also notes other aspects of being close to you, such as the strength of your perfume or after-shave lotion. As you pass through the door, the recruiter checks the back of you. Are your heels rundown? Does your skirt sag in the back? Are your clothes wrinkled and untidy? All these sights, sounds, and smells add up to the total picture you create.

By the time the interview starts, the recruiter already knows a great deal about you. Up to this point, the recruiter and you, the applicant, have not talked much, but information has been received and processed. Much of this information has come through nonverbal rather than verbal channels. Communication is certainly present.

PHOTO 6-1

A recruiter gains a mental picture of a job applicant from reviewing the applicant's written materials.

SILENT MESSAGES

In the illustration you just read, messages were communicated by a whole series of factors, not just speech. Language and speaking are important communication tools. The sense of hearing and the skill of listening are essential to these verbal messages, but this is only a part of communication. In our earlier study of perception, we were reminded that we respond to stimuli received through *all* our senses. Consciously or unconsciously, we pay attention to a variety of messages that are not spoken, as did the recruiter in the story.

Verbal messages, then, do not occur in a vacuum. Speech is created by muscular contractions, accompanied by eye movements, and frequently punctuated by gestures. Speech occurs in a setting, at a time, on an occasion. Our busy sensory systems select from a tapestry of sights, sounds, and smells as we examine the context of verbal messages. These silent messages communicate too.

Definition of Nonverbal Communication

Because the term nonverbal communication includes messages from a wide range of channels, we will define it generally. For our purpose, nonverbal communication can be defined as those communications not written or spoken. This then includes all the ways human beings communicate with each other except for words.

Nonverbal Message Channels

You were first made aware of nonverbal communication channels when you studied Figure 1-2 on page 8 in the first chapter. Refer again to this diagram. Note the many channels for messages: words, voice, body language, space, time, personal appearance. Think of these categories as channels through which messages are communicated rather than as messages themselves. Remember, the messages are what we make of the stimuli received through the senses.

Through nonverbal message channels we gather information about other people. These channels include the following:

Physical characteristics: height; weight; age; sex; body structure; beard or mustache; skin color and texture; blemishes; handicaps; color, length, and style of hair; etc.

Body movement or stillness: posture in sitting, standing, or reclining; movement of the torso, arms, legs, head, hands, shoulders; and more subtle movement of face and eyes.

Personal appearance: choices of clothing; shoes; glasses; jewelry; etc.

Personal possessions: desk equipment; living quarters; furnishings; automobile; etc.

Personal preferences about spending time: working; sleeping; vacationing; committee work; social activities; etc.

Preferences in the use of space: size; shape; texture; arrangement; lighting; color; temperature; etc.

As you talk business, you do more than speak and listen. You use your eyes to actively decode a variety of nonverbal messages: forming impressions, paying attention to unexpressed feelings and attitudes, and developing sensitivity toward others. The messages you send and receive through nonverbal channels are essential to business talk.

Difference Between Verbal and Nonverbal Communication

Consider two major differences between verbal communication (spoken or written words) and nonverbal communication (actions and behavior).

1. **Verbal messages** are language-based. We are taught precise ways of using words to convey abstract types of information.

Whether written or spoken, verbal messages require that people share a common language system if they are to communicate. Through this language code, complex kinds of information such as math concepts, alternatives for problem solving, and data for analysis can be transmitted. Note the number of years you have had to study the English language in order to use it well. Verbal messages are important, because much of our knowledge comes through symbol systems that are used in reading, writing, and speaking.

2. **Nonverbal communication** is rooted in cultural experience, learned through social imitation, and absorbed through living. These messages provide information not often expressed in words.

Human beings produce and receive communication within a framework of behaviors that give meaning to what people say and how people understand. You have learned these behaviors unconsciously and without training or special instruction. For example, you are aware of the acceptable distance between people during different types of interactions, the type of touching that is tolerated, patterns of looking at another person, and who sits where in certain situations. All these behaviors are rooted in the way we grow up, and these patterns are different in each culture. You have learned to read the people you deal with through nonverbal communication. And they read you.

Nonverbal Communication Affects Verbal Communication

Because nonverbal communication accompanies the spoken word, it affects verbal communication in three ways: by strengthening it, by changing it, or by substituting for it.

1. **Nonverbal communication** strengthens verbal messages.

It was stressed in Chapter 5 that the vocal sound accompanying the words spoken is a powerful indicator of feelings. If the recruiter in the story said, "I'm very happy to meet you," and delivered that verbal message with a warm and friendly sound, the applicant would probably feel very welcomed. If the recruiter gave the applicant a firm, eager handshake, the verbal message would be further reinforced.

2. **Nonverbal communication** changes verbal messages.

"Those who work in the print media often envy those of the electronic media. Those in the electronic media—by a change in tone, by a lifted eyebrow, by a sudden laugh—can give an unexpected meaning, a 'touch of innuendo' as it were, to something they are saying or reading."

Robert Bentley

If, however, the recruiter had said the same words in a flat, unenthusiastic voice and had given the applicant a limp handshake, the nonverbal message would have contradicted the verbal message. Because these nonverbal messages are so deeply rooted in our experience, we often believe them rather than the words we hear. As the applicant, you would react to the lack of consistency between the words and actions. You might assume the recruiter was not glad to meet you for some unknown reason. You are more likely to believe what you see (or sense through other channels) than the words being spoken. You trust your eyes more than your ears. So, silent messages can change the interpretation of verbal messages. If the verbal message says one thing, but the nonverbal message contradicts it, the nonverbal will be the message believed. People often mask their feelings behind words, but when others are sensitive to silent messages, it is difficult to cover up feelings. Think of the people you most trust. Don't their words and nonverbal messages match? We call these *consistent messages*. So, silent messages can strengthen words by being consistent with the words, or can change meanings of words by being different from the verbal message.

3. **Nonverbal communication** substitutes for verbal messages.

What happens when four drivers arrive simultaneously at a four-way stop? Who goes first? second? Through nods, smiles, shrugs, pointing, etc., the decision is communicated without words.

Consider how each of these gestures substitutes for words: a hitchhiker's thumb, a baseball umpire's outstretched arms, palms down signalling "safe," or a traffic officer's wave telling you to move along. In an interview, a recruiter may signal the end of the meeting by standing up. Though no words are spoken, you read the silent message and know that it is time to make a graceful exit.

Nonverbal Communication Regulates Communication Situations

Communication happens in a particular geographic location—someplace, somewhere. This environment often prescribes the kinds of communication that will take place. For example, some surroundings invite oral communication; other settings seem to discourage it. Note the different seating arrangements in Figure 6-1. Speculate on how the arrangement of the space affects who speaks, the topics talked about, and the kind of listening.

FIGURE 6-1

The arrangement of a room affects the way people speak and listen.

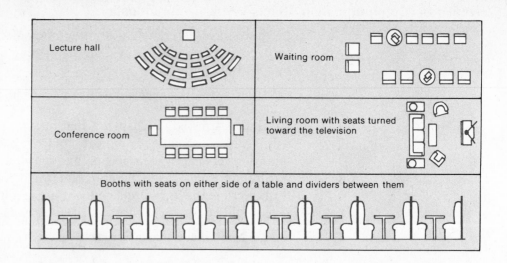

Space is used also to indicate power and status within business organizations. Powerful people are allotted larger offices, seats at the head of the table, and greater distances from others. Furthermore, the way a room is decorated, ventilated, and lighted regulates the kinds of communication situations—formal, informal, casual, business, social, etc. Carpeting, drapes, and comfortable seating produce positive feelings and cooperative attitudes. The use of wood and dark red colors in expensive restaurants encourages relaxation and intimate conversation. It is more difficult to talk if the area is noisy, the seats are too far apart, or there is so much clutter it is impossible to sit down. Soft, low lights seem to encourage social talk, while brighter lights are needed for business-oriented conversation.

These silent messages regulate communication situations and influence how we deal with each other.

NONVERBAL CODES

In the culture of the United States, as in other cultures, there are unwritten rules that guide nonverbal behavior. These rules, known as **codes**, are based on expectations people share about the behavior of others. Through the channels of personal appearance, physical movement, and the use of time and space you express your individuality, identify with groups, and clarify your position or status. By your adherence to the codes of dress and behavior, or by your disregard of them, you send messages about how you think and feel.

The business you work for is a small cultural society within a larger one. The company will have certain codes they will expect you to observe. This is natural, because any company is represented to the world by its employees. Clearly the higher up in the company you go, the more vital your role in representing that company. What are these unwritten codes that your company expects you to meet?

Personal Appearance

Your personal appearance is an important part of how you present yourself to others. As a matter of fact, it is one of the first things people notice. Your own individual style is reflected in your clothes, hairstyle, grooming, and personal accessories, and the more attractive your appearance, the greater impact, influence, and credibility you will have.

Now, this is not to suggest that you should spend money on new outfits to impress others. What is important is to discover and conform to the appropriate dress for a particular job or business. Clothes show group identification, status, and self-image.

> "Dress has a lot to do with how people act toward you."
>
> *Anonymous*

Group identification: Uniforms identify certain categories of workers—nurses, police officers, airline pilots, surgeons, people in the military, etc.

Status: College students dress more informally than office workers. People in service positions often wear smocks, aprons, coveralls, or other types of protective clothing. People in executive or managerial positions follow current trends in appropriate clothing such as the currently fashionable three-piece suits.

Self-image: Although styles emphasize the freedom to express personal identity through choice, there are still certain expectations on the job. Clothes that are conspicuous or too different from those of other employees are considered inappropriate: too casual, too bare, or too formal.

The more you know about the dress code of the organization, the more assured you will be about correct choices on the job. Hairstyles should be consistent with the required clothes. For example, a casual hairstyle that looked right for school may not fit the position you would like to have with your company. Thus, knowledge of what a business expects of its employees is essential to the individual who wants to succeed with that company. It means dressing for the part you want to play or for the role you would like to fill.

> "Dress does not make a man, but it often makes a successful one."
>
> *Benjamin Disraeli*

But clothes and hairstyles are not the only nonverbal messages you send. Nothing is more basic than personal grooming. Hygiene—cleanliness and care of personal belongings—is a must if you are to build relationships with people. Soap and water, razors, deodorants, toothpaste, shoe polish, and dry cleaning are standard requirements for a favorable impression.

In short, how you personally care for yourself sends messages about how you regard yourself. Often your clothes, hairstyle, personal grooming, and accessories (jewelry, shoes, purse, belt, watch, tie, etc.) are perceived by others as clues to your own self-image. Indeed, your personal appearance implies messages about not only how you feel about yourself but also how you relate to others. To feel confident about your appearance in a work situation, pay attention to what others are wearing. Note the clothes of the person at the next higher level. Read current magazine articles on dressing for the workplace. Ask your teacher for the names of authoritative books on the subject.

Body Movement

Of course, there is more for others to observe than just what you wear. Your body sends messages whether you speak or not. Think about posture, walk, gestures, facial expressions, and eye movements. Through these kinds of nonverbal behaviors, people reveal their feelings and attitudes.

Overt Body Movements. There are some kinds of movement that are overt (easily open to view) and quickly recognized as clues to feelings. These are an individual's walk, body position, and use of hands.

Walk. Just as you have an individual body frame—soft, heavy, and round; muscular, sturdy, and hard; or slender and fragile—so do you have an individual walk. Although you may dress to change the appearance of your body shape, the way you walk, sit, or stand often reveals your attitudes and feelings. For example, the rate of your pace or the length of your stride may change depending on whether you are in a hurry, reluctant to arrive, or terribly tired. When you are sad, your body reflects this inner state. When you are preoccupied with a problem, your body shows it. But when you are alert and enthusiastic, the whole muscular tone changes.

Positions. The position of your body in relation to another person is a powerful clue about your feelings. For example, leaning forward, using an open position (arms and legs uncrossed), and facing directly toward someone often indicate your openness to another person. Conversely, unwillingness to participate, a feeling of being threatened, a defensive attitude, or boredom show up in other body positions. What messages do people send when they cross their arms, sit turned away, choose a seat at some distance from others, cover part of their faces with their hands, or drum restlessly with their fingers? Often the body says what words do not say. Or perhaps the words say one thing while the body silently screams something else. When messages conflict, do you believe the verbal or nonverbal message?

Gestures. Hands are extremely important when they are used in nonverbal communication. They often are illustrators that serve to emphasize a point; sketch a path or direction of a thought ("from here to there"); point to objects directly; show size or spatial relationships ("The fish was *this* big"); show an action ("The boat was wobbling like this"); or demonstrate something by drawing it in the air ("It looked like this").

Touching. As useful as the hands are in substituting for speech or in helping to make words clear, they probably communicate more through the sense of touch. Because unwritten rules govern body contact, people in our culture are less likely to touch each other than are people in some other cultures—Latin America, for example. But when hands reach out to comfort a friend, extend a greeting, seal a bargain, or offer congratulations, these gestures often say more than words.

Because business relationships are more formal and impersonal than friendships, a somewhat rigid code about touching exists. Handshakes are very important. Men do it almost automatically—indicating a meeting between equals. Women in business have learned to extend their hands when they are introduced, thus establishing the equality of their positions.

Generally, however, little touching goes on in the workplace between co-workers because touching involves moving into another person's territorial space and making body contact. We do this with words rather than touching. If any touching is initiated, it is probably a higher-status person touching someone of lower status—rarely the reverse situation.

Covert Body Movements. We've been talking about easily observed overt movements revealing nonverbal messages. Equally or perhaps more important are the covert movements over which individuals have little control. As receivers we use these channels to help make sense of words.

Facial Expression. It is far easier to control the large movements of the body than the covert (disguised or hidden) messages sent by the face and eyes. The face is tremendously important in conveying nonverbal messages. In fact, it may be the most important way that feelings are expressed. Albert Mehrabian states that a person's nonverbal behavior has more bearing than her or his words in communicating feelings or attitudes to others. He presents this equation:

$$\text{Total feeling} = 7\%\ \textbf{verbal}\ \text{feeling} + 38\%\ \textbf{vocal}\ \text{feeling} + 55\%\ \textbf{facial}\ \text{feeling}[1]$$

Usually you read the face of someone who speaks to you. In fact, when you can hear the words but cannot see the speaker's face, you may miss the real message that is being intended. These small, fleeting changes in facial expression are often involuntary. But you watch for them to understand the speaker's intention or emotional state. Think for a minute of the twitch of an eyebrow, the curl of a lip, the flaring of nostrils, and the tightening of the lips. These movements send messages to the careful observer.

Eyes. A large percentage of facial expression is revealed through the eyes. What is there about the movement of the eyes, the intensity of a gaze, or the dropping of eyelids that provides messages? You are probably aware of a number of unwritten rules: "Don't stare." "Look at me when I'm talking to you." "Look at the audience—not over their heads or out the window." You may have heard these statements as rules of proper behavior. Furthermore, you are conscious that when you look at someone, you are generally expected to acknowledge her or his presence if the person looks back. When you do not want to speak, you avoid eye contact. Are you aware that you do this?

People who are concerned with getting along with others tend to exchange mutual glances more often. When someone looks away, you may think the person is concealing something. It might be considered a signal of, "I don't want you to know what I am feeling." When you find yourself looking away from someone with whom you are talking, check what you are feeling inside.

Again, this kind of nonverbal communication is important in public speaking. Maintaining eye contact with your listeners urges them to acknowledge you by looking at you directly. Eye contact is generally interpreted as a willingness to be open and receptive to another person, and it is worth practicing. But you cannot look at everyone all the time. Your audience may be sizable. Try focusing your visual contact in different areas of the room. Include those people sitting at your far right or left. Look directly at a person long enough to tighten an invisible line of communication between you. As you practice your speech beforehand in the privacy of your room, concentrate on the imaginary listeners sitting before you. Look at them and talk with them.

Space and Time

In addition to your personal appearance and the movements you make, your use of space and time conveys personal messages to others.

---

[1] Albert Mehrabian, *Silent Messages*, 1st edition, © 1971 by Wadsworth, Inc. Reprinted by permission.

Space. Your body occupies space. Furthermore, the space around you is your **territory**. There are probably areas that you consider personally yours: your seat in the car, your place at the table, your side of the bed, your closet, or your armchair. When you are on the job, the place where you regularly work such as your office, your desk, or your work station makes up your territory. You may find yourself upset when someone uses your typewriter without your permission.

In business there are a number of unwritten codes regarding the way you handle the territory of others. These generally are based on courtesy and regard for others. For example, a supervisor may walk into a subordinate's office unannounced. But you may feel you must knock on your boss's closed office door and wait to be invited to enter. You are entering the boss's territory, and the position or status of the person indicates how you approach this office. Indeed, you may have noticed that as an executive becomes more important to a company, her or his office is likely to become less accessible and to occupy more space. The power and authority of a businessperson is often judged by the size of her or his office, its location, and the number of secretaries who guard it.

One other comment about space will help you understand why it is so important. The relationship between you and another person, as well as the subject matter you are discussing, will often determine the physical distance between you as you communicate. Think about your own experience. You probably recognize at least three kinds of space for communicating:

1. Your **personal space** (very close to you and controlled by you) is the area that you share for intimate conversation.
2. Your **social space** (across a desk or table) is the area for communicating with friends and business associates.
3. Your **impersonal space** (a greater distance between you and others) is an area for public communication.

Note the importance of these spatial distances in communication. Whom do you permit into your intimate or personal space? How does this work in business? Often a salesperson invited into your home (insurance, real estate, etc.) will suggest that you sit together around the dining table. This reduces the space between you and puts you across from each other or next to each other. It allows the salesperson to enter into a more personal space than he or she might have in the living room and permits closer contact. Accordingly, your understanding of the use of space as nonverbal communication (a way of sending personal messages) will be helpful in handling your speech encounters.

Time. Finally, the way you use time on your job is part of your nonverbal communication. Americans seem to live in a wristwatch society. Businesses operate on a time schedule, and clearly time is valuable to business. Work schedules are set according to time. Appointments are made for a certain time. Time clocks are punched in and out. Your company will have certain expectations as to how you use your time. For example, you will be expected to arrive on time, to attend meetings and conferences on time, to keep appointments, to use work hours for company work (not your own personal business), and to scrupulously observe the amount of time allotted for coffee breaks and lunch.

What kind of personal messages are conveyed by your positive use of

"Politeness is like an air cushion; there may be nothing in it, but it eases our jolts wonderfully."

Samuel Johnson

"Lost, yesterday—somewhere between sunrise and sunset—two golden hours each set with sixty diamond minutes. No reward is offered, for they are gone forever."

Horace Mann

time? Other employees will recognize that you are willing to be an equal member of the team. Your supervisors will appreciate being able to count on you. Your customers will be impressed with your promptness in arriving for appointments. Your nonverbal message conveys your attitude of cooperation and respect for the time of others as well as your own.

BUSINESS ENVIRONMENTAL CODES

When do you ask your boss for a raise? At your convenience or his? Where does your supervisor criticize your work? At your desk? In her office? In front of others or privately? How does business get done on the golf course? What has any of these questions to do with talking business?

Business meetings, whether sales, reporting, problem solving, etc., happen in a particular environment. In other words, people talk business in a specific location, in a public or private setting decorated in a cheerful, ugly, or neutral manner, with a limited or unlimited amount of space arranged with chairs and tables in formal or informal positions, at a specific time of day or night, and for a business reason. These circumstances contribute nonverbally to the *climate* or the atmosphere of the meeting. Let's define each of them.

"Just as every act in a man's life occurs in some definite geographical place, so does it occur in an organizational place, a particular location in the invisible geography of human organization."

Alvin Toffler

Place—within the company building, in a particular territory, outside of the organization in open territory, etc.

Setting—the physical arrangement of tables, desks, chairs, etc.

Space—the amount of seating or working space available.

Time—the time of day, length of time available, pressure of deadlines, etc.

Occasion—the reason for the meeting or business talk.

Environments create nonverbal codes of behavior in business meetings.

Let's set up some business situations and apply our knowledge of the effect of environment on communication. What can you assume about the participants, the topic, and the style of meeting if the following situations exist?

1. You have a scheduled appointment at 3 p.m. with a banker in her gray-blue private office. You are shown in at 3:20 and asked to sit across the desk from her. There are four other people waiting outside her office to see her.

2. You work in a large general office with eight other people in the immediate vicinity. Your supervisor leans over your desk at 9:30 on a Tuesday morning to give you some new data for a report you are writing. She stands, you remain seated; you both look at the papers.

3. You and another businessperson meet for lunch in a public restaurant. You sit across from each other in a booth. He has asked you to meet him there. Neither of you is limited to an hour for lunch.

Ask your instructor for the analysis of each of these three situations given in the teacher's manual. Compare your perception with the description given. Can you identify codes of behavior relating to where people sit, who leads the conversation, the type of topics discussed, time codes, and the degree of formality in each situation?

FIGURE 6-2

The physical circumstances surrounding a business talk influence the climate of the conversation.

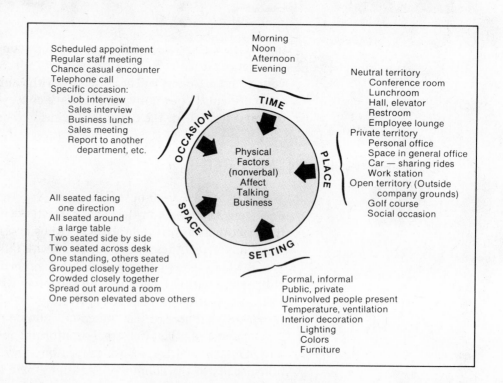

Chapter 6   Integrating Your Nonverbal Skills

IMPROVING NONVERBAL COMMUNICATION

This chapter has made you newly aware of the importance of nonverbal messages. To improve your own message sending and receiving, try these tips:

1. *Be aware that you send messages on many channels.* Everything about you gives information—the way you look, the way you move, and the things with which you surround yourself. Your sensitivity to your nonverbal as well as your verbal messages will help improve your communication.

2. *Keep your messages consistent.* If your voice gets louder and higher as you say, "But I'm not angry"; if you perspire profusely but claim you're not nervous; if you say, "That was a great play" in a sarcastic tone; if you remark, "I'm glad to meet you" and extend a limp handshake, your nonverbal communications contradict your verbal messages. Be a trustworthy communicator. Match your verbal, vocal, and nonverbal messages.

3. *Avoid nonverbal communication barriers.* Often first impressions can mislead you. Wait to judge. Don't be guilty of:
   a. Stereotyping a person based on appearance alone.
   b. Making a hasty assumption based solely on nonverbal behavior.
   c. Judging a person because of the person's behavior in a single incident.

4. *Decode verbal messages more accurately.* Watch for the nonverbal clues that accompany the message.

5. *Be sensitive to the nonverbal messages of others.* Remember that people don't always say exactly what they are thinking or feeling.

6. *Remember that nonverbal behavior—like words—may have many meanings.* Rather than guess, ask:

   "You're smiling, Ann. Does this mean that you agree?"
   "Do you want to say something, Yoko?"
   "These suggestions don't seem to be going over with you, Jane. Is this true?"
   "Does that head shake mean that we are not in agreement, Juan?"
   "Something seems to be bothering you. Am I right?"

In brief, there is no sure way to understand the nonverbal messages sent by another person unless you ask. The trick is to be aware of nonverbal messages and then to validate the message you are getting.

CHAPTER SUMMARY

The words you speak *and* a whole series of nonverbal messages make talking business possible. All the ways you communicate that are not verbal are collectively called nonverbal communication. These messages come through such nonverbal channels as physical characteristics, body movement, sensory stimulation, clothing, accessories, possessions, personal preferences, facial expressions, and eye movements.

Verbal messages are language-based and taught, while nonverbal communication is culturally based and learned through observation. Unwritten codes of behavior have developed as nonverbal message systems, but verbal and nonverbal communication are bound together, and both have many meanings.

Nonverbal communication strengthens, changes, or substitutes for verbal communication. It often regulates communication situations. In talking business, the place, setting, space, time, and occasion each affect business communication. Suggestions for improving nonverbal communication are given.

BODY LANGUAGE *(Individual Activity and Pairs)*

Purpose: To write verbal messages that are consistent with nonverbal body language.

Briefing: Study the pictures below. On a separate sheet of paper, write the words that each person might say based on the body language you observe in each picture. Then write your response to the verbal message. Share your answers with a partner. Identify points of disagreement. On what clues did you base the verbal message in each picture?

EXPECTATIONS BASED ON WORKING CLOTHES *(Individual Activity and Pairs)*

Purpose: To identify the role of clothing in our expectations of working people.

Briefing: Study the illustrations below. Answer the questions on the next page. Compare your answers with a partner.

Working Clothes

A   B   C

D   E   F

Rick Norton/King's Island

EXPECTATIONS BASED ON WORKING CLOTHES *(Individual Activity and Pairs)*

Purpose: To identify the kinds of information provided by working clothes. To check assumptions based upon clothing and appearance.

Briefing: Study the illustrations on the preceding page. Then read the statements below. Mark "Yes" if you agree with the statement, "No" if you disagree, or a question mark "?" if you are in doubt. Share your answers with a partner. Clothing will not supply all the answers. Identify previous personal experience that has influenced the answer you give.

Illustrations of Working Clothes

	A	B	C	D	E	F
1.						
2.						
3.						
4.						
5.						
6.						
7.						
8.						
9.						
10.						
11.						
13.						
13.						
14.						
15.						

1. Has been trained for a particular job.
2. Makes a high salary.
3. Attended college.
4. Married and has a family.
5. Specialist in a particular occupation.
6. Is flexible and open-minded.
7. Is patriotic.
8. Is interested in public service.
9. Is dependable and reliable.
10. Will be polite to me.
11. Votes in local, state, and national elections.
12. Pays bills promptly.
13. Will listen to me carefully.
14. Would make a good boss.
15. Gives a full day's work on the job.

BUSINESS DRESS CODES *(Pairs)*

Purpose: To examine a variety of company dress code guidelines, and to role play the reactions of new employees to a required code.

Briefing: Choose a partner. Person A is employed by a company and has the responsibility for explaining the company dress code guidelines to a new employee. Person B is the new employee who listens, asks questions, and seeks further explanation.

Person A: You are the company representative. You will present one of the dress code guidelines to the new employee. Read the one assigned to you carefully. Decide on a name for your company and the type of position the new employee will fill. Be ready to explain the guidelines and answer questions the employee asks you.

Person B: You are the new employee. Listen carefully as the company representative explains the company dress code guidelines to you. You may ask questions, ask for definitions, reasons, and further explanations, or challenge the company's stand.

> *Guideline #1:* "Our company sets up dress standards for our employees. We are not trying to all look alike, nor are we trying to stifle individuality. But we are concerned with the image of our company. Since the employees represent the company to the public, we have some pretty specific requirements."
>
> *Guideline #2:* "Our dress standards are unwritten, and we do not even talk about them. Employees know what is expected of them, and they dress accordingly."
>
> *Guideline #3:* "Each person is expected to dress appropriately for his or her work. Good taste is the governing factor at all times."
>
> *Guideline #4:* "Our dress code is very strict. Women must wear dresses or skirts—no pants—at all times. Men must always wear ties and dress shirts. No sport shirts are allowed."
>
> *Guideline #5:* "Our dress guidelines are to wear what is contemporary with the times and what you think the customers expect you to wear."
>
> *Guideline #6:* "One of the problems in society today is that there is such a widely varying standard of what constitutes good taste that a dress code is more important now than in the past."

Debriefing: Role play your conversation for the class. What general conclusions can be drawn from these dramatizations? What can you do to prepare to meet the dress guidelines of a company that you may work for in the future?

BUSINESS SPEECH SITUATIONS *(Group Discussion)*

Purpose: To discuss business situations and how the context affects the speaking exchange.

Briefing: Work together in groups of five or six. Discuss these questions. Apply them to each of the following situations:

1. What business topics might be discussed?
2. Who would talk? Who would listen? Would there be interaction?
3. Describe how time, place, etc., affect communication.
4. What can be done to improve the nonverbal environmental factors?

   Situation #1: The place is the telephone company building; the setting is the cafeteria, a room with long tables. The time is noon; the lunch period is 30 minutes. The occasion is an everyday, on-the-job gathering of employees for lunch.

   Situation #2: The place is the small office of an administrator. The occasion is a report from a state inspector after an unscheduled inspection. Four department heads are seated. The administrator sits behind a cluttered desk; the inspector is positioned in a chair at the side of the desk where she can see everyone. It is 4:00 p.m. on Wednesday.

   Situation #3: The place is the jewelry counter on the main floor of a department store on a Tuesday at 5:00 p.m. It is a hot summer day, and the air-conditioning system has been turned off several hours for repairs. A number of customers are waiting for service from the one salesclerk at this location.

   Situation #4: The place is the company staff room at 9:00 a.m. on Monday. There is a long conference table with 12 leather chairs arranged around it. Seven people are meeting together for a regular Monday meeting. The department head generally sits at the end near the door; the others usually take the same seats each time.

   Situation #5: The time is 2:30 p.m. on Thursday. The occasion is a special meeting of employees that is being held in a crowded, smoke-filled, and poorly ventilated conference room with 10 to 15 chairs. The executive in charge of the meeting is standing at the front. The purpose of the meeting is to explain new safety rules of the company. Twenty employees are standing or sitting. One shift of workers is just leaving work, another shift of workers made a special trip for the meeting, and a third shift of workers is just reporting for duty.

   Situation #6: The place is a popular restaurant at 1:00 p.m. on a Friday. One businessperson has invited another to talk business over lunch. The two are seated across the table from each other. The restaurant is crowded with other customers located within hearing distance.

Debriefing: Summarize your conclusions for one situation. One person may represent your group and make a brief report to the whole class.

NONVERBAL CLUES *(Group Activity)*

Purpose: To discover how nonverbal behavior reveals feelings. To identify how nonverbal behavior affects feelings.

Briefing: Divide into groups of five or six. One member of the group serves as the volunteer and leaves the room.

Each group reads the situations listed below and chooses one. When the volunteer returns to your group, you may talk about anything you like (not necessarily the situation at hand), but your nonverbal behavior must communicate a particular attitude toward the volunteer.

Continue talking for three to four minutes. When the instructor stops the conversation, discuss the questions in the debriefing section.

You may select another volunteer and make up your own situation for the second time.

Situation #1: Be very honored and impressed. Without the volunteer knowing who he or she is supposed to be, pretend that the person is a celebrity and that you are most honored to have him or her join your group. Create this impression nonverbally while you talk about something else.

Situation #2: Be very reserved in your behavior. Pretend you have a secret that you don't want to share with an outsider (the volunteer).

Situation #3: Be very friendly. Pretend that you want to have a party and would like to hold it at the volunteer's house.

Situation #4: Be very condescending or ignore the outsider. Pretend that the person is not suitably dressed for the occasion. Act superior.

Situation #5: Be very unfriendly in your nonverbal behavior. Pretend that the volunteer is different from other people in the group.

Situation #6: Be highly suspicious of the volunteer. Pretend that you believe the person is a spy who is trying to get secret designs.

Debriefing:

1. As the volunteer, how did you feel about the group behavior? What specific actions made you feel this way? Which group member most effectively communicated nonverbally?

2. As a group, did you find it easy to send inconsistent verbal and nonverbal messages?

WHO, WHAT, WHEN, WHERE, WHY? *(Individual Activity)*

Purpose: To identify a real business situation and analyze the verbal and nonverbal elements in it.

Briefing: Think of a real situation for a business discussion. Around the circle below, specify a particular time, setting, place, and occasion for a particular meeting. Identify the participants in the speaking exchange, their status, and their relationship to each other.

Occasion (why?)   Time (when?)

A Business Discussion   Place (where?)

Space (how arranged?)   Setting (what?)

Participants (who?): names, positions, relationships

Write a paragraph in the space below that gives the following information: the status of each of the participants, where they will sit, why they have come together, who will lead the talking, and the topics they will cover or the goals they plan to achieve. Include an analysis of the nonverbal behavior that will take place (shaking hands, choosing seats, etc.). How will the participants know when the meeting is over?

TIME MANAGEMENT *(Individual Activity)*

Purpose: To identify specific behavioral aids in managing time successfully. To make a plan for personal improvement.

Briefing: Select five of the following time-saving techniques. Then rank the order of each technique from 1 (most valuable) to 5 (least valuable). Take into consideration your own activities and personal habits in regard to time management.

_____ *Use a scratch list.*
Keep a list of things to be done. Scratch off each one as you do it.

_____ *Throw things away.*
Keep a wastebasket near at hand. Develop the habit of tossing things in the wastebasket rather than putting them into drawers.

_____ *Clear your desk or work area.*
At the end of each day, put everything away. Make decisions about what to keep or throw away. Start fresh each day.

_____ *Control your reading time.*
Skim things you must read. Mark for closer reading only the most important segments.

_____ *Schedule your activities graphically.*
Use a large calendar with plenty of space. Keep it where you can see it easily.

_____ *Set up a "tickler" file.*
Use a card file to tickle your memory about important dates, bills that are due, deadlines, etc. Plan far in advance.

_____ *Rearrange your work area.*
Put everything that you need regularly within easy reach.

_____ *Limit your phone calls.*
Keep a list of calls you need to make. Do these all at one time. Use a two-minute egg timer. When the phone rings, turn the timer over and try to finish before the sand runs through.

_____ *Write short notes.*
Keep a note pad handy along with envelopes and stamps. Jot short notes to people, rather than long, detailed letters.

_____ *Sort your mail standing up.*
Go through your daily correspondence quickly. Throw away all the circulars, ads, and unwanted items. Take action immediately on memos, bills, etc.

_____ *Write down your daily goals.*
Jot down things that must be done each day. Number these in order of priority.

_____ *Set an alarm for deadlines.*
Give yourself 20 minutes to finish a particular job. Try to beat the clock.

_____ *Say no to things you cannot do.*
Avoid putting off making a decision. Know your schedule and your limitations. Say no, and do not feel guilty.

NEW IDEAS VS. THE OLD WAYS *(Group and Individual Activity)*

Purpose: To discuss a company problem as a member of a business firm. To role play a point of view verbally and nonverbally.

Briefing: Divide into groups of seven or eight. One group member will be an observer. The observer will complete the Observer Report below and share these observations with the group after it has finished the task.

Task: You are all employees of a particular company. Decide on the name of the company and identify the type of business. Now imagine the following situation. You have been called together to make a decision on one of the following matters:

1. Revision of the company dress code. (First, decide what it has been in your company.)

2. Changing the method of scheduling work hours. (At present, your company uses a nine-to-five time clock punch-in system. The president has asked you to consider "flextime," which would permit a variable schedule for all employees.)

Caution: Assume that half of the group are employees who have been with the company for more than 15 years. The other half of the group have worked at this company for three years or less. Decide which individuals will represent old-timers and which will represent new employees. You have 40 minutes to present both sides fairly. Speak and act as you believe old-timers and newcomers would speak and act.

Debriefing: What kinds of nonverbal behavior did you respond to during this discussion? Was there a real difference of opinion? Invite your observer into the group to make an observer's report.

Observer Report

Names of Group Members: _____

_____

Briefing: Answer the following questions on a separate sheet of paper as you observe your group. Report the answers to the group when it has completed the task.

1. As the group began setting up the company and choosing the problem, did you see any nonverbal behavior that indicated enthusiasm, responsiveness to others, eagerness, or willingness to participate? List the *behavior*. What did the person *do*?

2. In the beginning steps, did you note any nonverbal behavior that indicated confusion, resentment, withdrawal, or frustration? List the behavior.

3. After the group began role playing the employee discussion, what nonverbal behavior did the old-timers exhibit? What nonverbal behavior did the new employees exhibit?

TALKING BUSINESS IN A DIFFERENT CULTURE: A BUSINESS COMMUNICATION PROBLEM *(Group Discussion)*

Purpose: To examine the problems involved in talking business with people from another cultural background.

Briefing: Work in groups of five or six. Your instructor will set up a situation described in the teacher's manual. Have one person read the commentary below to the group.

Commentary: The basic difference is that the Arabs are different from North Americans in that they are highly "contexted." (The people have developed a need to know more about you before a relationship can develop.) They examine the entire circumstance in which events are happening in order to understand them. In the Middle East, if you aren't willing to take the time to sit down and have coffee with people, you have a problem. You must learn to wait and not be too eager to talk business. You can ask about the family or ask, "How are you feeling?" But avoid too many personal questions about wives, because people are apt to get suspicious. Learn to make what we call chit-chat. If you don't, you can't go to the next step. People will be watching you, getting to know you, and developing feelings about you. They're probably even watching the pupils of your eyes to judge your responses to different topics. Eckhard Hess, a psychologist at the University of Chicago, discovered that the pupil is a very sensitive indicator of how people respond to a situation. When you are interested in something, your pupils dilate; if I say something you don't like, they tend to contract. But the Arabs have known about the pupil response for hundreds, if not thousands, of years. Since people can't control the response of their eyes, which is a dead giveaway, many Arabs wear dark glasses. These are people reading the personal interaction on a second-to-second basis. By watching the pupils, they can respond rapidly to mood changes. We're taught in the United States not to stare, not to look at the eyes that carefully. If you stare at someone, it is too intense, too sexy, or too hostile. That's one of the reasons why they use a closer conversational distance than we do. At about five feet—the normal distance between two Americans who are talking—we have a hard time following eye movements. But if you use an Arab distance—about two feet—you can watch the pupil of the eye.

Overall, what they're doing is coding, sort of synthesizing their reactions. They say to themselves, "How do I feel about this person?" In contemporary American terms: "What kind of vibes am I getting from him?" They are also responding to smell and to the thermal qualities of the other person. . . . So they're picking up thermal, olfactory, and kinesthetic cues also. A lot of touching goes on during conversations in the Middle East.*

Discussion Questions:

1. You are to sign a contract with an Arab company within the next two weeks. Identify the way you will go about it. Make a specific plan for talking business.

2. List your expectations of the people with whom you will deal.

3. List the specific behavior changes you will make.

4. How successful do you predict you will be?

---

* Edward T. Hall, "Learning the Arabs' Silent Language," *Psychology Today* (August, 1979), pp. 47-48. Reprinted with permission from Psychology Today Magazine. Copyright © 1979 (APA).

COOPERATIVE SQUARES* *(Group Activity)*

Purpose: To work with a group to finish a task without breaking the rules. To operate as a team with limited communication opportunities. To observe types of nonverbal behavior that are continually operating.

Briefing: Divide into groups.

1. Each group must have only five members.

2. Each group must be separated from the other groups.

3. Members of the group may sit on the floor or around a table.

4. Each group needs at least one observer.

5. Each person will receive an envelope that contains pieces of a puzzle. Wait until the signal is given to open the envelope.

Object of the exercise:

Complete **five** squares of **equal** size. Each person must have one square in front of him or her.

Rules of the exercise:

1. No one may speak.

2. No one may signal by pointing, looking, sighing, etc.

3. No one may reach for another piece or take a piece from another.

4. Anyone may *give* puzzle pieces to another at any time.

Observers: Look for the following:

1. Who is willing to give?

2. Who finished a square and then withdrew?

3. Who continually struggled, yet did not give away any pieces?

4. How many people were actively engaged in putting pieces together?

5. What kinds of nonverbal behavior signaled frustration and anxiety?

---

* Adapted with permission from "An Experiment in Cooperation," *Today's Education*, Vol. 58 (October, 1969), p. 57, and included in D. Nylen, J. R. Mitchell, and A. Stout, *Handbook of Staff Development and Human Relations Training: Materials Developed for Use in Africa* (Washington, D.C.: National Education Association, 1962).

SAMPLE CONTRACT FOR PERSONAL COMMUNICATION
IMPROVEMENT *(Individual Reference)*

1. Identify your goal. (Think about thorny communication relationships in your own life. Write down what you would like to achieve as a goal.)

    "I would like to eliminate the conflict between my father and me when we discuss money."

2. Describe the present problem. (In clear statements of observation, write down the specific behaviors that you would like to change.)

    "My dad raises his voice and gets very loud and red-faced whenever the subject of money comes up. He projects an "allness attitude" by making rigid Parent statements. He never seems willing to listen to me. He ends the conversation abruptly. I seem to bring up the subject at inappropriate times. And I find myself saying the same things over and over each time. I get very defensive and cross my arms to protect myself. We both interrupt each other and contradict each other."

3. Set up a plan for your own behavior changes. (Since you are responsible only for your own behavior, list those specific things that you can do differently.)

    "a. I will not bring up the subject of money unless I notify him in advance that I would like to discuss it. I might ask him if I can make an appointment at his convenience.
    b. I will not respond to his ideas or what he says without first restating what he has said and get him to OK my understanding of his message.
    c. I will use empathy (try to see why he feels as he does).
    d. I will ask him to hear me out before he interrupts me.
    e. I will try to listen actively to what he says.
    f. I will not interrupt.
    g. I will sit with my arms behind me and hope this position will clue him that I am receptive to his feedback."

4. Write a method of determining when your goal is reached. (State a specific way of knowing when you will be satisfied that you have completed this contract.)

    "I will be satisfied that I have achieved my goal when:
    a. I can state my father's arguments as he would like them to be heard. I'll get his OK.
    b. I can have a conversation with my father about money without getting upset.
    c. My father can give me a positive statement about my changed behavior as feedback."

Signed _____ *Sara Boyd* _____

Date _____ *October 12, 19--* _____

CONTRACT FOR PERSONAL COMMUNICATION
IMPROVEMENT *(Individual Activity)*

Purpose: To set up a specific plan for personal communication improvement.

Briefing: Let's talk about the business of making specific improvements in your speaking and listening skills. You can do this by signing a contract to work on improving a particular area of your personal communication. Identify your problem, set your goal, work out a step-by-step plan to change your behavior, and clarify when you will be satisfied that you have completed the contract and achieved your goal. (See the sample contract on page 205.)

Contract

1. Identify your goal.

2. Describe the present problem.

3. Set up a plan for your own behavior changes.

4. Write a method of determining when your goal is reached.

Signed _____

Date _____

CHECKLIST OF COMMUNICATION TERMS *(Quiz)*

The terms used in this chapter form a vocabulary about nonverbal communication so that we can talk about it. To check your understanding write the number of the correct term in the blank preceding its definition. Note there are more terms than definitions.

Definitions	Terms
a. _____ The nonverbal message channels that include the way in which you move and the movements themselves (or lack of movement).	**1.** nonverbal communication
	2. physical characteristics
	3. body movement or stillness
b. _____ The distance across a desk or table between communicating businesspeople.	**4.** personal appearance
	5. personal possessions
	6. preferences about spending time
c. _____ The reason for the meeting or business talk.	**7.** preferences about use of space
	8. verbal messages
d. _____ Messages without words.	**9.** consistent messages
	10. group identification
e. _____ The physical arrangement of table, desks, chairs, etc.	**11.** social status
	12. self-image
f. _____ The areas where you sleep, keep your clothes, and sit to eat, etc.	**13.** overt body movements
	14. walk
	15. positions
g. _____ Communications in which voice, words, and nonverbal movement send the same message.	**16.** gestures
	17. touching
	18. covert body movement
h. _____ Unwritten rules based on behavior expected by others and related to courtesy and regard.	**19.** facial expression
	20. eyes
	21. business environmental codes
i. _____ Large, easily seen nonverbal messages provided by movement.	**22.** time
	23. place
	24. setting
j. _____ Uniforms and identifying emblems worn in business and industry.	**25.** space
	26. occasion
	27. personal space
	28. social space
	29. impersonal space
	30. territory

CHAPTER 7

Let's Talk About the Business of Designing and Developing Your Business Presentation

Now that you have studied perception, listening, language, speech, and nonverbal communication, you are ready to put all these skills to work in a formal presentational situation. Chapters 7 and 8 provide a step-by-step explanation of this process. Pretend that you have been asked to be a presentational speaker in a business situation. After studying this chapter, you should be able to do the following:

Chapter Objectives

1. Prepare an analysis of your audience and a statement of the purpose of your speech.
2. Use research sources for material to add to your presentation.
3. Move through the steps in designing and developing your presentation.
4. Outline a presentation including the introduction, body, and conclusion.

Oral presentations are an essential part of business. Here are examples of informative presentations designed to secure understanding. Rosa Ortega reports on shipping problems at the plant managers' meeting. Dr. Mary Guilbert briefs the production staff on changes to be made in textbook E92, which she is editing. Ron York, public relations vice-president for Oliver News Service, explains careers in newspaper publishing to high school students on Career Day. Gary Dayton conducts software training sessions for all employees using the new computer systems.

Here are examples of persuasive presentations seeking to influence decision making. Gina Andrews proposes a new flextime schedule for her consumer relations department. With his proposal for marketing Fiber-Fill, Robert Jamison will seek approval from the board of control for the manufacture of a new cereal. Clyde Anderson recommends a new insurance program to the board of directors. Both informative and persuasive oral presentations are used in business.

ORAL PRESENTATIONS MEET BUSINESS NEEDS

Presentations are business messages which are prepared to serve business goals and are to be delivered orally in a variety of situations and to audiences of various sizes. The speaker frequently supports his or her ideas by using visual aids such as charts and graphs. Often a company prepares its business message on videotape or film. The message is introduced by a speaker who then follows the presentation with a question-and-answer period. In this chapter, we will discuss the preparation of business messages that (like public speeches) are designed to be delivered orally.

PHOTO 7-1

A business presentation can be as informal as a meeting in someone's office.

Business audiences are specific targets. The size of an audience can vary in number from one listener to a large group. For example, your boss may ask you to present a plan for solving a production problem. You deliver the presentation while seated across the desk from each other in the boss's office. Or, you may be asked to explain a new procedure to the members of your department (7-10 people) or demonstrate a new product to the entire sales staff (35-40 people).

Because presentations are given when a need arises, the subject matter varies from training new employees in company policy to reporting technical information or presenting proposals to the management. These in-house presentations are delivered to people whom you may know personally within the company.

An effective company speaker may be asked to speak to audiences outside the organization. When you speak to groups outside your company, you are your company's voice. You may be explaining your company's position on price increases, selling your company's goods or services, or creating goodwill. In any case, you speak for the company, and the audience sees your company through your presentation.

The important point to remember is that presentations are given because there is a need. You speak to achieve a business goal. It is important to know exactly why you are speaking and what you hope to accomplish as you make your presentation.

Whatever the business occasion, there must be some logical reason for you to speak before an audience. You may have more information than others about a particular business area. You may feel strongly about a proposal that needs your support in order to justify it. Or you may seek agreement or action from your listeners. For whatever reason you make a presentation, it is essential that you present yourself and your ideas in the most effective way possible. Your upward mobility may depend on it.

Oral Presentations and Public Speeches

As an audience member, you have listened to public speeches that are similar to business presentations. They are similar in the following ways:

1. Both are prepared by a speaker for delivery before a group.
2. Preparation of both requires an analysis of audience and occasion.
3. Both are carefully planned and organized to achieve the speaker's goal.
4. Audience members are presented with ideas that they will associate with the speaker who presented them.
5. Both provide the opportunity for a delivery style that can be appreciated by an audience.

The differences are listed in Table 7-1 on page 212.

Basic Principles

An oral presentation is a carefully planned and organized event, not a casual act. It is designed around a central purpose, and the speaker's words, ideas, and actions are directed toward achieving the intended results. Because the speaker's reputation is often enhanced or lessened with fellow workers by the quality of an oral presentation, the stakes are high. Consequently, the speaker examines the message to be given and the individuals to whom it is to be delivered. The speaker then shapes the message accordingly.

There is no recipe to guarantee a successful business presentation, but there are basic principles that can be learned. Like investing in the stock market, the secret of a good presentation is to predict the results accurately. This ability to forecast how people will respond to you is based on a careful analysis of six important questions. Ask yourself:

1. What needs and circumstances lead me to speak to this audience at this time and on this subject?

Public Speeches	Business Presentations
1. Designed for a general audience	1. Designed for a specific business audience.
2. Planned for listeners who are not necessarily known to the speaker.	2. Within the company: planned for listeners who are company employees. Outside the company: planned to represent the company to listeners who are not necessarily known to the speaker.
3. Goals are general.	3. Goals are related to specific business needs.
4. Purpose is to inform or to persuade.	4. Purpose is to create understanding in order to influence thinking and generate action.
5. Organized logically so listeners can follow the lines of reasoning.	5. Organized to meet a specific business need and to propose and justify solutions.
6. Delivered to audiences of varying sizes but often open to anyone.	6. Often delivered to audiences of one or two, or to small groups. All audience members have common company interests.
7. Delivered to audiences who do not necessarily make decisions on the validity of the speaker's ideas.	7. Delivered to business listeners who frequently have the authority to accept or reject the speaker's proposal.
8. Usually express the speaker's personal views.	8. Adhere to the company's views and policies.
9. Usually prepared by the speaker and/or an assistant.	9. Frequently prepared from information submitted by various departments.
10. Often one person speaking to many with little interaction between speaker and listeners unless a question-and-answer period follows the speech.	10. Frequent interaction between speaker and listeners during the presentation and following it. Questions and answers are expected.

2. What information, means of explanation, argument, or method of persuasion should be used for this particular group of listeners?
3. What facts will determine my method of developing, ordering, and arranging my ideas?
4. Why will I choose certain words and use them in a particular way?
5. How will I sound and act to suit the particular situation?
6. What specific attitude or action do I want from my listeners as a result of my presentation?

TYPES OF ORAL PRESENTATIONS

Whatever the business occasion, there is a need to present material either to secure understanding or to influence decision making. Often the two goals are combined in one presentation. A successful businesswoman recently said: "In my experience, there is no such thing as a purely informative speech in business. All presentations are delivered to influence others. Information is used to secure understanding so that decisions can be made."

We might think of oral presentations on a continuum with greater or lesser amounts of information included depending upon the speaker's purpose. The importance of this point is that presentations at opposite ends of Figure 7-1 require a different kind of speaker preparation. Informative speeches require an investigation of the listeners' level of knowledge about the topic; persuasive presentations demand that the speaker research those factors that motivate an audience to behave in desired ways. Let's examine these two kinds of presentations separately so that their special characteristics can be identified and compared.

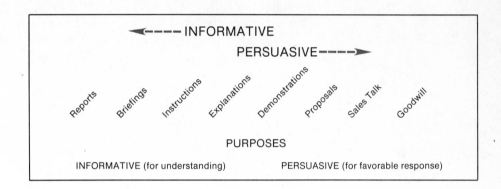

Informative Presentations

Three major types of presentations are included in this category, because they clearly provide a great deal of information in order to secure the audience's understanding.

Reports. An oral report is often a brief version of a longer written report. The speaker does not read the written document, but prepares a summary of it. The advantage of the oral report is that the speaker can highlight sections that are important to a particular group of listeners. The full written report may be distributed at the same time so that the listeners can check their understanding of the material later. **Reports** present results; they tell what has already happened.

There are many kinds of reports. The major types include:

Statistical reports—use more numbers than words.
Fact-finding reports—present data and omit comments.
Research reports—cover the search for new information or knowledge.
Progress reports—presented between the start and completion of a project.
Analytical reports—identify a problem, analyze data, present conclusions, and offer recommendations for action.
Technical reports—convey information between specialists with similar training.

Reports deal with factual material. They should be accurate, systematically organized, and nonargumentative. The report may be made to listeners who are experts in several fields, or to executives and personnel from a variety of departments. The language of the report must be geared to the audience members and their specialized areas of work. The use of charts, graphs, and other visual aids helps the speaker make the findings clear.

Briefings. Whereas reports tell what has happened, **briefings** tell what will happen or what is expected. As the name suggests, this type of presentation is a summary of goals, a list of details, or a short set of explanations or instructions. A briefing may combine a progress report with an explanation of how the listeners should regard the information. It briefly fills in gaps of information for some and updates information for others. For example, squadrons of fighter pilots are briefed before a mission; squads of police officers are briefed on the situation before they go out on riot control; salespersons are briefed before they take a new product to customers in their territories. Briefings are often informal presentations with a great deal of interaction between the speaker and the listeners. Briefings are prepared with care to include all pertinent information, and they are delivered orally to provide open channels for feedback and questions.

Explanations, Instructions, Demonstrations. "How to" information comes alive through oral presentations that *show* as well as explain and instruct. These presentations often include a demonstration of the object or procedure being discussed. Any information-giving presentation begins with the common level of listeners' knowledge. The material is arranged to lead the listeners step-by-step to a higher level of understanding.

PHOTO 7-2

Effective oral presentations should show as well as explain and instruct.

Sorbus

An effective way to begin a presentation is to start with an overview and move into specifics. For example, when demonstrating a new office machine, begin with an explanation of the jobs that the machine will perform and how this will improve work in the office. Then explain the parts of the machine. Instruct the employees in the step-by-step method of its use, and demonstrate each step as the operation is explained. Or, you can present the same information but reverse the procedure: begin with specifics and conclude with a general overview. Of course, which method works best is determined by knowing the office staff, understanding how the machine will be used, and suiting the arrangement of the material to the particular case. It is helpful if the speaker and listeners interact during the explanation. Questions should be encouraged and answered as the speaker moves through the presentation. Listeners may be invited to perform each step as it is demonstrated. Remember, the purpose is to secure understanding so that the machine will be used properly. Encouraging "hands on" experience will test the listeners' understanding of the instructions and demonstration.

Informative presentations rely on accurate collection of data, reliable research, and statements of observation in speaking. Remember that the goal of informative presentations is to tell others what they do not know in a way that they will understand. You cannot safely assume that you are understood. Devise ways to get feedback: ask questions, encourage comments, or find ways of getting the listeners to participate actively. Finally, remember that you are providing information with an ultimate goal in mind. If you ask yourself why you are relating the information, you will discover the purpose of your presentation.

Persuasive Presentations

Persuasion is one of the most important functions of language. A **persuasive presentation** seeks to influence the thinking, beliefs, or actions of the audience. Persuasive presentations may fall into one of several categories:

1. **Sales presentations.** The purpose is to move listeners to buy, subscribe, sign up, or act in a specific way. The presentation provides essential information, includes a demonstration of what the product or service will do, creates a need for the item, and makes it easy for the listeners to behave in the manner the speaker suggests.
2. **Presentations that justify a proposal.** These speeches seek a favorable response from groups that have decision-making power. The speaker adapts the message to individuals in the group, supports or defends the proposal against opposing views, and often lays the speaker's professional reputation on the line before company superiors.
3. **Goodwill presentations.** Designed to improve the company's reputation or represent the company's views, these presentations establish a positive attitude toward the company and its policies.

Persuasive Strategies. Persuasion is a consciously planned effort by the speaker to change the attitudes and/or behaviors of others. To do this, the speaker must figure out the attitudes, beliefs, and needs of the audience in advance. We call this an **audience analysis**, and it is used as a blueprint for building a speech presentation.

Armed with this blueprint, speakers can consider strategies to win acceptance for a proposal. People do not accept change easily or quickly. They resist change. A wise speaker sets a specific goal that the audience must consider and supports this goal with three basic appeals:

1. **Speaker appeal.** People are often persuaded to believe the speaker's message because they are attracted to the speaker. Physical appearance and

certain personality qualities attract listeners. The following qualities increase the speaker's **credibility** or believability:

a. **Competence.** The speaker seems thoroughly prepared and is armed with evidence, facts the audience will believe, and personal illustrations that apply to the listeners. The speaker cites sources of information and is willing to explain details, thus building the audience's belief in the speaker's expertise.

b. **Trustworthiness.** The speaker comes across as sincere in his or her support of the proposed goal, with no suggestion of a personal stake in the outcome. The speaker communicates in a caring way with the listeners and works to build rapport with them.

> "An audience will forgive a speaker almost any lack if he is manifestly earnest about his proposal. . . . Earnestness moves our emotions, thaws our indifference, and gives us the faith which a leader must create."
>
> James A. Winans

c. **Poise.** The speaker displays a comfortable degree of confidence and the listeners respond positively to the speaker's mannerisms, posture, movement, and ideas. The speaker talks fluently, but a sense of control is evident.

d. **Enthusiasm.** The listeners perceive the speaker as friendly and outgoing as well as spontaneous and excited about the ideas presented.

2. **Logical appeal.** Listeners tend to seek information that supports what they already believe, and avoid that which contradicts their existing beliefs and attitudes. A logical appeal begins at a point where the audience is already in agreement. With carefully marshalled arguments, the speaker leads the audience toward an acceptance of the proposal. Opposing points of view may be presented and carefully refuted; emotional language is avoided; well-documented statistics, testimony, and clear reasoning are thoughtfully presented.

3. **Emotional appeal.** Each member of the audience has personal needs for survival, good health, safety, appreciation, and recognition. The speaker recognizes the individual needs of the listeners and personalizes the benefits of approving the proposal. Listeners identify with the speaker's personal experience, anecdotes or stories, description, sharply drawn comparisons or contrasts, and quotations. To win approval for any plan, the presenter puts the proposal in terms that make it vivid and alive to the listeners.

Review of Presentation Principles

So far, we have learned the following about business presentations:

1. They are designed with a specific audience in mind—most frequently, listeners within your own company.
2. They meet specific needs by providing information that is used for decision making.
3. They are usually designed to influence the business decision makers.
4. They may take the form of a formal presentation with a question-and-answer session immediately following.
5. They may be informal speaking situations with interaction between audience and speaker.
6. Informative presentations include reports, briefings, and "how to" information.
7. Persuasive presentations are sales or goodwill speeches, or presentations justifying a proposal and asking for a decision.

DESIGNING YOUR SPEECH PRESENTATION

There are four steps in the design process: **discovery, analysis, decision making**, and **research**. Let's examine one step at a time.

Step 1: Discovering Ideas

Presentations are packed with ideas and information. The first step in preparation calls for creative thinking. Put your pencil down for this first step. Let your ideas percolate. New insights will bubble up. You will not use all these ideas, but a presentation design begins with thinking about what you know. Then these ideas slowly shape into a plan with a goal or purpose. Think about the interests, needs, and concerns of your intended audience. Think about the place where you will speak, the time of day, the room arrangement. Think about previous speakers you have heard and how they have handled their presentations. Carefully consider the successful speaking events you have heard in the past. Ask yourself the following list of questions (the answers will aid you in designing your presentation):

1. Why am I giving this presentation?
2. Who asked me to give the presentation? Why was I asked instead of someone else?
3. What is expected of me?
4. What is the time limit?
5. What do the listeners want to know?
6. What do the listeners already know?
7. What do I know about the topic?
8. What more do I need to know?
9. Where can I get more information?
10. How can I keep the listeners interested, making sure that they get some value from the presentation?

Right now, of course, you will be making practice presentations in your classroom. Your classmates will be your audience. But if you have held or now hold a job, you might ask the class to listen to you the way a group of your fellow employees would listen. Describe the audience to the class. Design your presentation for that business group. Think about that particular audience and what they might need to know that you could tell them.

Step 2: Analyzing Your Purpose and Your Audience

Don't pick up a pencil yet. You are still thinking—generating ideas and focusing on specifics. You need to answer two major questions in your analysis. The first question is:

1. What do you want to achieve with your presentation?

Business presentations are given to achieve business goals. What is your goal? What is it that you want to achieve? This is called the **speech purpose** of the presentation. Let's consider a variety of purposes.

If your purpose is TO INFORM, you will explain, report, demonstrate, define, brief, show, tell, describe, etc. You expect your audience *to understand*, to know more, to see more clearly, to comprehend, to follow your reasoning, to gain additional details, to learn directly, to expand into new areas, etc.

If your purpose is TO CHANGE attitudes or beliefs, you will challenge, propose, advise, interpret, suggest, reason, appeal, persuade, justify, etc. You expect your audience *to be persuaded*—to shift, to consider, to reconsider, to be more open, to revise, to acknowledge, to accept, to lay aside, to replace, to modify, etc.

If your purpose is TO MOVE TO ACTION, you will sell, inspire, stimulate, motivate, sway, convince, win, etc. You expect your audience *to act*—to buy, to vote, to write, to join, to organize, to enlist, to contribute, to collect, to behave, to go, etc.

The design of your presentation starts with knowing your purpose for speaking and what you want your listeners to know, think, feel, or do when you are finished. For example, one purpose might be to demonstrate a word processor so that your listeners can understand how it works. But if you want to demonstrate and explain the operation of the machine so that each of your listeners can operate it, this is a different purpose. The first purpose is just to get your listeners to understand. The other purpose is to move them to action. So if you are to persuade your listeners, you will show them the steps in operating the machine, ask them to perform the steps, convince them that they will do it right if they follow your instructions, and leave them believing you.

Now you need to consider the answer to the first question in analyzing your presentation: What do you want to achieve? Answer this question, and you will have the purpose to achieve through your presentation. Here are some examples:

"I want to convince the employees that buying company stock is a wise financial move."

"I want to persuade the audience to take their clothes to Sun Dry Cleaners next time."

"I want to describe the uses of Fiber-Seal to the class."

"I want to persuade the class members to consider working for city government."

"I want to stimulate the listeners to think about learning to fly."

"I want to demonstrate the way to take blood pressure."

"I want to explain the steps in preparing a résumé."

"I want to convince the audience that gas engines can be converted to propane fuel."

"I want the employees to invest in beeper services."

"I want to demonstrate the analysis of a financial statement."

At this point, you may be confused as to what you want. You now need to consider the second question in the analysis step:

2.   What does your audience want?

Before you begin your presentation, you must do an **audience analysis** to gain information about your group of listeners.

Figuring out your audience is similar to scouting the opposing football team. It pays to know what you are up against. In most business presentations, you will be speaking to people within your company, and you are likely to know many of them. If your job is selling to the public, however, you will be speaking to strangers, and your first job is to make friends with them. Whether with co-workers or with strangers, you will want to know as much as possible about them. Refer to Figure 7-2.

One reason for knowing your audience before you develop your presentation is that you need to know where to start. How much do audience members already know? How much do they need to know before they will accept your proposal? A second reason for knowing your audience is that you need to get them involved. Each of us has needs, interests, habits, goals,

FIGURE 7-2

The design of a presentation begins as the speaker thinks through the occasion, the audience, and the reason for speaking. David Harlan, a training manager for Continental National Bank, prepared this initial analysis of a presentation on "Negotiable Instruments" for a training seminar.

PRESENTATION REQUIREMENTS: *Bank Teller Training Seminar*

PLACE: *Training Seminar Room. Has conference table, 9 chairs, couch on one side of room, table with videotape equipment and coffee pot on other. End of the table where I'll be speaking, has a blackboard on the wall and pull-down movie screen. Other end has Teller training cage for practice demonstrations which can be videotaped for replay.*

AUDIENCE ANALYSIS: *Five women, three men, 30-40 years old. All will wear required coat and tie or dress. All are new employees of C.N. Bank except for one woman who is transferring from another department in our bank. Three of the new ones have had previous experience at other banks. All are being paid and are "on the job" now. All are here to listen because at our bank all new tellers, bookkeepers, etc., must go through a one-week training session. This is the second day of training. They have all read the textbook and will be examined on the material. They feel comfortable with each other by now, and I know each by name.*

TIME: *9-19-87, 2:00 p.m.*

PRECEDING MATERIAL: *I have done the introduction. Peggy Bulott has shown two films: "The Banking Industry," and "The Teller's Job." Tellers need to know documents and*

DECISION ON TOPIC: *I'll talk now about "Negotiable Instruments"—items that serve as mediums of exchange.*

RESEARCH NEEDED: *Better look up the history of money, mediums of exchange. Refer to* Principles of Banking.

desires, and wishes that pressure us daily. We are motivated by speeches that take these pressures into account. If your message is geared to meet the audience's particular needs, the audience will listen and respond. Probably the most important reason why you will want to analyze your audience is to increase your ability to forecast their responses. Use the following three categories as a basis for your analysis so you will be better able to predict your audience responses.

Basic Needs. People get hungry, thirsty, tired, restless, and bored by lack of stimulation. These common **basic needs** regularly require attention. For example, it's hard to listen to a presentation that overlaps your lunch hour, especially if you skipped breakfast. It is difficult to concentrate on a speaker's message if the room is too hot or stuffy or if, at the other extreme, the air conditioning is too cold. A wise speaker recognizes the audience's physical needs and adjusts to them.

But even more important, people share common psychological needs. To satisfy these needs, listeners often pay close attention to speakers' messages. What are some of these basic human needs?

"There are four ways of examining men—by their conversation, disposition, family and conduct."

Hindu proverb

1. Security and protection
2. The esteem of others
3. Relaxation and recreation
4. Personal money gain
5. Recognition and praise
6. Prestige
7. A sense of personal accomplishment

These are common threads that can be used to relate your message to your audience. By considering carefully the strongest needs of the people in your audience, you can find ways of relating your subject to them. An analysis of your listeners' common needs can serve as a focus for planning what you will say. For example, let's say you are to give a presentation to employees about the company's new insurance plan. You know that you can meet their needs for security and protection and that the listeners will be interested. But they won't want to listen to you at 4:00 p.m. when they are tired from a day's work. So you should schedule your presentation for another time.

Factual Information. What other information about your listeners will help you in planning your presentation? There are specific things you can find out about the group you will address. And, of course, the more you know about your listeners, the easier it will be to direct your message to them. Consider the checklist below.

1. Number of people in the audience
2. Number of men and women
3. General age group
4. Economic level
5. Educational level
6. Specific occupations
7. Status in their organizations
8. Racial or ethnic groups
9. Political affiliations
10. Marital status

Not all of this information is important to each presentation. But you'll want to refer to this list as you think about a speech you are to give. To illustrate, you have been appointed United Fund chairperson for your company. You are asked to make an appeal to various groups of employees. Your presentation to a group of long-time employees will be different from the presentation you give to a group of new workers. For one thing, each group's reasons for giving will be different. Their earning capacity clearly is different, so their ability to give is not the same. You will need to adjust your appeal and gear your presentation to persuading the particular group to whom you are speaking.

Attitudes and Beliefs. There is one other area to consider in analyzing your audience before planning your presentation. Although you will speak to an audience as a group, each member of the audience will listen individually. In other words, they bring their attitudes with them when they listen to you. For example, what are their attitudes toward you as a speaker? Are they present because they want to be or are they required to attend this session?

The answers to these questions will indicate some of the audience's basic attitudes.

Since your central concern is to achieve your purpose (to inform or to persuade) with this particular group of people through your message, you should consider their beliefs and attitudes. You can do this by shifting to their point of view in any of three ways:

1. Think about your receivers' attitudes toward your subject. Are they interested? concerned? indifferent? uninformed? curious? hostile? angry? What questions run through their minds as they listen? How do they stand on this topic?
2. Reflect on your listeners' relationship to you. Are these people co-workers? friends? strangers? Do they know you well? Do they respect your knowledge? your position? your concern for them? Do they like you as a person? On what basis can you win them over to your ideas? What common factors provide a meeting ground for you and your audience?
3. Consider your audience as a group. What are their business goals? What values are important to them? How willing are they to risk or change? What are their special interests?

If you are speaking to persuade, you must have some accurate idea of whether or not your listeners favor your proposal. If so, to what degree do they favor it? Your audience probably can be classified into one of three categories:

1. No opinion—has either no information about your topic or little interest in it.
2. In favor—is already sold on the idea.
3. Opposed—holds an opposite point of view.

How would you approach an audience in each of these situations?

First, if you are fairly sure that your listeners hold no opinion on your topic, it may be that the lack of opinion results from a lack of knowledge. Your job will be to approach the group directly and fill in the knowledge that they need in order to understand the topic. When they have this basic understanding, you can create interest by presenting your arguments in favor of your proposal. You must arouse them by relating the topic to their special interests. Remember, explanation must come before you try to persuade them.

In the second instance, your audience is already in favor of your proposal. This can be tricky for a speaker because the listeners are not interested in hearing what they already know and believe. Your job will be to focus their attention on some meaningful action that will solve the problem or on an approach that is new and different.

In the third instance, you may speak to an audience that is opposed to your proposal, or holds another view of the topic. They may hold slightly negative attitudes, or they may be downright hostile to your proposal. Your task in this case is to present logical reasons and evidence in order to move them toward a positive attitude. If they are unwilling to even listen to your arguments, all you can do is present yourself as a capable, willing speaker with an interesting message. Leave a favorable impression, if possible.

To win your listeners requires a keen insight into how they think, feel, and behave. Your task is to get their attention, focus their interest, move them toward involvement, and create a good relationship with them. By knowing who they are, what they do, what they believe, what they have in common, and what benefits they will get from accepting your proposal, you will be armed with the information to design your presentation.

Step 3: Decision Making

Now it's time to pick up your pen or pencil and get to work! The next major decision you will need to make is to choose a topic. When you enter the business world, your presentation will depend on a particular business need. You will make a presentation because it is an efficient way of informing all members of a group at one time. Or you will present a proposal because action must be taken. Right now, however, your concern is to find topics for your classroom presentations.

If you are to give a demonstration, what could you bring to class and show as you discuss it? Try writing down two or three topics. Consider these: the special features of a Kirby vacuum cleaner; selecting proper running shoes; the use of beepers for the businessperson; different types of filters for 35-mm. cameras. Now try writing two or three ideas of your own.

Do the same thing for a briefing on a process you know about. Remember, you are explaining to encourage understanding, so your purpose is to inform the listeners. Consider these topics: the process of developing pictures; setting type; preparing a tax return; bookkeeping; selling radio advertising time; operating a firewood business. Don't read on until you have two or three good ideas.

If you are to give a persuasive presentation, you will need to think carefully about the audience. What might you persuade them to do? What idea might you convince them of? Again, write down several ideas that will help document your thinking. Here are some ideas: "Use this method of keeping your checking account balanced." "Make a good impression in your next job interview." "Learn how to spot fraudulent checks." "Use these techniques to prevent fires and ensure customer safety in your business." "Buy these Stanley products." Now try jotting down some persuasive topics of your own.

Many students put off the decision of topic choice. This is no time to procrastinate! The sooner you make this decision, the more quickly you can get into the important work of developing your idea.

A tip that proves most useful for a novice speaker is to limit your topic. Narrow the subject to one simple idea. Try to state the idea as concretely as possible. You will not be able to tell all you know about the subject within the time limit. For example, instead of talking about "Company Policies," you might limit your subject to "Know the Company Code on Employee Dress and Conduct"; instead of "Labor Unions," you might limit your subject to "Union Membership Gives You Four Benefits."

Hang onto this list you have just started. Keep it handy as you read the rest of this chapter. Ideas will pop into your head as you go along. WRITE THEM DOWN. If they don't get recorded, you may lose them forever. Find a place to keep them so you will have them for reference. But do it now. Think of some topics. Make some decisions. Collect at least one topic in each area we have discussed.

Step 4: Researching for Additional Material

As a part of the design of your presentation, you will want to know some sources of information that you can use. On the job, you can easily go to informed people for material to fill in the gaps of your speech. In class you will want to obtain up-to-date information for your oral presentation. Below is a list of information sources:

1. Interviews with knowledgeable people
2. Radio and television
3. Books
4. Magazines
5. Newspapers
6. Government documents
7. Advertising pamphlets

The library is the quickest source for most of these references. The following section explains how to use the library efficiently.

Research is an organized process of seeking facts about some problem or question. The most efficient and convenient place to find answers is often the library. Your most important contact is the librarian, who will consider your questions and direct you to the proper reference works. The librarian is a key resource in helping you with research. But it is your job to plan your questions well. This makes hunting for answers less time-consuming and frustrating.

The following information will arm you against much wasted time in the library, so read carefully. The principal function of a library is to organize a great body of diverse information in such a way that you can retrieve this information efficiently when needed.

The first step in research is to think of the library as a group of collections: books, serials (magazines called periodicals, newspapers, documents, abstracts, etc., all of which are published periodically), maps, directories, encyclopedias, etc. Most of these collections have tools for locating materials. Let's look at the four collections you will use most:

Books. The tool used to dig out information about a book is the *card catalog*. These drawers of cards list all the books owned by the library. Each book is catalogued three ways: under the author's last name, by the title, and by subject. If you know only one of these pieces of information, you can locate the book you want. The cards, three for each book, will give the same information—author, title, place and date of publication, publisher, number of pages, and the call numbers so that you can find the book on the shelf. Be sure to write down all the numbers when you look up a book. In many libraries, card catalog information is now available on computer.

Periodicals. The tool used to unearth information from magazines is an *index*. An index is a listing of articles from various magazines. It lists the authors, subjects, magazine titles, issues, dates, and page numbers so that you can ask for the right magazine. Your library will have the back issues of these periodicals bound in volumes.

Newspapers. These valuable information sources are difficult to store and hard to handle; you may find them on microfilm in your library. Indexes to articles in issues of a newspaper will give dates and section, page, and column numbers of the articles you need. The index will be in hardback form, even if the newspapers are stored on microfilm. Examples are the *New York Times Index*, the *Wall Street Journal Index*, and *Index to the Times* (London).

Government Documents. The U.S. Government is the largest publisher in the world. The index to government documents is the *Monthly Catalog*. The material is arranged by subject matter.

The second step in research is to consider which of these collections will serve you best for your topic. Ask yourself these questions: "Who is writing about my subject?" "Will it be found in business sources? in general periodicals? in encyclopedias? in journals? in books?" "How is my subject being treated?" Remember that it can take several years to produce a book. You may require very current material for your speeches. Below is a list to help you become acquainted with the indexes that are the key to the most recent information. You should become familiar with these valuable sources:

Readers' Guide to Periodical Literature—lists articles in more than 100 well-known magazines under specific subject headings and authors. Current issue indexes are printed in paperback volumes; the accumulated information is printed in bound index volumes.

The Public Affairs Information Service—lists publications in economics and public affairs and covers a great deal of material published currently. It is catalogued by subject and by author.

Business Periodicals Index—contains an index to business periodicals arranged by subject. Articles describing companies are indexed under the name of the company. An author listing of book reviews is included.

The Business Index—lists 325 business periodicals including the *Wall Street Journal, Barron's*, and the financial section and business articles of the *New York Times*.

Funk and Scott Index of Corporations and Industries—lists articles in major business, financial, and trade magazines and key newspapers, analytical reports of investment and advisory services and stockbrokers, and bank newsletters.

The Magazine Index—lists, by company name and industry, 370 popular publications in a computer information service that is up-to-date and easy to use. Information about issues of magazines may be as recent as two weeks. Since this is an expensive service on microfilm, your library may not have it. If it does, however, search by author and by subject.

The New York Times Index—contains condensed, classified history of the world as it is recorded daily in the *New York Times*. Headings are arranged alphabetically. Articles within a heading are listed chronologically. Each entry is followed by a precise reference—date, page, and column of the item it summarizes.

The Wall Street Journal Index—lists articles that have appeared in the *Wall Street Journal*. The first section is corporate news; the second is general news. Within the sections, entries are arranged alphabetically, using the letter-by-letter system without punctuation.

Because libraries store large quantities of printed information, new methods of storage and retrieval are constantly being developed. Microform is a general term for this technology and includes such methods as micropiece, microfiche, microprint, and micro-opaque. Again, your librarian is your best source for helping you locate and retrieve material in your library.

To locate an article in a periodical or newspaper, use one of the published indexes described. Search by subject and/or author until you locate an article that sounds useful. The index will give the name of the article and the name of the magazine in which it was published; it will also give the date, volume number, and pages on which the article appears. Because each index has its own method of recording information, it is essential that you write down the information to aid the librarian in locating the material for you. For current topics or data on any subject, begin with the latest paperbound number of the index and work chronologically through the hardback volumes.

If you do not find the material you want, consult the librarian for the location of specialized periodicals on such topics as accounting, insurance, labor and labor relations, law, marketing, office management, personnel, retailing, or transportation. Each field has its own publications.

As you consider your speech design, remember that nobody knows everything about a particular subject. But everyone likes to get information from someone who is willing to check the accuracy of facts. So, look up additional information and use it in your speech by indicating where you found it. Rather than thinking less of you, your audience will appreciate knowing the source of the material. Cite your sources with such remarks as, "In an article from the November 11 *New York Times* . . . ," or "Roger Ward reports in a *Motor Trend* article of October, 1983 . . . ," or "From the July, 1982, issue of *Business Week*. . . ." By clarifying where you read the information, by quoting someone directly and giving the speaker credit, and by reminding the audience of the sources of information, you avoid plagiarism—passing off someone else's words or ideas as your own.

Now we are ready to review the next steps in preparing your presentation.

DEVELOPING YOUR SPEECH PRESENTATION

Like an engineer building a piece of equipment for a special job, you design your presentation for a particular group. Now you will need a carefully drawn blueprint to speak from—an outline of your key ideas effectively arranged, well supported, and carefully summarized. Listed below are the five steps for developing your ideas into such a blueprint.

Step 1: State the thesis.
Step 2: Organize main points into a pattern.
Step 3: Link the parts of the pattern.
Step 4: Add supporting material.
Step 5: Plan opening and closing remarks.

This is the time to begin jotting down your own ideas—step-by-step. Know your assignment and keep your audience clearly in mind as you work.

Step 1: State the Thesis

The thesis statement in your presentation can have many names: proposition, purpose sentence, or central idea. Whatever it is called, it is the central statement of the entire presentation in capsule form. The thesis must be thoughtfully worded, because it is the speech in a nutshell and says exactly what you plan to demonstrate or prove. It phrases the idea that your audience will remember.

This thesis should:

1. Link the subject to your purpose and your audience.
2. State what you are going to discuss.
3. Express the idea in simple, precise words.

You must work to perfect your thesis—the central statement. Its importance should not be underestimated, for it determines the shape of the whole presentation. Indeed, the main portion of your presentation must develop or unfold this statement. You must be willing to strip away any ideas that do not help to make this central idea clear. Below are some examples of thesis statements. Many of these have been used to set up actual business presentations.

1. Microfilm systems have a number of advantages over existing paper systems.
2. Our new insurance plan will be aimed at the young graduates of drivers training programs.
3. With the increase of oil-to-gas heating conversions, our company should market a new line of gas heaters.
4. By 1999, the national standard will be a 36-hour workweek.
5. Let's try using more hand tools to provide a better finish on our sheet metal.
6. Our company products could be most effectively sold with billboard advertising.
7. Let me demonstrate the simplicity of the Lanier Pocket Caddy tape recorder.
8. A media specialist will provide four major benefits for our company.
9. Let's run a national photo contest as a marketing promotion.
10. Attend the company picnic at River Run this weekend.
11. If we are to remain competitive, we must increase our research budget.

Step 2: Organize Main Points into a Pattern

When you have worded your thesis statement to express the exact message you want your presentation to convey, you will develop this central idea. **Main points** form the major portion, or the body, of your speech. They explain why your thesis is true, why you believe it, or what you mean by it. If they are carefully arranged, they will justify your argument, make your proposal clearer, or win your audience to agreement or action.

Plan the body of your speech—the development of the thesis—in **outline** form. Indicate the main points with Roman numerals; label the supporting ideas with capital letters. Limit the main points to two or three. Your audience can remember three well-stated main points. More than three can be confusing.

Stating your main points so that they are similar in wording will help your audience recognize and understand the development of your thesis. Arranging your main points in a logical order will also aid your listeners, and incidentally help you to remember them. In the outline for an informative speech shown in Figure 7-3, note that each main point begins with the words "Mean Jeans" and then gives a particular type of information about the simulation activity.

FIGURE 7-3

Sample outline for an
informative speech.

```
THESIS:  Mean Jeans Manufacturing Company is a simulation
activity used in teaching.

BODY OF THE SPEECH:
    I.  Mean Jeans is designed to be used in teaching
        business courses.
        A.  Everything is included in the package.
            1.  Directions
            2.  Work sheets
            3.  Illustrations
        B.  Designed for 11-31 students
        C.  Can be expanded to 35 students
        D.  Can be completed in 6-9 weeks
        E.  Suitable for a variety of courses:
            1.  General business
            2.  Consumer education
            3.  Business dynamics
            4.  Free enterprise
            5.  Economics
            6.  Marketing
            7.  Distributive education
   II.  Mean Jeans simulates an actual model business
        community.
        A.  Mean Jeans is one company in a community of
            16 businesses.
            1.  Manufactures fashion denim apparel
            2.  Must depend on other 15 businesses for a
                variety of goods and services
        B.  The interaction between companies makes this
            simulation unique.
  III.  Mean Jeans reinforces basic business concepts for
        the students.
        A.  Economic side of business
        B.  Managing money
        C.  Using banking services
        D.  Making credit decisions
        E.  Investing money
        F.  Shipping goods
        G.  Selling goods and services
        H.  Purchasing goods and services
        I.  Communicating orally
        J.  Communicating in writing

CONCLUSION:  I've told you three things about Mean Jeans
Manufacturing Company: it is an activity designed to teach
business, it simulates an actual model business community,
it reinforces basic business concepts.  I hope you can use
this information.
```

For informative speeches, there are some familiar patterns of arranging ideas in a logical order that will help your audience to follow you:

Topical Order. The thesis is divided into a series of subtopics: reasons, benefits, advantages, categories, etc.

Thesis: There are three reasons to own this pocket calculator.

    I. It is slim and easy to hold.
   II. It performs many functions.
  III. Its cost is reasonable.

Space Order. The main points are arranged according to position in space or geographic location.

Thesis: Our company is spread from coast to coast.

    I. There are three major plants in the East and South.

II. Company headquarters and branch offices are in the Midwest.

III. Four regional offices are in the West.

Time Order. The main points are arranged according to when they happened (chronological order).

Thesis: Entract Company is celebrating 60 years of growth.

   I. We grew slowly but steadily in the '20s and '30s.

  II. We expanded rapidly in the '40s and '50s.

 III. We began our overseas growth in the '60s and '70s.

These main points form the skeleton of your outline. On the bones of this skeleton you can hang interesting material that develops each point. As you write your main points in outline form and number them with Roman numerals, be sure they are stated in parallel form. This helps your listeners to recognize your pattern of organization. In the following example, the points are *not* parallel:

Thesis: Interesting materials for speeches come from several sources:

   I. Personal experiences enliven presentations.

  II. You can find material in the library.

 III. Current business publications update presentations.

Which point in the above example needs rewording? Would the outline be better balanced if the second point were restated, "Library research strengthens presentations"?

There are also some well-known patterns for arranging your main points in a persuasive presentation:

Deductive Pattern. This might be called "state-your-case-and-prove-it." It arranges the main points by topic as shown above for an informative speech, but since the purpose of a persuasive presentation is to change an audience's thinking or to move an audience to action of some sort, the emphasis is different. In the topical outline for an informative speech given above, the desirable features of a particular calculator were simply listed. In the outline below, the features are listed *and* found superior to those of competing models so that listeners may be persuaded to buy.

Thesis: This pocket calculator is superior to others on the market.

   I. It is slimmer and easier to hold. (compare to others)

  II. It performs more functions than others of its size. (compare to several others)

 III. It costs less than the other three. (compare prices)

Inductive Pattern. This pattern cites a specific case plus another specific case plus another case and then draws a general conclusion. This is the pattern used in the sample outline for a persuasive speech shown in Figure 7-4. This pattern is also used if the listeners may be hostile to the thesis, as in the example below:

Thesis: (The electric company is justified in proposing a rate increase.)

   I. The cost of operations has increased.

  II. The demands on generating capacity have increased.

 III. The research for new energy sources has increased.

FIGURE 7-4

Sample outline for a
persuasive speech.

```
AUDIENCE:  Business teachers

SPEAKER:  Salesperson from South-Western Publishing Company

INTRODUCTION:  "There's been nothing like it--up to now!"
You are wondering if I'm talking about a new book.  No, but
have I got a teaching aid for your business courses!

THESIS:  (Order Mean Jeans Manufacturing Company for your
classes.)

BODY OF THE SPEECH:
    I.  You want to involve your students in learning in a
        meaningful, creative way.
        A.  Mean Jeans simulates a model business community
            of 16 businesses.
        B.  Mean Jeans is a modified flow-of-work, multi-
            station simulation.
        C.  Mean Jeans is designed for 11-35 students; can
            be completed in 6-9 weeks.
        D.  Mean Jeans is a simulation activity in which your
            students take an active part.
   II.  You want business concepts to be more than just book
        theory.
        A.  Your course can become a practical laboratory.
            1.  Mean Jeans manufactures fashion denim apparel.
            2.  15 other businesses provide goods and services
                to Mean Jeans.
            3.  Interaction among all the companies makes
                Mean Jeans unique.
        B.  Business concepts come alive as students partici-
            pate in:
            1.  Managing money
            2.  Using banking
            3.  Making credit decisions
            4.  Investing money
            5.  Shipping, selling, and purchasing goods
            6.  Communicating
  III.  You want an activity that can be adapted to your
        particular courses:
        A.  General business
        B.  Consumer education
        C.  Business dynamics
        D.  Free enterprise
        E.  Economics
        F.  Marketing
        G.  Distributive education

CONCLUSION:  Order Mean Jeans Manufacturing Company for your
classes.  Order to involve your students in learning, to
provide more than just book learning, and because this
activity can be adapted to your particular course.  I'll
take your orders now, or contact your regional South-Western
office and ask for Stock No. G10.  Your business classes
will never be the same again.
```

As the listeners hear and agree with the main points, they will be more open to the suggestion which is the thesis. Note that the thesis statement in the above example and in Figure 7-4 is enclosed in parentheses. Parentheses around the thesis in the outline indicate that it will be withheld until the end of the speech.

Problem-Solving Pattern. Arranging ideas in problem-solving order works very well for many presentations. However, you might not want to reveal the solution, which is your thesis, until you have carefully explained the problem. If the audience is not aware of the problem, you may want to discuss the causes and effects of the problem and then present the solution you want them to accept. Your pattern might be:

Introduction
    I. Presentation of the problem
   II. Causes and effects of the problem
  III. (Thesis) The solution I recommend is . . .
      A. It will reduce the cause.
      B. It will eliminate the effects.
Conclusion: Summarize and focus on your solution.

Note that you save your central idea until the last point in the speech. Be sure to develop this point, however, if you seek to have the audience accept your solution.

Meet-the-Audience-Needs Pattern. This pattern is well known to persuasive speakers who use logical and emotional appeals to win their listeners. The thesis is in the middle of the speech. The speaker presents the effectiveness of the idea and tells the audience what they must do to achieve this effect. The outline would look like this:

Introduction
    I. Arouse the audience.
   II. Dissatisfy the listeners with present conditions.
  III. Present your thesis as a way to alleviate the conditions.
  IV. Picture your idea and how it will work.
   V. Move the audience to take action.
Conclusion: Action Step

"Your thoughts are like pearls, but you need a thread to string them on."

Anonymous

Any of these patterns of developing an idea can be used. They are the strings that tie your presentations together. Simply decide which of these patterns will work best for your audience.

Step 3: Link the Parts of the Pattern

No matter how clearly *you* see the pattern or organization you are following, your audience must recognize it, too. Therefore, plan **transitions** between the parts of your outline. These may be word clues, such as "First," "Second," "Third," or "The next point I'd like to make is. . . ." Transitions are like highway signs to clue an audience as to where you both are. Other transitions are:

"Now let's consider . . ."
"Furthermore . . ."
"In addition to . . ."
"Finally . . ."
"In summary . . ."

Transitions help to take the audience with you as you move from one point to the next. For example, "I've been discussing the problem caused by lack of marketing research, and now I would like to offer a plan to solve this problem."

As a reminder, it is a help to write the transitional words on the note cards you use when delivering the speech. You may know where you are in the outline, but share that information with the audience by using transitions. This is vital!

Step 4: Add Supporting Material

Your carefully constructed pattern is the blueprint for your presentation. But this skeleton alone is dull. It is the information you put on the bones that draws an audience to your ideas. The following types of supporting material will add interest and clarity to the main points and subpoints that you have selected. To make your ideas vivid and memorable, try to use some of each type.

Definitions. Clarify what you mean when you use a specialized term that your listeners may not know. Put it in a general category or describe the essential qualities that clarify your meaning.

> "Poise is the art of raising the eyebrows instead of raising the roof."
> "Diplomacy has been defined as the art of letting someone else have your way."
> "By *transition*, I mean 'a few words that clue an audience about the idea to come next.' "

Examples. Use stories, personal experiences, illustrations, or specific instances to illuminate a point. Clue the audience with such words as, "For example," or "To illustrate, let me tell you a story. . . ."

> "Dr. Albert Einstein once explained how, under his relativity theory, time is not absolute. He said, 'When you sit with a nice girl for two hours, it seems like only a moment. But when you sit on a hot stove for a moment, it seems like two hours. That's relativity.' "

Comparison and Contrast. Show the similarities between what you are talking about and what the audience already knows. Or contrast two things by showing the differences.

> "A job is something you go to from 8 to 5. Work is something you give yourself to."
> "Your smile is your personal piece of sunshine."
> "Life is like an onion," said Carl Sandburg. "You peel it off one layer at a time, and sometimes you weep."

Quotations and Testimony. Use the ideas of someone else who expresses an idea vividly or whose expert opinion adds authority to your point. Give credit to the source.

> "Congressman George Mahon gave this advice to new and ambitious members of Congress: 'Don't talk too often, do your homework, don't ever lose your credibility by using statements that are tricky or deceitful.' "

Factual Data. Include numbers, statistics, and accepted facts. Because this information is often useful to businesspeople, it is important to present it accurately and clearly so that the audience knows the precise interpretation of the figures. Visual aids are often helpful. Using a comparison may make statistical data meaningful.

> "Rather than merely giving the facts, engineers at the space center explained their work in terms of comparison. The 182-foot first stage of the Saturn I is 'three feet taller than the White House,' its thrust is 'equal to the power re-

FIGURE 7-5

Full outline of the
presentation on "Negotiable
Instruments" given by David
Harlan, training manager for
Continental National Bank.

PURPOSE: To give the tellers a background on the documents and language of banking and show how to apply this information on the job.

THESIS: In the past, there were a variety of negotiable instruments; in the present, there are requirements for negotiability and bank handling that are important to know.

DEVELOPMENT OF THESIS:

Main Point I. In the past, there were a variety of negotiable instruments.

    A. Barter--early history, found clay tablets when digging into old Babylonian temple, *(story)* found one to be a "promise to pay" back to the temple priestess for borrowed seed, payment to be corn.

        examples Later--cobblers traded shoe repair for side of beef; tailors traded new coat for a sheep or goats.

    B. Mediums of exchange--salt, fish hooks, precious jewels, metals, early coins (cut *examples* coins in half, then in eighths = expression "two bits")

    C. Credit balances--English ships taking load to trade for spices in India often robbed *illustration* by pirates. English began sending double loads with letter of instructions. If ship got through, English would have credit. Paperwork began = bill of exchange = draft =

    D. Negotiable instruments--letter of instructions streamlined to modern check; information first *explanation* included owner of account, receiver of amount, and finally the bank as handler.

Transition: (The speed of travel and commerce increased the need for uniformity.)

Main Point II. In the middle of the last century, requirements were set up.

    A. Uniform Commercial Code--began because of need:
      1. Banks were issuing their own money.
      2. Money varied from state to state. *illustration* Couldn't get money in Laramie, WY, with draft drawn on NY bank.
      3. Passed National Banking Act, 1863, to *explanation* regulate money size, etc. = uniformity

    B. Five legal requirements for checks to be negotiable instruments:
visual aid on blackboard
      1. Signature handwritten
      2. Sum must be certain (unconditional promise to pay)
show check written on T-shirt
      3. Payable on demand (demand account = checking)
      4. Must have a payee
      5. Name of bank clearly indicated

    C. If there is to be negotiation, there must be:
      1. Delivery
definition of terms
      2. Possession
      3. Holder in due course
      4. Endorsements--payee puts name on back to make transaction, shows instrument has been exchanged, payee accepts responsibility, previous endorsements, can restrict.

Transition: (And now let's look at the bank's role.)

Main Point III. In the present, there are rules for the bank to follow.

    A. Transit and routing numbers (show check, explain numbers)
visual aid B. MICR (computer language--Magnetic Ink Character Recognition)
definition C. Cash items--how a teller handles a check
explanation D. Collection of noncash items--special handling of checks

CONCLUSION: If an item is missing ANY ONE of the five *Focus on Purpose* requirements, DO NOT CASH!

quired to drive 100,000 Cadillacs,' and the concrete in the 400-foot-high test stand 'would be sufficient to build a four-lane highway from Dallas to Fort Worth.' "

Visual Materials. Use charts, drawings, flannel boards, pictures, slides, films, overhead projectors, flip charts, models, diagrams, or chalkboards to illustrate points visually. A good presentation will almost always include visual aids. But it is important to remember that the visual aid must amplify, support, or enhance the verbal message. Use of visual aids will be covered extensively in Chapter 8.

When you decide on the supporting material you will use in your speech, note it on your speaker cards in the appropriate space. An important quotation should be fully written out and perhaps read from the notes, but you will remember the other materials by simply jotting down a few key words in your outline.

FIGURE 7-6

Reduced outline of David Harlan's presentation on "Negotiable Instruments."

```
INTRODUCTION

THESIS:  In the past, there were a variety of negotiable
instruments; in the present, there are requirements for
negotiability and bank handling that are important to know.

DEVELOPMENT OF THESIS:
    I.   In the past, there were a variety of negotiable
         instruments.
         A.   Barter
         B.   Mediums of exchange
         C.   Credit balances
         D.   Negotiable instruments
              1.   Promise to pay
              2.   Order to pay
                   (a) Bills of exchange
                   (b) Drafts
                   (c) Checks
Transition:  (The speed of travel and commerce increased
the need for uniformity.)
    II.  In the middle of the last century, requirements
         were set up.
         A.   Uniform Commercial Code
         B.   Five legal requirements
         C.   Negotiation
              1.   Delivery
              2.   Possession
              3.   Holder in due course
              4.   Endorsements
                   (a) Types
                   (b) Functions
                   (c) Liabilities
Transition:  (And now let's look at the bank's role.)
    III. In the present, there are rules for the bank to
         follow.
         A.   Transit and routing numbers
         B.   MICR--computer machine language
         C.   Cash items--characteristics
         D.   Collection of noncash items--characteristics

CONCLUSION:  If an item is missing ANY ONE of the five
requirements, DO NOT CASH!
```

Step 5: Plan Opening and Closing Remarks

A presentation has three parts—the opening or introduction to the thesis statement, the development of the central idea or the body of the speech, and the closing. Let's discuss the closing first because you have already prepared the body of the speech and know how to end it.

Closing. This is the climax of your presentation. At this point you will tie the ideas together and then focus on your purpose for speaking. Your conclusion should do three things:

1. Summarize your central statement and main points in a brief, concise restatement.
2. Focus on the purpose of your presentation.
   a. Restate your belief or position.
   b. Appeal to your listeners for acceptance.
   c. Explain what your listeners can do with the information you have provided.
   d. Zero in on what you would like your listeners to do.
3. Develop a sense of completeness.
   a. Use a strong final statement. Write it out in advance.
   b. Clinch your ideas in the listener's mind.

Opening. Now you are ready to prepare the beginning. This is the introduction to the speech. Its purpose is to grab your audience and to let them know what is coming. You have waited until last to prepare this introduction because you needed to know what ideas you were going to introduce to the audience. So now you know! Your introduction should do three things to set up your thesis:

1. **Begin by getting your listeners' attention.** Start with a story, a quotation, an unusual statement, a series of questions, or whatever you believe will hook this group's attention. Of course, acknowledge the person who introduces you (if this is the case), but then start out strongly. Be sure that what you say is related to your topic and will lead your receivers in the direction you have in mind.
2. **Involve the audience.** Think of the needs, attitudes, and beliefs of the particular group and relate your thesis to their concerns.
3. **Establish your credibility.** Clarify your position, knowledge, or experience that qualifies you to speak. Share a bit of yourself and pull the group to you.

Now **identify your thesis**. Lead your listeners to your core idea. If you want them to take a particular action ("Join the Christmas Club"), you may withhold this until later in your speech. However, your purpose in speaking should be clear. State positively, "I am convinced that our department needs a new image" rather than the blunt "I'm going to convince you that. . . ."

You probably will want to write out your introduction. There is security in having the first ideas written on your note cards. But if you are thoroughly familiar with what you want to say, you may not have to write out whole sentences—except for your central idea. Key phrases will do.

Now review your blueprint. Speak through it aloud. A presentation is designed to be heard, and you should be the first one to hear it. Ask yourself these questions:

1. Am I satisfied that this is what I really want to say?
2. Am I satisfied that the body of the speech unfolds the central idea clearly?
3. Do the ideas flow? make sense? hold interest?

There is still time to make changes, reword transitions, and smooth out rough spots. Practice your presentation orally again and again. Prepare a final set of note cards and write on one side only. Use as few as possible. You know what you want to talk about, so the cards are only a guide for your thinking as you speak.

CHAPTER SUMMARY

This chapter began with examples of oral business presentations and stressed that such presentations play an important role because they are designed to meet business needs. A comparison of oral business presentations and public speeches revealed important similarities and differences between them. The different types of informative presentations (reports, briefings, explanations, instructions, and demonstrations) and persuasive presentations (sales, justifying proposals, and goodwill speeches) were described. Six important questions requiring careful consideration before undertaking any type of speech presentation were listed.

Business presentations are: (1) directed to specific audiences; (2) designed to create understanding or to influence decision making in business; (3) presented in formal situations followed by questions and answers, or in less formal situations with interaction during the presentation.

The four steps in designing a presentation include: (1) discovering ideas; (2) analyzing your purpose and your audience; (3) decision making about your topic; and (4) researching for additional material.

The five steps in developing the presentation are: (1) wording the thesis; (2) organizing main points into a pattern; (3) linking parts of the pattern; (4) adding supporting material; and (5) opening and closing the presentation. Sample outlines of both informative and persuasive presentations are included.

WORKSHOP ACTIVITIES

CLASS AUDIENCE ANALYSIS *(Individual Activity)*

Purpose: To analyze your classmates as a potential audience for informative and persuasive speeches.

Briefing: When you speak to a group of people, you should know as much as possible about them in order to plan your speech message to fit the group. Think about the members of your speech class. Fill out this sheet. Be sure to include your instructor as a member of your audience.

Listener Analysis:

1. How many people?_____ Males?_____ Females?_____

2. What is the average age level? _____ Other age levels present?_____

3. What general educational background? _____
   _____

4. What social groups or other affiliations do the class members belong to outside the classroom? _____
   _____
   _____
   _____

5. What general beliefs do they hold about business? about money? about speaking? about working, etc.?
   _____
   _____
   _____

6. What topics will be interesting to them? _____
   _____
   _____
   _____

Setting Analysis:

1. Will the physical arrangement of the room affect my presentation?_____
   _____

2. Can all students see and hear from where they usually sit? _____
   _____

3. Can I arrange the speaker's stand, table, etc., to be more comfortable for me and the audience?

_____

4. If I plan to use visual aids, have I checked to make sure that electrical outlets work? charts and graphs are legible? that there are sufficient materials such as thumbtacks, tape, etc.?_____

_____

Time Analysis:

1. Will there be a timekeeper?_____   How will I know how much time I have left to speak?_____

_____

2. Can I cut down the size of my topic to fit the allotted time? _____

_____

Business Audience Analysis

If you choose to prepare a speech for a business audience, you will need to answer the following *additional* questions as a part of your analysis. This will be a "pretend" situation, of course, and you will brief your classmates on who they are, who you are, why you are speaking, etc. They will listen to you as members of your business audience. Perhaps they will ask the questions your business audience would.

1. Who is the speaker?

2. What is the relationship between the speaker and audience?

3. What are the common bonds between audience members?

4. Do members of the audience know each other?

5. Why is the audience present? Are they listening during work hours?

6. Where are we meeting?

7. What does my audience know about my subject?

8. Why do I think my audience should be interested in my subject?

9. What does my audience know or think about me?

10. What specific strategies do I need to use to be sure my audience will respond as I want them to?

SPEECH FRAGMENTS: MAIN POINTS *(Individual Activity)*

Purpose: To practice arranging ideas logically.

Briefing: Practice dividing a central statement into two or three parts. Each part should explain or develop the central idea according to a recognizable pattern. Write one part for each type of arrangement (topical order, space order, or time order) listed below and on the next page.

Topical Order

Some ideas divide easily into topical categories. You may decide to organize a topical arrangement according to aspects, qualities, reasons, steps, branches, or departments. Choose one. Write the thesis statement and the main points in full sentences. Consider these suggestions for thesis ideas: the qualities of a good manager; the duties of a bookkeeper; the branches of government; the aspects of marketing; or choose any other topic that interests you.

Thesis Statement:

Main Points:

I.

II.

III.

Space Order

Sometimes it is convenient to explain a subject through its geographic relationships (space order). Choose one. Write a thesis statement and the main points in full sentences. Consider these suggestions for thesis ideas: the arrangement of buildings in an industrial complex; the location of various departments on different floors of an office building; the sales areas around the country for a particular company; or any other subject that lends itself to geographic arrangement.

Thesis Statement:

Main Points:

   I.

   II.

III.

Time Order

Some subjects are more effectively explained in a time sequence (chronological order). Choose one. Write the thesis statement and the main points in full sentences. Consider these suggestions for thesis ideas: the history of instant printing; the development of the shoe industry; the growth of popular, recorded music; the growth of citizen's band radio; or any other topic you choose.

Thesis Statement:

Main Points:

   I.

   II.

III.

SPEECH FRAGMENTS: SPEECH OPENING *(Individual Activity)*

Purpose: To prepare and deliver the introduction of a speech.

Briefing: The introduction of a presentation should prepare an audience to hear the discussion of the thesis idea. An effective introduction should do the following:

1. *Arrest attention and interest.* You can do this by creating curiosity, by showing an object, or by presenting striking facts, a graphic description, a personal incident, a dramatic opening illustration, an unusual quotation, etc. These must relate to the central idea.

2. *Involve the audience by the use of the word "you."* Think of the audience's needs, attitudes, or relationships to the subject. Focus on the listeners by such questions as, "Do you remember . . . ?" "How many of you have . . . ?" or such statements as, "Because you are all professional people . . ." or, "You each carry personal identification. . . ."

3. *Establish yourself or your concern with the topic.* This identifies your reason for speaking on the particular subject and clarifies the depth of your concern, the basis for your knowledge, or the reasons for your interest.

4. *Create a strong thesis sentence.* State the central idea in one short, simple, and effective sentence. Use words that can be remembered.

Your Opening

Select an idea for a presentation. The purpose of the idea may be either to inform or to persuade. Carefully word the thesis statement. Write it in the space for *Thesis Statement* below. Now plan and write the way you would introduce this statement in a speech to your class. Fill in the three steps below. Deliver this introduction, which may be as short as 30 seconds, to the class. Do not give the speech; just give the introduction to it. If the audience is sorry not to have the opportunity to hear the whole speech, then you have successfully accomplished the assignment.

Attention Step:

Audience Involvement Step:

Establish Credibility Step:

Thesis Statement:

SPEECH FRAGMENTS: SPEECH CLOSING *(Individual Activity)*

Purpose: To plan, prepare, and deliver the closing of a speech presentation.

Briefing: The closing of a speech should summarize the thesis statement and the main points that unfolded or developed it. The closing may begin with such transition statements as:

"In brief . . ."	"To sum up . . ."
"Finally . . ."	"To conclude . . ."
"To put it all together . . ."	"In summary . . ."

Also, the closing should focus on the purpose of the speech and the desired audience response.

Example 1: Purpose—To Inform

Summary: "To summarize, the steps for operating the roof air conditioner on your motor home are: turn on the generator controls in the proper sequence; turn on the air conditioner controls in the proper sequence; and then turn them all off in the reverse order."

Focus: "I hope you will remember this information for trouble-free operation. Enjoy your motor home air conditioner while it's sweltering outside."

Example 2: Purpose—To Convince

Summary: "Finally, we've been talking about the advantages of this slim, pocket brand *S* calculator—its functions, its price, and its reliability—based on my personal experience."

Focus: "When you are in the market for a pocket calculator, I hope you will remember these remarks and consider brand *S*."

Example 3: Purpose—To Move to Action

Summary: "Let me conclude by reminding you that there are thousands of people with undetected diabetes. You may be one of them. This condition cannot be corrected until it is discovered."

Focus: "I have brought a package of reagent test tapes for urinalysis. There is one test tape for each of you to take home. Do this simple test. Dip in urine and then note if the tape changes color. If this yellow test tape changes color from yellow to shades of green, there is an indication of sugar in the urine. It could be diabetes. You should see your doctor. But if the tape remains yellow, you have the assurance that you are not one of the thousands of undetected diabetics. Do this test today."

Your Closing

Prepare the closing steps to a speech. Summarize the thesis and the main points; then focus on your purpose and the response you want from your audience. Deliver this speech ending to the class just as though you had given the entire speech.

TICKLER FILING SYSTEM: A SCRAMBLED OUTLINE *(Individual Activity)*

Purpose: To arrange the following puzzle pieces into an outline form.

Briefing: When put together in the right order, each of the statements below forms a part of an outline. Cut up the entire page into separate statements. Find the thesis, main points, and supporting ideas and label them. Paste the parts back together on a separate sheet to make a speech outline on the subject of preparing and using a tickler filing system.

_____ If there are only 28, 29, or 30 days in a particular month, the remaining folders are ignored for that month.

_____ File routine matters for the current month according to the date when action is required.

_____ You will find this filing system invaluable—*if* you check it regularly the first thing each day, and *if* you take immediate action on the business matters filed there.

_____ A reminder of events that occur yearly.

_____ Get 43 letter-size file folders.

_____ Second, set up the following procedure for filing business material.

_____ Check the dated files at the end of the month to be certain nothing has been overlooked; then remove items in the next month's folder and redistribute them in the dated folders according to the date on which the item is due.

_____ First, gather together and arrange the following materials.

_____ Payments that occur periodically.

_____ File each piece of correspondence or business item requiring future action in the folder of the month ahead when attention is required.

_____ Arrange the folders in a drawer or file, dated folders in front.

_____ Third, use this file to tickle your memory about a variety of important future business matters.

_____ Notes on matters to call to the attention of someone else.

_____ You will use this filing system for many important items:

_____ Label 12 letter-size folders for each month from January through December.

_____ Notes for recurring future meetings.

_____ File items that require more than one working day of the current month in the dated file several days ahead of the required completion date.

_____ Annual meeting arrangements.

_____ Number 31 folders consecutively from 1 to 31 to represent each day of the current month.

_____ A tickler file is a chronologically arranged system of file folders used to control records and to tickle your memory about future business matters.

PERSUASIVE SPEECH TO THE CLASS *(Individual Presentation)*

Purpose: To change the attitudes or behavior of your audience.

Briefing: Think of a topic on which your classmates may have a variety of opinions. Select one side of the topic to persuade your class to believe or act upon. Stick to business topics; for example, a device to reduce shoplifting in retail stores, giving blood to the community blood bank, buying company stock, recommending company fitness programs, or the importance of dressing appropriately for a particular position.

Plan a speech of 5 to 6 minutes in which you try to persuade your classmates to do as you suggest. You may stimulate, convince, or try to move them to an action. Use your audience analysis to help you select the appropriate appeals.

Jot down your ideas on a separate sheet of paper. Review the patterns for arranging ideas for a persuasive speech. Use the outline form suggested below. Be sure to include your purpose. Practice your speech orally a number of times using a visual aid if you can design an effective one. Stay within the time limit.

Introduction

Attention Step   _____

Involve Audience   "you" _____

Establish Credibility   "I" _____

Thesis: (Complete sentence written out. May be stated here or later in the presentation.)

Development of Thesis

Transition (First . . .)

Main Point   **I.** _____

Supporting   **A.** _____
Material

              1. _____

              2. _____

       B. _____

Transition (Second . . .)

Main Point   **II.** _____

Supporting   **A.** _____
Material   **B.** _____

              1. _____

              2. _____

Transition (Finally . . .)

Conclusion

Summary _____

Focus on Purpose _____

Name _____ Class _____ Score _____

PERSUASIVE SPEECH CRITIQUE SHEET *(Instructor's Evaluation)*

Briefing: Tear out this page and give it to your instructor before you speak.

SUBJECT OF SPEECH: _____ SPEAKING TIME_____

POSSIBLE POINTS: 50   (Each question: 5 points)

The Verbal Message (25 points):

1. Did the speaker begin by getting attention and involving the audience in the subject?   _____

2. Was the purpose of the speech clearly stated?   _____

3. Was a pattern of arrangement of ideas clear?   _____

4. Did the conclusion summarize the ideas and focus on the desired purpose?   _____

5. Were the ideas well supported?   _____

The Nonverbal Message (15 points):

6. Did the speaker maintain eye contact with all members of the audience?   _____

7. Was the speaker fluent and conversational?   _____

8. Was there free, easy, natural movement?   _____

Effectiveness of Communication (10 points):

9. Did the speaker relate the material to the needs and interests of the audience?   _____

10. Did the speaker have poise and enthusiasm and work to persuade the audience?   _____

                                                                    Total   _____

Instructor's Comments

Words of Praise:

Suggestions for Improvement:

INFORMATIVE SPEECH TO A BUSINESS AUDIENCE *(Individual Presentation)*

Purpose: To deliver an informative presentation to your classmates as if you were addressing a specific business audience.

Briefing: Use the ten questions suggested for the Business Audience Analysis on page 238. Now prepare an informative speech for the group you have chosen.

Select a topic that you can explain or demonstrate to the audience you have selected. Outline your presentation in the form suggested on page 245. Use a visual aid.

Limit your presentation time to five to six minutes. Before delivering your speech, however, take an extra minute or two to explain your audience analysis to your classmates. They are then to listen to your presentation as if they were the business group you have selected.

SUGGESTIONS:

	Topic	Prospective Audience
1.	How to address business envelopes	secretarial students
2.	How to balance cash receipts	cashiers
3.	Sanitation requirements	janitorial or maintenance employees
4.	Use of price markers	stock clerks
5.	Selling television advertising time	sales personnel
6.	Purpose of job descriptions	all employees
7.	Reducing inventory costs	stock department employees
8.	Using a dictionary	clerical personnel
9.	Minimizing shipping costs	shipping department employees
10.	Recognizing counterfeit currency	bank tellers
11.	Reading a schematic	radio and television repairpersons
12.	Writing a résumé	job seekers
13.	Dress codes for your company	all employees
14.	Improving safety habits on the job	assembly-line employees
15.	Fire prevention and safety	all personnel

Name _____ Class _____ Score _____

INFORMATIVE SPEECH CRITIQUE SHEET *(Instructor's Evaluation)*

Briefing: Tear out this page and give it to your instructor before you speak.

SUBJECT OF SPEECH: _____ SPEAKING TIME_____

POSSIBLE POINTS: 50   (Each question: 5 points)

The Verbal Message (20 points):

1. Did the speaker begin by getting attention and involving the audience in the message? _____

2. Was the purpose of the speech clearly stated? _____

3. Did the ideas follow a logical sequence? _____

4. Did the conclusion summarize the ideas and focus on the desired purpose? _____

The Nonverbal Message (20 points):

5. Did the speaker maintain eye contact with all members of the audience? _____

6. Was the speaker fluent and conversational? _____

7. Was there free, easy, natural movement? _____

8. Was the visual aid used well? _____

Effectiveness of Communication (10 points):

9. Did the speaker have poise and enthusiasm and show a desire to communicate? _____

10. Did the speaker accomplish the assigned purpose? _____

Total _____

Instructor's Comments

Words of Praise:

Suggestions for Improvement:

CHECKLIST OF COMMUNICATION TERMS *(Quiz)*

Check your understanding of the communication terms used in this chapter. Write the number of the correct term in the blank preceding its definition. Note that there are more terms than definitions.

Definitions

a. _____ The parts of an outline numbered with Roman numerals.

b. _____ Arrangement of ideas according to chronological order.

c. _____ A type of supporting material making an idea clear by relating an unknown thing to something already known.

d. _____ Sign posts or markers linking parts of the outline and tying ideas together for the speaker and the audience.

e. _____ The information about a group of listeners that begins the preparation of a speech presentation.

f. _____ The sentence that summarizes the whole idea of a presentation.

g. _____ Speeches that seek to influence the thinking, attitudes, or behavior of the audience.

h. _____ A pattern that presents cases or reasons and then draws a general conclusion.

i. _____ The audience's perception of a speaker's competence, trustworthiness, poise, and enthusiasm.

j. _____ Speeches that seek to get audience understanding by providing information.

Terms

1. report
2. briefing
3. persuasive presentations
4. sales talks
5. justifying a proposal
6. goodwill presentation
7. audience analysis
8. trustworthiness
9. poise
10. logical appeal
11. emotional appeal
12. discovering ideas
13. research
14. to inform
15. to move to action
16. basic needs
17. attitudes and beliefs
18. government documents
19. thesis statement
20. main points
21. topical order
22. time order
23. deductive pattern
24. inductive pattern
25. problem-solving pattern
26. meet-the-audience-needs pattern
27. transitions
28. examples
29. quotations and testimony
30. comparison and contrast
31. visual materials
32. informative presentations
33. credibility

CHAPTER 8

Let's Talk About the Business of Delivering Your Presentation

When delivering a speech presentation, you must carefully consider: (1) the efficient use of such channels as visual aids to help carry your message; (2) the effective delivery strategies; and (3) the reception by your target audience. After you have read and discussed this chapter and participated in the workshop activities, you should be able to do the following:

Chapter Objectives

1. Prepare speaker notes as delivery aids.
2. Design visual aids to enhance the delivery of the verbal message.
3. Deliver a presentation.
4. Handle question-and-answer sessions efficiently.

You have studied how to select a topic, research it, and organize it into an outline with your particular audience in mind. Now you are ready to think about the oral delivery of your presentation. **Delivery** refers to the manner in which the speech is prepared and communicated.

Perhaps the first task is to look at a bit of inspiration from a wise teacher, James Winans:

> Let us imagine all speeches and all memory of speech-making to be blotted out, so that there is no person in the world who remembers that he has ever made a speech, or heard one, or read one; and there is left no clue to this art. Is this the end of speech-making? Here comes a man who has seen a great race, or has been in a battle, or perhaps is excited about his new invention, or on fire with enthusiasm for a cause. He begins to talk with a friend on the street. Others join them, five, ten, twenty, a hundred. Interest grows. He lifts his voice so all may hear; but the crowd wishes to hear and see the speaker

better. "Get up on this truck!" they cry; and he mounts the truck and goes on with his story or plea.

When does the converser become a speech-maker? When ten people gather? Fifty? Or is it when he gets on the truck? There is, of course, no point at which we can say the change has taken place. There is no change in the nature or spirit of the act; it is essentially the same throughout, a conversation adapted, as the speaker proceeds, to the growing number of his hearers. There may be a change, to be sure, if he becomes self-conscious; but assuming that interest in the story or argument remains the dominant emotion, there is no essential change in his speaking. It is probable that with the increasing importance of his position and the increasing tension that comes with numbers, he gradually modifies his tone and his diction, and permits himself to launch into a bolder strain and a wider range of ideas and feelings than in ordinary conversation; but the change is in degree and not in kind. He is conversing with an audience.[1]

The point to remember from Winans is that speeches are conversations *with* an audience. Although his example relates to public speaking, the same principle holds true for presentational speaking. Specifically, presentations are conversations adapted to a particular audience. This means the speaker takes the audience into account—both in the presentation of ideas and in the delivery. This chapter is designed to boost your confidence in your delivery strategies.

Remember that when you speak, you deliver three messages simultaneously:

1. The verbal message you have prepared.
2. The nonverbal message that strengthens the verbal message.
3. The vocal message that communicates your attitude toward your topic and your audience.

All three of these messages will be discussed in this chapter.

THE VERBAL MESSAGE

Words delivered orally possess the potential of a strong impact on listeners. They catch the ears, engage the attention, create mental images, and generate audience responses. Yet speakers often dread setting this process in motion. "What if I forget?" is the worry of many beginning speakers. Security measures to set this fear at rest result from finding and practicing an effective style of delivering verbal messages.

Styles of Delivery

As a speaker, you can choose one of several styles of delivery for your verbal message. Your presentation may be spoken without any previous planning, read word for word from a completely written-out manuscript, memorized, or spoken with occasional reference to note cards. Each of these four styles of delivery has its advantages and disadvantages.

---

[1] James Albert Winans, *Public Speaking*, Revised Edition, © 1917, pp. 20-21. Reprinted by permission of Prentice-Hall, Inc., Englewood Cliffs, N.J.

"The trouble with people who talk too fast is that they often say something they haven't thought of yet."

Anonymous

"Vice-President Alben W. Barkley confessed he made only three errors in his first political speech: (1) he read it from a prepared manuscript, (2) he read it poorly, (3) it wasn't worth reading at all."

Anonymous

"By failing to prepare, you are preparing to fail."

Anonymous

Impromptu speeches are made on the spur of the moment with little or no advance planning. Because an individual is recognized as an expert in a particular area, that person may be asked to comment on an issue or present well-founded views without prior warning. This presentation is not specifically prepared for the occasion, but years of experience and expertise make it worth hearing. Because the person has done no advance preparation, however, an unprepared speech is rarely well organized, designed for a particular audience, or delivered fluently. A beginning speaker will rarely choose this style of speaking, because it creates too much pressure.

Manuscript speeches are completely written out, usually typed double-space for easy reading, marked for accurate phrasing and effective pauses, and delivered from the copy word for word. The advantage of this style of speaking is that the language can be carefully chosen, the ideas can be carefully structured, and a copy can be released to the news media. There are some disadvantages. Reading is not speaking, and an audience may feel that the manuscript itself creates a barrier between speaker and listener. Also, maintaining eye contact is difficult for the speaker. Practice in reading aloud is essential if a speaker is to communicate effectively from a manuscript.

Memorized speeches are carefully prepared, written out, studied, and committed to memory. Less frequently used than other styles, this type of presentation places a tremendous pressure on the speaker. While there is no manuscript to serve as a barrier, there is the obstacle of remembering the words and the ideas to be presented. This often causes the speaker to concentrate on the message and limits the amount of feedback received. Like the manuscript speech, the memorized presentation restricts the speaker in adjusting the speech message to feedback from the listening audience.

Extemporaneous speeches are carefully prepared in advance. The speaker researches the subject, analyzes the audience, outlines the major ideas, adds supporting materials, plans the opening and closing, and rehearses aloud before the occasion. The speaker may use note cards with main ideas and key phrases outlined to trigger her or his memory. Usually these brief notes serve the speaker as an aid rather than a barrier. The speaker is able to concentrate on communicating with the audience, maintaining eye contact, reading feedback, and clarifying with further examples when audience feedback indicates that it is necessary. Although the speech is carefully thought out in advance, the delivery style sounds spontaneous and conversational.

Of these four styles of delivery, you have probably surmised that the extemporaneous style is the most effective for business presentations. While a memorized style is useful for a brief ceremonial speech, and the manuscript speech might be necessary for a long, technical paper, the extemporaneous method fits the principle of "talking with an audience" best. It does require that a speaker be completely prepared. Before the speech, the speaker thinks through an audience analysis and then follows the steps outlined in Chapter 7. During the presentation the speaker will use note cards to serve as memory clues, but the actual speaking will be in a conversational style. The wording may not always be the same as it was during oral rehearsal, but the ideas may be further expanded if audience feedback indicates this is needed. The extemporaneous style permits the speaker a wonderful flexibility and gives the audience a sense of direct "on the spot" communication.

Speaking Notes as a Delivery Aid

No one expects a well-prepared speaker to deliver an entire presentation completely from memory. On the other hand, listeners are not fond of having a speaker read an entire presentation from notes. This can happen if the speaker has too many notes. So, how much do you need to put on your note cards? You need just enough to give you confidence, and not so much that you create a barrier between yourself and your listeners.

Your **speaker note cards** are clues that remind you of things you want to say and of the order in which you want these things said. Here is one way you can prepare note cards. Rehearse your speech orally several times from your outline. Concentrate on getting the main points of the presentation clearly in mind. Then sit down and brief the speech onto cards. Many speakers like to use 3″ x 5″ cards and number them to keep them in order. Cards are helpful because they are small and easy to handle, and do not rustle like paper. It is helpful to have your introduction, attention step, audience involvement step, reasons for speaking, thesis, and each of your main points on separate cards. Supporting material can be noted in legible key phrases that will trigger your memory. A final card may summarize and focus on your purpose.

In delivering your presentation from note cards, use them only when necessary. When quoting directly from some authority or citing specific statistical information, speakers know that listeners expect accuracy and will not mind the speaker's reference to notes. The best procedure is to use the notes openly when needed but to beware of twisting or rumpling them while talking. This distraction can focus the audience's attention on the cards rather than on the ideas being expressed. The fewer the number of words on the cards, the less likely you are to read from the cards.

After you have prepared your cards, rehearse again orally using the notes. You can add a few words or adjust the phrasing as you practice. Remember, in practice and in delivering your presentation, talk *with* your listeners by looking at them. Speak directly and eliminate all possible barriers between you and your audience. Sample notes for a speech presentation are given in Figure 8-1.

After reading through the outline notes in Figure 8-1, you could probably deliver the presentation yourself. The notes on the cards are very complete. After practicing the speech using these note cards as reminders of the main points and supporting ideas, this speaker could probably cut the material on the cards considerably. A series of key words might be all the reminder needed. The labels at the left could certainly be omitted. The speaker must be sure that the supporting material is of a variety of types and that it covers all the questions the audience might want to ask.

Handouts as a Delivery Aid

For long meetings or all-day training sessions, rather than preparing note cards or a manuscript to speak from, many training managers outline their whole presentation and then photocopy this outline with the subheads and supporting material omitted, but with the capital letters and numbers indicating where material is left out. Copies of these incomplete outlines are distributed to the audience members as the session begins, and the speaker delivers the presentation point-by-point from his or her own completed out-

FIGURE 8-1

Sample notes for a speech presentation.

INTRO		CARD 1
	A.	Fast, easy money...
	B.	You can start a small, profitable business...
	C.	I turned my hunting hobby into a small business that helps pay my college tuition. (SHOW STUFFED PHEASANT)
THESIS	D.	I will explain the process of making and selling feather hat bands.

	CARD 4
(When you have completed several hat bands...)	
	III. Find interested buyers for your product.
	A. Where and how to sell
EXPLANATION	1. word of mouth
	2. take orders
	3. speak to groups
	4. bazaars
	5. find stores to display
	B. Pricing
STATISTICS:	1. cost
WRITE ON BOARD	2. profit

(First...)		CARD 2
	I.	Gather the essential materials.
	A.	Feathers
EXPLAIN		1. stripping the bird
DESCRIBE		2. sorting feathers-- length, colors
SHOW FEATHERS		
IN BAGS		3. storing feathers
DEFINE	B.	Velcro for fastening
DEMONSTRATE		1. how it works
		2. how to buy
	C.	Felt for the band
VISUALLY SHOW		1. colors
		2. lengths
EXPLAIN		3. buying it, where, amounts

	CARD 5
(In conclusion...)	
SUMMARY	A. I have told you the process I use for making and selling feather hat bands--
	1. gather the materials
	2. assemble materials creatively
	3. find interested buyers
FOCUS	B. I hope you consider how you can turn one of your hobbies into a profitable small business.

(After you have gathered your materials...)		CARD 3
	II.	Assemble the material creatively by using your imagination.
EXPLAIN	A.	Sewing the velcro and felt
		1. proper size
		2. adjustable
DEMONSTRATE	B.	Adding the feathers in different patterns
CONTRAST AND		1. color coordinates
COMPARE		2. variety of styles
VISUALLY SHOW	C.	Finished product (SHOW SEVERAL DIFFERENT ONES)

line. As they listen, the members of the audience fill in the missing information on their handout sheets. Using this incomplete outline form as a handout has several advantages:

1. Audience members can follow the speaker's presentation easily because they have the thesis and main points in their hands.
2. Listeners become involved with the speaker and actively participate in the presentation.
3. Each listener has something to see, hold, write on, and take home. Listening is not just passive.
4. Listeners can refer to the handouts at a later time.

A sample of this type of handout appears on pages 282-286.

Once you have determined the content and delivery style of your presentation, you should consider what your audience will see as they listen to you. The term **visual aid** describes those things you show an audience to assist them in understanding your verbal presentation.

First and foremost, you are your own best visual aid. Your audience sees how you are dressed, how your face and body movements reflect what you say, and how you handle your notes. But it is usually not enough just to let your audience listen and watch as you speak. You want them to focus on the ideas you are presenting. To do this, you must plan to bring your audience and your ideas together with as much impact as possible by using visual aids.

"Tell me, I forget; show me, I remember; involve me, I understand."

Chinese proverb

People in business have learned the value of making their listeners partners in their presentations. Seldom does a businessperson rely on words alone to inform colleagues, to persuade management, or to sell products and services to customers. The wise presentational speaker strives to actively involve the audience by providing direct and purposeful experiences that require listener participation. For example, a car salesperson shows a vehicle, demonstrates its features, and invites the customer to try it out. The customer sits in the car, inspects the dashboard, turns the steering wheel, feels the upholstery, smells the newness of the car, peers into the engine, slams the hood and doors, and finally takes the car for a drive. This active participation does as much to sell the car as the salesperson's presentation. All of the customer's senses are stimulated by the experience. But it is more difficult to provide this direct experience when the audience is composed of a larger number of people. Presentational audiences usually sit, listen, and are passively involved. It is up to the speaker to plan audience experiences that engage the eyes as well as the ears.

Adding Visual Impact to Your Ideas

Visual aids are chosen to meet presentational needs: to clarify or support ideas, to increase audience interest, to improve retention of ideas, and to develop understanding. When choosing visual aids for a presentation, the speaker must remember that elaborate visual materials distract an audience unless they serve the speaker's purpose. If they do not enhance the message, even the best visual aids should be omitted.

The speaker will consider three factors when planning visual aids. First, consider the speech material:

1. Which ideas can be illustrated according to appearance—size, shape, color?
2. Which topic can be demonstrated according to function—how it works, how it is used, how it is related to something else?
3. Which numbers, trends, or comparisons can be graphed or charted?
4. Which main points, ideas, or relationships can be listed or diagrammed?

Second, consider the audience and the speaking situation:

1. How many people will be in the audience?
2. How far will the audience sit from the visual aids?
3. How large must the visual aids be to be seen easily by the entire audience?

PHOTO 8-1

Visual aids can clarify the
speaker's message.

4. How can the visual aids be available when needed and out of the way when they are not being used?
5. What audiovisual equipment is available?

Third, consider the preparation and cost of the visual aids:

1. Which visual aids will communicate the presentational ideas most effectively?
2. What facilities are available for preparing these materials?
3. How can color, lettering, and interesting layouts clarify main points in the message?
4. Which visual aids can be prepared easily and inexpensively?

Types of Visual Aids

In selecting visual aids, there are two general types to consider:

1. **Empirical**—the actual object or a model, mock-up, or cutaway of the object.

   Advantage: provides lifelike experience.

   Disadvantages: may be too small to be easily seen or too cumbersome to transport; may be difficult to obtain.

2. **Symbolic**—pictures, illustrations, charts, graphs, films, slides, or videotapes.

   Advantage: can show what cannot be actually brought to the presentation.

   Disadvantage: time-consuming to prepare, hard to make large enough, must have proper equipment.

Objects, Models, and Cutaways. To provide the most direct experience for your listeners, make your visual aids as concrete as possible. If you are selling a vacuum cleaner, have the machine present to demonstrate its features and to show it in action. Real objects provide direct experience.

If it is not possible to have the object itself, then have a **model** to demonstrate its special features. Examples include models of buildings, aircraft, or the geographic features of a locale. The value of a model is that it can reduce or enlarge real objects to observable size and often can be assembled during the presentation.

Cutaway models are useful because they eliminate or cut away parts in order to reveal details of a complex interior. An example of a common cutaway model is the human anatomy with the skin removed to show the skeletal structure and internal organs.

These objects create interest, focus the audience's attention on the ideas being presented, and require the listeners to use several senses to build their understanding.

Illustrations, Charts, and Graphs. If you cannot bring an object to your presentation and a model is not available, you can use symbolic representations. To be effective, however, they must be professional in appearance. Charts and graphs often are too cluttered with detail and are improperly lettered. Illustrations or drawings are often too small and too complex to see. Photographs or pictures, even when mounted for display, are generally ineffective because they are also too small to be seen by the entire audience. Each of these weaknesses is a drawback to effective communication.

However, well-designed charts and graphs convey a professional visual message in a direct, economical way. Because they are displayed to make a point, the audience sees the information as well as hears the point being discussed. Material that is seen is remembered 55 percent better than material that is only heard. Since charts or graphs are designed to be self-explanatory, they are also a timesaver for the speaker.

Follow these general rules when preparing charts and graphs:

1. Be sure they contain the precise information you want conveyed.
2. Design them in size, shape, and color to be easily read at a distance of 25 feet.
3. Make them simple and clear, and focus on one idea only. Use another aid to show separate parts of an idea.
4. Provide a key or legend that explains the data.
5. Use a good layout design. Divide the area into thirds vertically and horizontally. Place the center of interest at one of the four places where the lines intersect.
6. Keep colors bright and simple. Use vivid colors on white or pastel poster board, or white on black or a dark background.
7. Make letters large and clear.

Charts and graphs may be prepared on large sheets of poster board, carefully drawn with a pencil, and inked with a variety of colors. Dry-transfer or vinyl letters are uniform in size and give your visual aid a professional appearance.

Graphs are diagrams of various sorts showing a system of relationships between items. The purpose of a graph is to convey an idea speedily and accurately. There are a variety of types of graphs: line graphs, bar or column graphs, circle graphs, and pictorial graphs.

Line Graph. A line graph like the one shown in Figure 8-2 is useful for showing changes over a period of time, a comparison between several things, or a trend with a time base. The points are connected in order by a straight or curved line. Several data points can be represented on a single graph, but the separate lines must be differentiated in some fashion. In Figure 8-2, for example, the solid line represents women employees, the dashed line represents men. The following are some general suggestions for preparing a line graph.

1. Prepare a rough copy of the graph material first.
2. Compare no more than three to four lines on a single graph.
3. Label the horizontal base line to show time. Indicate the zero point.
4. Give each line a different color or symbol and identify it horizontally for easy reading.
5. Record quantities or numbers up the side on the vertical scale.
6. If the graph has a title, center it above or below the graph with large letters.

FIGURE 8-2

Line graph comparing the number of men and women hired by the XYZ Company over a six-year period. A line graph is a useful way to show a trend.

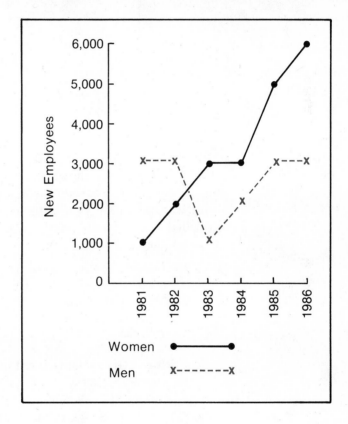

Bar Graph. The information presented in Figure 8-3 is represented by horizontal or vertical bars that compose a bar or column graph. This type of graph, which often includes a time series, is used to compare a limited number of items or to show a frequency distribution. To design a bar graph:

1. Arrange the data in order from the smallest quantity to the largest, or vice versa.
2. Leave space between the bars for ease in reading the information. Label each bar clearly.
3. Print the title, captions, and the key to reading the graph in large, distinctive letters.

FIGURE 8-3

Bar graph. Information
represented by solid and
dashed lines in Figure 8-2 is
here represented by solid
and open bars to facilitate
year-by-year comparison of
the data.

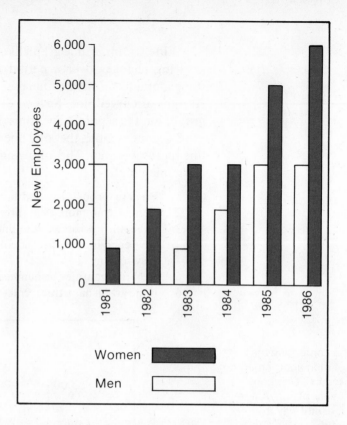

Circle Graph. A circle graph is an effective way to show a whole quantity, represented by a circle, divided into parts. This type of graph, as illustrated in Figure 8-4, shows the relationship of each part to the whole as well as each part to the other parts. Use this type of graph to show how the sales dollar is spent, how profits are divided, how an employee's working day is divided into different tasks, etc. Circle graphs are often called pie charts. Follow these suggestions for making a circle graph:

1. Label the complete circle to represent the total quantity (hours, dollars, an organization, etc.).
2. Mark off the parts within the circle.
3. Shade or color the segments to show differences between them and label each clearly.

Pictorial Graph. This attention-getting visual display uses pictures or symbols to represent the elements being graphed. For example, one donkey might represent 100 Democrats, and one elephant 100 Republicans. In Figure 8-5, the biological symbol for female represents 1,000 women, the biological symbol for male represents 1,000 men. To make a pictorial graph, find a symbol to represent the elements being graphed. As in a bar graph, the symbols in pictorial graphs may run vertically or horizontally.

Charts and Tables. Charts are combinations of words and numbers that quickly convey an idea visually. One of the simplest visual aids is a word chart on which a speaker lists the key points to be remembered and refers to it during the presentation. A **table** lists precise data and specific information. For example, a table may condense a great deal of statistical material into an organized list that can be referred to quickly. Comparisons between and among statistics can be made easily. The listener can follow visually

FIGURE 8-4

Circle graph or pie chart.
The information graphed in
Figures 8-2 and 8-3 is here
converted into percentages—
pieces of the total pie.

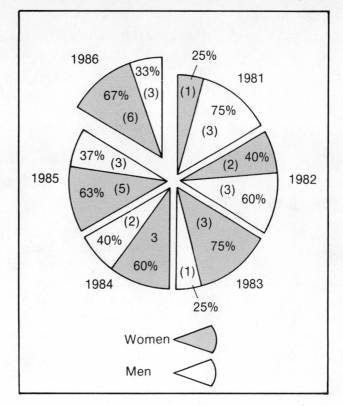

FIGURE 8-5

Pictorial graph using
symbols to show the XYZ
Company hiring data.

while a speaker communicates a number of quantitative ideas and uses the table as a reference point. The following are general rules for constructing a table:

1. Head each vertical column clearly and concisely.
2. Place comparative data horizontally from left to right for easy reading.
3. Standard terms should be used for each item (yards, meters, decimals) in the table.
4. The total design should incorporate careful alignment of data, plenty of white space, and clear titles.

Displaying Visual Aids

The most professionally designed chart or poster is of little use if you arrive at the speaking situation unprepared to display your visual aids. If you plan to design charts or graphs on poster board, be sure to arrange for a way to display them. Every company usually has an easel (see Figure 8-6) with sturdy legs and a tray to support your chart. Be alert to spot one in your company conference room or art department. Another useful support for your visual aid is a **tripod** with a tray to support large poster-board visuals.

FIGURE 8-6

An easel makes it easy to display charts, graphs, or other visual aids prepared on poster board.

A second way to display a poster-board visual aid is to prepare it on a simple three-sided display that stands alone or can be suspended on a stand and easily rotated. Figure 8-7 illustrates this interesting visual aid, which provides three surfaces for charts yet shows the audience only one chart at a time.

Another way to display a series of charts is to prepare them on a **flip chart**, which resembles a large notebook with the pages fastened at the top so one page can be flipped over and the next chart displayed. (See Figure 8-8.) Flip charts can be prepared professionally for repeated use in business presentations, or they can be made by hand for class presentations. A flip chart is also useful to a speaker if there is no chalkboard available in the room where the speech is delivered. Blank pages provide a space for the speaker to write, draw, or diagram spontaneously.

FIGURE 8-7

FIGURE 8-7

A three-sided display can stand alone or be suspended on a stand and rotated to show each surface.

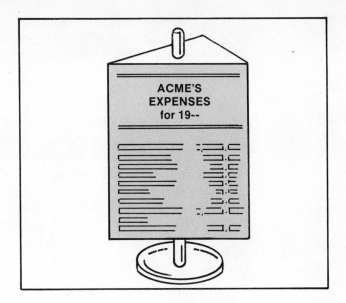

FIGURE 8-8

Visuals can be prepared in advance on a flip chart, or the blank pages can be written on during the presentation.

Some speakers like to use poster-board charts that are covered with several strips of white paper. The paper is taped over the main points to be discussed. As the speaker reaches a particular point in the presentation, he or she can tear off a section at a time until the whole chart is exposed by the conclusion of the presentation. This is known as a **strip chart**.

Projected Visual Aids. Some of the most professional-looking visual aids are those designed to be projected on movie projectors, slide projectors, filmstrip projectors, opaque projectors, and overhead projectors. In addition to these, your company may have videotape recording equipment and monitors, tape recorders for special sound aids in your presentation, and facilities for computer graphics. A whole world of technology is ready to help you create exciting visual aids. However, a word of warning! If you do not know how to operate any of this equipment, do not use it unless you ask someone to run the equipment during your presentation. The purpose of using a visual aid is to add to your presentation—at the time you need it—without distracting your audience or creating pressures for yourself.

Slide Projectors. You can easily produce slides for your presentation by photographing maps, charts, graphs, or pictures too small to use without projection. Insert the slides you will use in the carousel that is mounted at the top of the slide projector, and practice speaking as you flip each slide forward automatically. Remember, one disadvantage of using slides is that the room must be dark for the pictures to show clearly on the screen. The darkness cuts off your direct contact with the audience as you project the slides. You cannot check for the audience's level of interest, lack of understanding, or need for clarification. Thus, you must rely on a question-and-answer session after the slide presentation.

Movie Projectors. Companies or institutions often want the same presentation given to different audiences. Therefore, they frequently use 8-millimeter or 16-millimeter films (or slides with a synchronized audiotape). The projector presents the company's message, and the speaker handles a question-and-answer session which follows the showing of the film. Movies are not just used as visual aids in speaking situations. Coaches, for example, may rerun the films of games for their players and discuss the plays as they are shown. Generally, however, a film presents its own message, and the speaker uses this message as the basis for discussion. In any case, using a movie as a visual aid lends professionalism to business presentations.

Filmstrip Projectors. A filmstrip can supplement a speaker's message, provide a basis for interaction between speaker and audience, or may be used as the basis for a question-and-answer session following the projected presentation. Other types of visual aids may lend more dynamic amplification to a speech presentation. But filmstrips are advantageous because, as with slides, the speaker controls the amount of time he or she wishes to spend on each picture.

Opaque Projectors. Opaque projectors can enlarge already printed or prepared material by projecting it onto a screen without additional processing. Although awkward to handle and cumbersome to move, an opaque projector is valuable because it can be used to prepare large charts and graphs by projecting them from a book or magazine onto a sheet of poster board. The copied material can be drawn on the poster board and colored or inked in later.

Overhead Projectors. Material shown on this widely used type of projector can be prepared in advance by producing inexpensive **transparencies**. These clear or colored sheets of acetate are laid on the original material to be reproduced and run through a **Thermo-fax**® or a similar type of infrared copier. The design or illustration may be enhanced with water-soluble, felt-tipped colored pens. Or you can make your own transparencies by drawing on special sheets of acetate with colored pens, either in advance or while the presentation is being given. The material is projected on a screen behind the speaker, and the room does not need to be darkened in order to use an overhead projector effectively. The strength of using the overhead as a visual aid is that the speaker can maintain audience contact while presenting and discussing the visual. Special dramatic effects can be created by using transparency overlays. Each overlay can be added until the whole picture is complete. This gives an impressive cumulative effect. In using the overhead projector, place the machine where it will not obstruct the audience's view of the projected material on the screen.

Handouts as Visual Aids. An effective way to provide visual impact for your audience is to prepare pictures, samples, advertising materials, or brochures to hand out to your listeners. The trick is to choose the appropriate time to distribute these so they do not compete with your oral message. If handouts are distributed during your speech, they will distract attention from your presentation. The purpose is to reinforce your message by giving the audience something to take with them. It is often best to show your handout during your speech, discuss the relationship between the handout and the information in your presentation, and then pass the material out to the audience when your speech is completed.

Guidelines for Using Visual Aids

There are three major guidelines to keep in mind when using visual aids. First, plan the use of visual aids *after* you decide what you will say in your presentation.

1. Ask yourself where a picture, chart, or graph will make your presentation more interesting.
2. Ask yourself if the visual aid will support your ideas. Remember, pictures and projections must reinforce, not overshadow, the verbal message.

Second, practice using the visual aids. No matter how carefully they are prepared to convey a professional appearance, visual aids are not useful unless they work smoothly to illustrate your ideas.

1. If you are using objects or posters, they should not be visible until they are needed. Decide: (1) where they will be placed until you need them, and (2) what you will do with them after you have used them.
2. Practice your presentation orally at home and use the visual aids as you will display them in front of your audience.
3. Stand to one side of the visual aid and use a pointer to refer to details on it. Keep your eyes on the audience and do not block their view of the visual material.
4. If you are using projected visuals, practice using the equipment.
5. Use this checklist for projected visuals:
    a. Where are the nearest electrical outlets? Do they work?
    b. Are additional extension cords needed in order to position the projector where you want it?
    c. Is there a screen available?
    d. Can you use a blank wall instead of a screen?
    e. Will the audience be able to see without having to reposition themselves?

Third, follow that old maxim and *be prepared*. Arrive early for your presentation and be sure everything is ready. Bring along an emergency kit that contains such items as:

cellophane tape	extension cord
thumbtacks	extra bulb for projector
chalk	three-pronged adapter plug
pointer	masking tape
fuses	marking pen

Look at your visual aids as your audience will see them. Because a speaker's credibility is frequently judged by the visual support, use these questions as a guide to evaluate your visual aids.

1. Are they professional in appearance?
   a. Is the printing neat and completely legible?
   b. Are they attractive in form, design, and color?
2. Are they self-explanatory?
   a. Title?
   b. Key?
   c. Completely labeled?
3. Are they easy to see and easy to read for everyone in the audience?
4. Will they be easily accessible when needed during the presentation?

THE VOCAL MESSAGE

Your voice is one of your most valuable instruments in capturing your audience and holding them fast throughout your presentation. As the speaker, it is you who orchestrate the audience's attention; you set the tone and focus them on the argument you are advocating or the information you are sharing. In other words, you must concentrate on what you are saying. Your message is the reason that you are up front. If you shift focus to concern about yourself, your audience will sense this and worry with you. If you think about your nervousness rather than your ideas, your audience will be anxious for you. Your job is to think about what you are saying.

One of the ways to do this is to visualize your success as you practice. Imagine the scene exactly as you want it to be—you, up front, dynamic, confident, prepared, and in earnest about your topic, your audience deeply involved in your presentation.

Perhaps this is a good time to review the subject of stage fright discussed in Chapter 1. On page 11 there are suggestions for reducing stage fright. It may be helpful to review them at this point. Finally, you can pull your three messages—verbal, nonverbal, and vocal—into a unified whole by keeping these tips in mind:

1. **Dress the part of a speaker.** Your audience sees you before you say a word. Your appearance is in the visual spotlight. Your clothes should be appropriate, comfortable, and becoming. Choose your clothing wisely, dress carefully, and then proceed with confidence.
2. **Act the role of a speaker.** Approach the speaker's stand with poise. Acknowledge your introduction and greet any other people seated on the platform. Look at the people seated before you. Pause. Concentrate on the first words of your message. Take a deep breath. Relax and smile.

3. **Speak to the whole group.** The people at the greatest distance from you need to hear you with ease. Raise your volume to reach them. Fill the spaces between you and your listeners with the vibrant, enthusiastic sounds of your voice. Work to make your ideas stand out. But don't be afraid of silences. Use pauses to provide punctuation and to give the listeners time to take in ideas. Take time, pause, think, and then speak.

4. **Enjoy the opportunity to communicate.** Your enthusiasm, poise, and concern about your receivers ignite a receptive spark in those listening. As you carefully fan those sparks of attention and interest with your desire to communicate, you will discover that you and your audience are interacting. This is true communication!

"Poise is the appearance of be-ing at ease."

Anonymous

HANDLING A QUESTION-AND-ANSWER SESSION

When you have concluded your presentation, there may be a period of time left open for questions from the audience. The speaker is expected to answer in impromptu style any questions the audience asks. Many speakers dread this kind of give-and-take session because they fear being put on the spot.

One way to avoid getting questions that you might not care to answer is to deal with the topic in the main presentation before the question-and-answer session. If you think the audience will ask tough questions, prepare by asking yourself where the weakest link in your argument lies and what areas your proposal fails to cover. Then you must face these issues and cover them in your presentation. Here are questions that you can ask yourself *before* you deliver your presentation:

1. What do I know (as a person, as a company, as an industry)?
2. What don't I know? (Be sure of this area and do not be afraid to admit that there are areas in which you have little knowledge.)
3. What is being done to get the answers? (Find out if your company or industry is working on solving the problems. You need to be up on this information.)
4. What does the audience need to know? (You must be selective in giving information because you cannot tell all you know in the given time.)

If you are required to answer questions, it is wise to know something about the types of questions that are asked. According to Paul R. Edwards in an article published in the *Public Relations Journal*, nine out of ten questions people ask seek something other than information. He describes three categories of questions: *message* questions, *getcha* questions, and *answer-seeking* questions. Edwards describes these categories in the following ways:

1. A **message question** is one in which the asker is using a question to present an idea, state a conviction, or share information. The question will begin with such phrases as "Don't you think," "Have you ever considered," "Since," and "What would happen if." The asker of the message question is looking for affirmation of her or his position. Message questions account for about 45 percent of the questions asked.
2. The **getcha question** is used to reveal a flaw in the speaker's character or material. The goal of the getcha questioner is to be "one up" by making the speaker appear inadequate, anxious, embarrassed, guilty, or angry. Getcha questions often begin with "Why" or "How come" and account for about 45 percent of questions asked.

3. The **answer-seeking question** is the only one in which the questioner truly is looking for an answer. These questions begin with "How" and account for only 10 percent of questions asked.[2]

How do you, as a speaker, handle your responses to these questions? First, listen carefully to the questioner. All the nonverbal clues that you have studied will help you determine the speaker's intent. Focus on how the question is asked. Listen to the vocal tone, watch the facial expressions, posture, and gestures. Carefully figure out if the questioner is seeking information or whether the words carry a hidden message. If you fail to identify the type of question, you may handle the answer improperly. Take time to consider all these factors before you answer.

Here are some suggestions for responding to the questions you are asked:

1. Message questions. Handle these questions by listening carefully and agreeing with the questioner if you can. Often the person is seeking affirmation of a particular position or idea. When you cannot agree, strengthen your message by rephrasing the question and framing it in light of your speech purpose. You can give recognition to the questioner to make that person feel better yet strengthen your own position.
2. Getcha questions. Handle this type of question in a positive manner. Try not to be defensive or hostile. Never argue with the questioner, because neither of you can win. If the questioner has made a good point, admit it. You might try to disarm her or him by asking a question yourself. As with a message question, you can redefine the question in terms of the purpose of your presentation. Finally, you can agree with part of the question and then present factual evidence or differing opinions to gently disagree with the balance of the question. If the questioner is persistent, maintain your sense of humor and permit the pressure of the group to control the questioner.
3. Answer-seeking questions. Give your answer in a way that reinforces your speech purpose. If you don't know an answer, admit it. Offer to get the answer but then be sure to follow up on the offer. This shows that you are sincerely interested in helping the questioner. Don't worry that not having an answer immediately affects your credibility. This actually enhances your credibility because your audience will perceive you as honest. When you do know an answer, the audience will believe you. Remember, it is all right not to know everything about your subject.

One last point: Whenever you respond in a question-and-answer session, be as polite as possible. As a result, you will be a respected speaker.

> *"Ten out of ten questions require a response."*
>
> Les Crain

CHAPTER SUMMARY

When you deliver an oral presentation, you are unifying your verbal, nonverbal, and vocal messages so your listeners will regard you as a competent, trustworthy, poised, and enthusiastic speaker. From the four delivery styles (impromptu, memorized, reading, or extemporaneous), you select the appropriate style for the occasion. For most presentations you are encouraged

---

[2] Paul R. Edwards, "Nine out of Ten Questions Don't Need an Answer." Reprinted with permission from the July 1976 issue of the *Public Relations Journal.* Copyright 1976.

to use an extemporaneous style by carefully outlining and supporting your ideas in advance, then reducing this outline to notes from which you speak in a conversational manner with the audience.

To add visual impact to the verbal message, you select appropriate visual aids: empirical ones such as real objects, models, or cutaways; symbolic visuals such as pictures, charts, and graphs; or projected visuals such as film, videotape, or slides. By practicing your presentation orally using the visual aids, you can control all the messages you send. A question-and-answer session can reinforce your message if you listen carefully, identify the type of question (message, getcha, or answer-seeking), and phrase the answer in terms of your presentation.

MODEL PRESENTATIONS *(Individual Practice)*

Purpose: To practice delivery of two manuscript speeches. To learn an effective presentational technique.

Briefing: The following presentations are designed for different audiences and have been delivered by businesspeople. For Presentations #1 and #2, first review the audience analysis and the outline. Then stand and practice delivering the manuscript orally. Imagine the audience before you. As you speak, maintain eye contact, keep your voice projected to every listener, vary your vocal rate and pitch, and keep up your energy level.

Presentation #3 will be read aloud to you by your instructor after you have reviewed the audience analysis. As your instructor reads the presentation, fill in the missing information on the handout sheets, pages 282-286.

PRESENTATION #1: "Your Credit Rating and You"

Audience Analysis *(Student Reference)*

1. Who is the speaker?

    Shari J. Dorris, loan officer of Southwest Mortgage Company.

2. Who is my audience?

    A group of 20-30 male and female high school seniors from an upper-middle-class background. All will graduate from high school in two months and plan to attend college. We are meeting in a high school classroom.

3. What does my audience know about my topic—credit rating?

    These students have some general knowledge of the topic. They may have shopped with their parents who paid for items with credit cards. They may even have charged purchases on their parents' credit cards.

4. Why do I think my audience is interested in my subject?

    This is a seminar that the students have chosen to attend during their high school Career Week. Their choice indicates their interest.

5. Why do I think my audience needs to know about my subject?

    Credit is a means of developing purchasing power and establishing oneself as a responsible citizen. These young people are ready to think of themselves as independent individuals. They need to be prepared for the future.

6. What does my audience know or think about me?

    Since the speakers for Career Week are invited from the business community to speak to various groups, they will recognize my credibility as a female loan officer in a local business organization. I assume they will be very open to the ideas I will present.

7. What specific strategies do I need to use so that my audience will react as I want them to?

    I will use logical reasoning and a variety of supporting materials. My purpose is to convince these students of the importance of credit.

PRESENTATION #1: "Your Credit Rating and You"

Outline *(Student Reference)*

INTRODUCTION

Attention Step	**A.**	How many of you live in a house? (Get show of hands.)
Involve Listeners	**B.**	How do you think the house was paid for?
Establish Credibility	**C.**	I have worked as a loan officer at a mortgage company for five years.
Thesis Statement, Preview of Main Points	**D.**	There are three things I want to tell you about credit: It is important to understand, establish, and maintain a good credit rating.

DEVELOPMENT OF THESIS (BODY OF SPEECH)

Transition (First . .)

Main Point	**I.**	Understanding the significance of a good credit rating is important.
Definition	**A.**	Credit rating is the evaluation of how you handle financial obligations.
Explanation	**B.**	Why a business wants to know your credit rating.
	C.	Credit rating is needed to finance wants and needs.
specific instances		1. Buy car, furniture, place to live
example		2. Invest in business opportunities—ski shop
explanation		3. Bail out of tight situation—hospital costs

Transition (A good credit rating is important. Now my second point . . .)

Main Point	**II.**	Establishing a good credit rating depends on two major factors:
Subpoint	**A.**	Permanency.
example, definition		1. In work—salary—collateral
example		2. In residence—moving about—"skip town"
Subpoint	**B.**	Reputation.
contrast		1. Solid citizen vs. less than reliable
contrast		2. Co-workers speak highly vs. unflattering character assessment
contrast		3. Involved in community work vs. lawsuit

Transition (In review, I've been talking about. . . . Now I would like to make a final point.)

Main Point	**III.**	Maintaining a good credit rating requires effort, caution, and common sense.
Subpoint	**A.**	Making payments on time requires effort.
explanation		1. Do not use the "grace period"
illustration		2. Can develop bad habits
Subpoint	**B.**	Do not cosign on a loan—use caution.
definition		1. Define cosign
illustration		2. Story of Joe and his brother
Subpoint	**C.**	Use credit cards with common sense.
visual aid		1. Show cards
illustration		2. Story of my roommate
explanation		3. "Playing the float"—Mrs. Smith

CONCLUSION

Summarize	**A.**	Review three main points: understanding, establishing, and maintaining a good credit rating.
Focus	**B.**	Start out right when you leave high school, and your credit rating will work to your advantage in the future.

How many of you live in a house? (ASK FOR SHOW OF HANDS.) Now, how do you think the house was paid for? (NO RESPONSE NEEDED.) Most people can't pay cash for a purchase as large and important as a house, so they take out a loan from a bank or a mortgage company. This is seldom a problem—if they have a good credit rating.

After working as a loan officer at Southwest Mortgage Company for the past five years, I am very familiar with how a credit rating affects a potential borrower. It is important for *you* to become familiar with this, too, because soon you will be establishing credit (if you haven't already). You need to understand three essential things: the significance of a good credit rating, how to establish a good credit rating, and how to maintain a good credit rating.

First, let me develop your <u>understanding of why a good credit rating is important</u>. A credit rating   I is defined as an evaluation by businesses of how you handle your financial obligations. A good credit rating indicates that you do not spend a great deal more than you receive, and that you pay your bills when they are due.

Now, note the importance of this credit rating. It is essential to finance your wants and needs. In our society, almost everyone wants a car and needs furniture and a place to live, but not everyone can pay cash for these things. Your credit rating determines whether or not you will be able to purchase these items and pay for them over a period of time.

Or suppose an acquaintance approaches you with an exciting business opportunity—say, setting up a ski shop! You have always wanted to combine business with a personal interest, so you seek a loan from a bank or from a savings and loan company to help finance this venture. The loan might be just the thing to help you get started! But your credit rating determines whether or not you will get it.

It is also important to realize that while most people are covered by life and health insurance in case of an accident, the insurance policy may not cover all the costs involved. Again, a loan, made possible because of your good credit rating, can bail you out of a tight situation.

I've given you several examples of the importance of having a good credit rating, so let me move along to my second point. Establishing a good credit rating depends on two major factors: permanency and reputation. When a lender examines the possibility of extending a loan to someone, the lender looks at the potential borrower's *permanency*. There are two areas in which permanency is desirable: in work and in residency. If a borrower constantly moves from town to town or changes jobs frequently, the lender interprets this as meaning the potential borrower is unstable. When a company lends money, it wants to make sure that the money will be repaid. If a person has moved around a great deal, the lender may suspect that the person will "skip town" without repaying the loan. In this case, the lender would take a substantial loss. Therefore, the lender carefully scrutinizes the borrower's residency and job record.

II

Permanency, in regard to a borrower's salary, is also important. Even though a lender may ask a borrower for collateral (property, such as a car or real estate, that is acceptable security for a loan), the lender is more interested in the borrower's ability to repay the loan through regular income. After all, why would a loan company want two or three cars that the borrower put up as collateral? The company that lends money is interested in being repaid in dollars—with interest.

We've been talking about permanency as a requirement for establishing good credit. Now let's consider *reputation*! Lenders are always more willing to lend money to solid citizens than to those whom they suspect as unreliable. For example, an individual who is spoken of in glowing terms by co-workers is seen as a better risk than someone who is spoken of in an unflattering manner. An individual who is involved in community work may have a better reputation than one involved in a lawsuit.

One final, important tip for establishing a good credit rating: Do business with the same bank over a number of years and develop a rapport with some of the employees. This can be valuable when you need to borrow money.

I've been talking about understanding the importance of a good credit rating and the criteria for establishing a good rating. Finally, I would like to stress that maintaining a good credit rating requires effort, caution, and common sense. As I mentioned earlier, it is important to be consistent in order to establish a credit rating. It is also important to make payments on your current debts when the pay-

III

ments are due. This requires effort on your part! In many instances a creditor will allow you a "grace period" of five to ten days, and in this time you will not be assessed a late charge. It is really best *not* to take advantage of this grace period; when the loan company orders a credit report on you (and it *will*), it will discover that you constantly put off making payments until the last possible day. I have personally seen people get so accustomed to taking advantage of this grace period that they begin making payments even after the period has expired. A creditor would much rather lend money to a person who makes payments *when they are due.*

In order to maintain a good credit rating, you must also exercise caution! Do not cosign a loan. When someone asks you to cosign a note, that person is asking you to share a debt in case she or he is unable to repay the loan. If the original signer does not make payments, the creditor will come to *you* for the money. Let me give you an example. I know a man we'll call Joe who had cosigned on a car loan for his brother. When his brother stopped making the car payments, the bank turned to Joe for the payments. In the meantime, however, Joe had invested a large sum of money in a business venture, so he could not afford the car payments. As a result, both Joe *and* his brother received bad ratings from the bank. These ratings negatively affected their buying power for years.

(HOLD UP CREDIT CARDS.) I suspect that all of you will recognize these cards: American Express, MasterCard, Visa, and a gasoline credit card. It is very important not to overuse credit cards if you want to maintain your credit rating. My roommate loved to spend money, and with credit cards it's so easy to do! After all, the money never goes through your hands, and you don't have to record the expense in your checkbook! My roommate had a credit card for every major store in town. After several months, every store was after her to pay her bills. She couldn't, of course, because she had charged purchases at so many places. Many people find themselves in this situation. So be careful!

One of the most common problems with maintaining good credit is incomplete recordkeeping of the checks you have written. It is important to keep accurate records so you don't overdraw the amount of money you have in your account. People who overdraw have difficulty with their credit ratings.

One final practice that gets people in trouble with their credit ratings is what we call "playing the float." Since you probably are not working and drawing a paycheck at this time, you may not be guilty of "playing the float"—but perhaps I am wrong. Let me give you an example. Mrs. Smith goes to the grocery store the day before payday, knows that she doesn't have enough money in the bank to cover the check she will write for her groceries, but writes the check anyway. She figures that when her paycheck comes the next day, she will deposit it before the grocery check goes through the bank and thus her personal check won't bounce. This is a perfect example of "playing the float"! When the next day rolls around, Mrs. Smith (like many others in similar situations) forgets that she needs to deposit the money immediately. As a result, her grocery check bounces! In order to avoid this problem, *never* write a check unless the money is already in the bank. This common-sense reminder will help you maintain a good credit rating.

I've been delighted to be one of your Career Week speakers. I hope you can see that it is important to understand the significance of a good credit rating, to establish a good credit rating, and to maintain one. By starting out on the right foot as you leave high school, your credit rating will work to your advantage in the future.

PRESENTATION #2: An Employment Screening Presentation

Audience Analysis *(Student Reference)*

1. Who is the speaker?

   Eddie Salazar, applicant for employment.

2. What is the occasion?

   XYZ Bank is conducting an employment screening for applicants to their Officer Candidate Training Program. I have submitted my application and résumé. They have invited me, along with many other applicants, to the pre-screening meetings at the bank offices. They will explain the training program to all of us and then give each applicant an opportunity to sell herself or himself.

3. Who is my audience?

   After the program is explained, each of us will be asked to meet with an employment recruiter to give a three-minute presentation. In this speech I am to sell myself to the recruiter explaining why I am qualified for the program. I will not know in advance whether the recruiter is male or female.

4. What is my audience expecting to hear?

   The recruiter will listen to my presentation and evaluate me in terms of communication skills, degree of preparation, and presentation content, according to the letter XYZ Bank sent me.

5. What does my audience know or think about me?

   The recruiter will be listening to a number of other applicants and, I am sure, will compare me with them. As I speak, the recruiter will have a copy of my résumé to refer to. The recruiter will be looking judgmentally at my communication skills because the recruiter will determine whether or not I will be invited to move to the next step in the screening process.

6. What specific strategies do I need to use so that I will be selected for the next step in the screening process?

   I want to be perceived as competent, trustworthy, confident, and dynamic. I need to give information other than that listed in my résumé; I need to give honest reasons why I want the job; I need to sound original and different from the other speakers. I will prepare my presentation in plenty of time so that I can practice orally and time the material accurately. I will use only three note cards. My purpose is to sell myself through my communication skills.

PRESENTATION #2: An Employment Screening Presentation

Brief Outline *(Student Reference)*

INTRODUCTION: Narration, establish credibility.

Thesis Statement: There are three things I want you to know about me.

DEVELOPMENT OF THESIS

Main Point **I.** I possess the characteristics to be a good banker.
Main Point **II.** I have effective leadership skills.
Main Point **III.** I have selected XYZ Bank as my first choice of employment.

CONCLUSION: Summary and focus.

Manuscript *(Individual Oral Practice)*

When I was a boy, I thought bankers were men with long, curly mustaches, eager to foreclose on the mortgages of defenseless widows. As I grew older, I began to understand the important role that the banker plays in the community.

My name is Eddie Salazar and I am here to be considered as an applicant for your 1986 Bank Officer Candidate Training Program.

There are three things I want you to know about me.

First, I possess the characteristics to be a good banker. To be effective in banking, an individual   I must have a firm, upright character. My family, my employer, and the people listed on my résumé can all attest to my character. A banker should also be a capable steward of the possessions of others. Working in banking over the last several years has taught me to carefully safeguard the possessions of others. And a banker must have sound judgment in implementing financial decision making. I offer my experience in a variety of positions at Sun City Bank for the past five years and the knowledge gained from a number of American Institute of Banking courses I have taken. All of these qualities—firm, upright character, capable stewardship, and sound judgment—are characteristics of a good banker.

Second, I want you to know that I have effective leadership skills. I was extremely active in student   II government at my university and served as student chairman for the Welfare and Grievance Committee—which was a big job. My fraternity chose me as treasurer and then as president of the chapter, and I presently serve as chapter advisor. I am highly motivated, work well with other people, and am eager to move into new and challenging positions.

Third, I want you to know that I have chosen XYZ Bank as my most desirable potential employer.   **III**

XYZ has a longstanding reputation as a leading regional banking concern. I am from Texas, and as you know, Texas is a unit banking state. Our banks are, by nature, small. We therefore respect and take guidance from a larger regional bank. XYZ has overcome adverse circumstances, and such experience serves as a tool for successful future strategic planning. As a sports enthusiast, I can appreciate a team with losses early in the season, but able to achieve an over-all winning season. I believe in XYZ Bank. For such a large commercial bank to continue to open its doors to the public, to service its markets in an efficient, profitable manner, this bank must employ the most capable and qualified management possible. I believe I fit this description.

I have told you how I fit the profile of a good banker, and I have discussed my leadership qualities and my sincere desire to become an XYZ Bank employee. It is my hope you will review my qualifications and choose me as a candidate in the Officer Candidate Training Program at XYZ Bank.

PRESENTATION #3: "Foreign Trade Zones—Get a Handle on It"*

Audience Analysis *(Student Reference)*

1. Who is the speaker?

   Dayton Ballenger, Zone Manager, Oakland International Trade Center, Foreign Trade Zone #56.

2. Who is the audience?

   30 members of MBA program, enrolled in International Marketing course at the University of California, Berkeley. Average age 28, all graduate students.

3. What do they know about the subject?

   Very little.

4. Why will they be interested?

   They are interested in international trade, importing, and exporting. Recent legislation creates more advantages and interest in a foreign trade zone.

5. What do I want the audience to know or feel?

   Increased enthusiasm and desire for increased knowledge.

6. What do I need for this presentation?

   Projector, screen, electrical outlet, easel for charts, sound system, pointer, handouts.

7. Where will this presentation be given?

   In a classroom at the University of California at Berkeley.
   Class break precedes, classes follow.

8. What is the purpose?

   To inform.

On the following pages is a handout for a speech. Fill it out as your instructor reads the speech to you. Note the effectiveness of this presentational technique.

---

* Used with permission of Dayton Ballenger, Zone Manager, Oakland International Trade Center, Foreign Trade Zone #56, Oakland, California 94621.

PART 1

FTZ

FOREIGN TRADE ZONES
Get a handle on it!

date: _____

Name _____

Company _____

Product(s) _____

_____

_____

WHAT: A U.S. Foreign Trade Zone:

○ is an enclosed area within the United States
○ it is considered outside the U.S. Customs Territory
○ all domestic/foreign merchandise can enter without a formal Customs entry or payment of Customs duties or Government excise taxes.

HOW: Merchandise activities:

☐ stored   ☐ displayed   ☐ assembled

☐ tested   ☐ repaired   ☐ manufactured

☐ cleaned   ☐ manipulated   ☐ salvaged

☐ sampled   ☐ mixed   ☐ destroyed

☐ relabeled   ☐ processed   ☐ re-exported

☐ repackaged

notes:

1

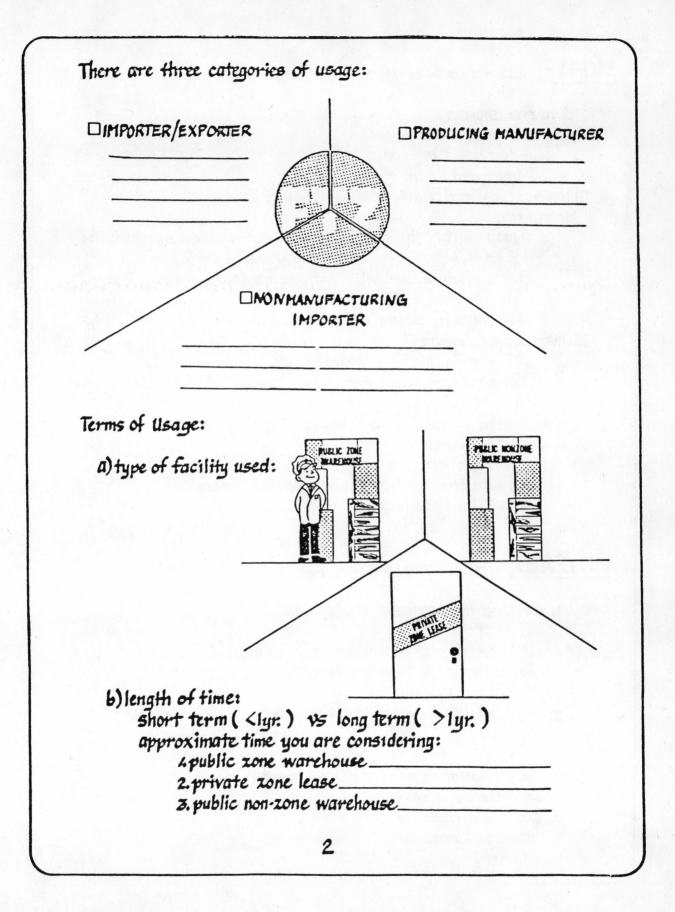

There are three categories of usage:

☐ IMPORTER/EXPORTER   ☐ PRODUCING MANUFACTURER

_____   _____
_____   _____
_____   _____
_____   _____

☐ NONMANUFACTURING
      IMPORTER

_____
_____
_____

Terms of Usage:

a) type of facility used:

b) length of time:
     short term (<1yr.) vs long term (>1yr.)
     approximate time you are considering:
          1. public zone warehouse_____
          2. private zone lease_____
          3. public non-zone warehouse_____

2

WHY: Advantages & benefits of FTZ use:

☐ duty free storage
    a) improved cash flow
    b) decreased insurance rates
    c) unlimited length of time
☐ lower taxes/tariff after manipulation of goods
☐ quota free
    a) may store, exhibit & merchandise then move merchandise
       into U.S. territory during next quota period
    b) manufacture/assemble with quota free merchandise
       to produce quota free product
    c) if manufacturing/assembly involved, US labor utilized
☐ inspection & repair
    a) maintain quality reputation of goods
    b) no duty on merchandise that cannot be repaired,
       is destroyed, or is re-exported.
☐ repackaging & relabeling (impact buying on various markets
☐ assembly & manufacture
    a) on very small to very large scales
    b) duty on resultant product could be lower
    c) US labor utilized

WHERE: FTZ#56's success due to many factors:

1. Oakland International Trade Center
    a) FTZ#56
    b) International Business Planning Center
    c) Exhibition & Display Center
    d) Trading Companies
2. strategic location to: Port of Oakland   Oakland Airport
                   Oakland Internat'l   Business Park
                   Airport   Major highways + rail
3. close association with the Department of Commerce
4. educational capacity
5. exhibition capacity
6. trading companies

3

PART 2

FOREIGN TRADE ZONES
Get a handle on it!

The following questionnaire is to determine if the program you have completed has increased your knowledge of Foreign Trade Zones. We appreciate your time & participation! Your responses will aid us in revising & improving our program.

Thank you!!

WHAT: define today's U.S. Foreign Trade Zone:

_____
_____
_____
_____
_____
_____

HOW: list the 3 categories of usage and at least 2 types of merchandise activities for each:

1._____
  a)_____
  b)_____
  c)_____
  d)_____

3._____
  a)_____
  b)_____
  c)_____
  d)_____

2._____
  a)_____
  b)_____
  c)_____
  d)_____
  e)_____

1

Name the 2 components of terms of usage.
a) _____
b) _____

For a) above, name + define the 3 options available

1. _____
_____
_____
_____

3. _____
_____
_____
_____

PRIVATE

2. _____
_____
_____

For b) above, name + define the 2 options available
1. _____
2. _____

Using your own product as an example, apply both the category + terms of usage to your situation, determining which is most appropriate + why.
_____
_____
_____
_____
_____
_____
_____
_____

2

CHECKLIST OF COMMUNICATION TERMS *(Quiz)*

Check your understanding of communication terms used in this chapter. Write the number of the correct term in the blank preceding its definition. Note there are more terms than definitions.

Definitions

a. _____ A type of visual aid that can be prepared in advance and used with an overhead projector.

b. _____ Ten percent of the questions asked after a presentation.

c. _____ A type of graph that uses pictures or symbols to represent data.

d. _____ A presentation carefully written out and read to an audience.

e. _____ A graph that demonstrates how a whole quantity is divided into parts.

f. _____ A visual aid with a number of pages that can be easily turned to reveal different charts or graphs.

g. _____ A machine used to make infrared film transparencies for an overhead projector.

h. _____ A presentation carefully prepared in advance but delivered from speaker note cards with a great deal of audience contact.

i. _____ A speech delivered with little or no preparation.

j. _____ An organized list of specific data such as statistics used as a visual aid.

Terms

1. impromptu speech
2. visual aid
3. manuscript speech
4. memorized speech
5. cutaway models
6. line graph
7. pictorial graph
8. transparencies
9. getcha questions
10. answer-seeking questions
11. flip chart
12. illustrations
13. bar graph
14. overhead projector
15. handouts
16. extemporaneous speech
17. speaker note cards
18. models
19. circle graph
20. Thermo-fax®
21. opaque projector
22. message questions
23. table
24. tripod
25. slide projector
26. movie projector
27. videotape
28. charts
29. strip chart

CHAPTER 9

Let's Talk About the Business of Communicating One-to-One

As you enter the world of business, you'll discover that much of your communication will be with one person at a time. And each one-to-one encounter will build your reputation as a skillful business speech communicator. This chapter introduces you to methods of applying your communication skills to these one-to-one situations. After reading the chapter, and participating in the workshop activities, you should be able to do the following:

Chapter Objectives

1. Adjust your sending and receiving skills in informal business speech situations.
2. Adapt your communication behavior to the unwritten rules of business etiquette.
3. Manage interpersonal conflicts resourcefully by understanding styles of conflict resolution and the stages of working out conflicts.
4. Plan and prepare for a variety of interviews.
5. Handle business telephone conversations skillfully.
6. Practice using speaking skills in dictation.

The office of tomorrow is here today. New and exciting tools for making the job easier have burst into the marketplace. Silicon-chip technology has developed desktop computers that turn stacks of complex statistics into easy-to-read charts; typewriters that recognize and correct misspellings; word processors that memorize, store, and retrieve documents; and copiers linked to teleprinters that print and duplicate a dictated memo, route it internally to offices around the country, and file it into electronic memory banks in field office computers. Information flows through the business community at an accelerated pace that makes information increasingly accessible. Time lags are measured in minutes, not days, as business extends itself from coast to coast, or around the globe.

Think of the direct effects on communication of dictation machines that can translate spoken messages into a typed page. In-house telecommunications branches have exchanges that are capable of handling audio data, visual messages, and interoffice work stations that can be connected electronically. To avoid the expense of travel, business meetings between executives in several locations can be conducted through telecommunication networks. Key company employees can confer with one another not only by telephone but visually with satellite hookups and wall-size projection screens in the teleconference rooms. Reports that were formerly written, reproduced, and distributed are now recorded for listening by telephone. Conference telephone calls, closed-circuit television, picturephones, videotapes, and voice-activated computers will all require the use of speaking and listening skills as never before. The ability to present yourself as an effective communicator is more important to business success than it has ever been.

But success in business is built on the use of communication skills in daily one-to-one human relationships in your personal life and your professional future. This chapter deals with one-to-one communication on the job: people-related message skills as well as job-related situations—interviews, business telephoning, and dictating.

ONE-TO-ONE COMMUNICATION

In communication terms, a one-to-one encounter is called a **dyad**, or two people talking together. In dyads, many important things will happen to you—someone will consider you for a job, your performance will be evaluated, you will build lasting friendships. All the communication skills you have learned will apply to one-to-one situations.

In face-to-face meetings, both people act as senders and receivers with feedback being adjusted as the two people watch each other. When one-to-one communication takes place on the telephone, both speak and listen, but visual communication is missing. Vocal inflections provide some feedback as to how the other person feels about what is being said.

The following factors affect dyads:

1. Each person's perception is that person's reality. Since no two people perceive an event in exactly the same way, common ground must be found.
2. Both people are affected by their own personal concerns. Sensitive awareness of the other person's current feelings increases an atmosphere of trust.
3. Each situation is different. Although two people may have talked together before, new events may have changed previous attitudes and feelings. Human relationships rarely remain static.
4. Subject matter varies from situation to situation. People are most concerned with topics that have a direct effect upon them.

Communication is the basis for human relationships, and you build your business success as you interact with your business colleagues one by one. You talk with others on the job for two major reasons: (1) to perform

PHOTO 9-1

In communication terms, a one-to-one encounter is called a dyad.

your job duties, and (2) to establish and maintain relationships with people on the job. Note the differences between these one-to-one conversations.

You ask a co-worker about the arrival of an expected shipment.
You discuss a company policy with your supervisor.
You transfer an outside customer's call to another department.

or

You chat a moment in the hall with a friend from another department.
You visit with an acquaintance during a coffee break.
You set up a golf game for Saturday afternoon with your supervisor.

The first group of messages are **job-related**, messages designed to get a task done; the second group are **people-related**, messages designed to establish and maintain human relationships. Let's discuss these personal encounters first and then consider job-related or professional one-to-one situations.

PERSONAL COMMUNICATION ON THE JOB

Some businesspeople who work together also socialize together; others keep their business lives separate from their personal lives. For many, the balance is somewhere in between. Whatever your job, you will need to feel comfortable with your fellow workers. Obviously some topics are inappropriate to discuss on company time, but there are opportunities to establish contacts on and off the job.

Developing Communication Levels

You maintain several levels of communication with others.[1] These levels depend primarily on how much of yourself you care to invest in the relationship. Consider these four levels of communication:

Recognition Level. There are many people whom you recognize and to whom you speak. With many of these acquaintances you communicate on the "Hi" and "How are you?" level. You acknowledge each other. You provide a verbal pat on the back for each other. This level of communication asks you to invest nothing but your awareness of the other person. It gives you social contacts and makes it possible to get better acquainted if you both would like to do so.

Chit-Chat Level. People with whom you communicate on this level are people with whom you spend time—at lunch, on breaks, or when sharing rides. You discuss people you know in common or general subjects, such as news items about places and things. You may gossip at this safe level of communication. Because you do not seek a closer or deeper relationship, you do not volunteer to share anything too risky about yourself.

Minor Investment (of Self) Level. On this level, you communicate with people whom you regard as friends—people you trust enough to share personal information. With these people you disclose a good bit of what you think, believe, or value. You invest a part of yourself in these relationships. You rely on the other people to accept your self-disclosure, and you open yourself to feedback from them. In turn, they share a part of themselves with you.

Major Investment (of Self) Level. There are some very special people in your life with whom you can reveal your deepest feelings. These are close friends with whom you have built a solid relationship based on mutual trust. You can expose yourself to these people and talk about your greatest concerns. You invest a very private part of yourself in these communication encounters—sharing mutually, willing to be open and caring about each other.

Investment of yourself in relationships with other people is a risky matter because you open yourself to another. But it is important to recognize that a positive communication climate is dependent on some degree of openness between people. It is also possible that too much openness (saying whatever you think without regard for the other person's feelings) will push relationships beyond the level that is acceptable to the other person. To understand the appropriate degrees of openness with others on the job is a delicate matter. It is possible to be friendly and outgoing and to serve as a good listener and a sympathetic receiver without becoming best friends. But trust is built by accepting and believing in others and by permitting them to respond to that trust.

"More psychotherapy is accomplished between good friends at coffee every morning at ten o'clock than all day long in doctors' offices. A good talk with a close friend can solve problems, or at least put them in perspective, before they become overpowering. One of the problems we face today is the scarcity of good friends."

Dr. Joseph D. Matarazzo

---

[1] For a useful analysis of levels of interpersonal communication, read John Powell, S.J., *Why Am I Afraid to Tell You Who I Am?* (Chicago: Argus Communications, 1969), pp. 50-85.

Practicing Communication Etiquette

There are several unwritten rules of **business communication etiquette** (generally accepted behaviors) used by successful businesspeople. Consider the following:

Use Simple Courtesy. For example:

1. Socialize on your own time, not on your employer's time.
2. Learn the names of the people with whom you deal. Call each one by her or his appropriate title (Mrs., Ms., Miss, or Mr.).
3. Introduce people to each other.
   a. Present a man to a woman (generally): "Caroline Barnett, this is Robert Schulte."
   b. Present a younger person to an older person: "Miss Ramirez, this is my friend Jane Ellen Boyd."
   c. Use titles of position: "Mayor Anderson, this is Dr. Ellen Kahn."

PHOTO 9-2

Knowing how to make introductions is an important part of business etiquette.

Avoid Offensive Behavior. It is inconsiderate to eat at your desk, smoke when it bothers others, chew gum as you talk, bring soft drinks into meetings, read magazines while on the job, etc. Remember that loud talking, playing a radio in your work area, or otherwise disturbing other workers is offensive behavior.

Choose Appropriate Subjects to Discuss. Try to be up-to-date and informed on current events. Read newspapers and news magazines and listen to news reports. It is a boost to your morale to be able to participate in group discussions. Try to make your contributions accurate by quoting your source of information. For example, "An article in *Business Week* says that small car sales are up." Identify your opinion by taking responsibility for it, saying, for example, "I tend to think . . ." "In my judgment . . ." "From what I have read, I believe . . ."

Avoid talking negatively about your job or about the people who work for your company. Negative comments may bounce back to you with connotations you did not intend. Remember that messages may be distorted when they are repeated.

Select Fitting Feedback Responses to the Messages of Others. Listen to the complete message. Hear the person out. If you find yourself about to argue, to disagree, to reject the message, or to get emotionally involved, stop and feed back what you heard before you respond. Restate the *content* of the message in your own words and ask the speaker if you are interpreting accurately. Or restate the *intent* (your perception of why the speaker said the message) in your own words. Ask for verification.

Phrase Questions Carefully. Don't probe. Word a question so that it does not seem evaluative or judgmental. Ask your questions in unthreatening or nondefensive tones.

In short, there are unwritten rules for appropriate business behavior in informal conversations. Guided by these rules, you will establish relationships with others at work. When the time and occasion are right, you and the other person can move your relationship into deeper levels of sharing and trust.

Managing Interpersonal Conflicts

Conflicts are inevitable when there are disagreements between people in the workplace. Handling conflicts through effective communication is important so that relationships can be maintained and strengthened.

Styles of Conflict Management. Different approaches to a conflict are described below, identified by the attitude of at least one of the participants, and followed by an example.

1. **Confrontation**—a "win-win" approach through which two people can work out their differences. This style assures good feelings about the solution and toward each other.

   "Look, I understand your problems and I know we don't agree about how fast we can get the product on the market. Since we do agree on the importance of a June shipment, what steps can we eliminate from the production process?"

"For you to win, somebody else does not have to lose."

Gary D'Angelo

2. **Competition**—a "win-lose" approach in which one person comes out on top leaving the other person with a sense of failure.

   "Listen, my department can't be ready to ship that merchandise by next month and that's final. Make other plans."

3. **Compromise**—a "lose-lose" approach leaving both people dissatisfied with the results.

> "Well, my department will work overtime to meet the June deadline, but you've got to contact the dealers and change the distribution orders."

4. **Accommodation**—a "smoothing" approach, known as "yield-lose," which requires one person to give in and leaves the other person with the sense of not achieving anything.

> "I'll go along with the date you want for shipping but we'll have to use the old packaging instead of your new cartons."

5. **Avoiding**—a "lose-leave" approach in which one person simply withdraws from the other.

> "Well, if you are going to make that decision, just leave my department out of your plans."

Studies of conflict management indicate that every person has the ability to use each of these five styles and must decide which approach is likely to be most effective in a particular situation. The confrontation style is recommended because it requires the application of interpersonal skills and results in a solution that is worked out by both people.

Stages in Conflict Management. Deborah Weider-Hatfield has formulated six stages that can be used in managing interpersonal conflicts:[2]

Stage 1. *Evaluate the conflict intrapersonally.* Both people try to evaluate the problem individually. Intrapersonal skills needed here are the ability to identify, own, and describe one's feelings; the ability to describe rather than to evaluate the behavior of the other person; the need to separate fact from inference; and willingness to empathize with the other person.

Stage 2. *Define the conflict interpersonally.* During this stage, both people need to help each other identify the causes of the conflict and agree on a definition. Interpersonal skills needed are the use of nonjudgmental questions; feeding back the comments of the other person; checking one's own perception of how the other person feels; sending verbal and nonverbal messages that correspond; and avoiding responses that go off on a tangent.

Stage 3. *Interpersonally identify mutually shared goals.* The purpose of this stage is to understand the needs and desires of the other person as well as to assert one's own desires and needs. This stage attempts to set goals from each different perspective and to identify goals that are shared by both people. Skills listed for Stage 2 are needed, as well as the ability to identify the positive aspects of the conflict management effort, and the ability to be problem oriented rather than controlling in one's communicative behavior.

Stage 4. *Interpersonally identify a variety of possible resolutions.* During this stage, both people generate a wide variety of ways to resolve the conflict between them. Additional communication skills needed include the ability to

---

[2] Deborah Weider-Hatfield, "A Unit in Conflict Management Communication Skills," *Communication Education*, Vol. 30, No. 3 (July, 1981), pp. 265-273.

communicate flexibly rather than dogmatically, and the ability to refrain from quick judgment of the other's solution.

Stage 5. *Interpersonally weigh goals against possible resolutions.* During this stage, both people weigh the goals outlined in Stage 3 against the possible resolutions in Stage 4. They try to decide which resolution satisfies the largest number of goals, and on which resolution they can agree. This requires all the interpersonal skills listed for the previous stages plus the ability to communicate spontaneously when reacting to the relationships between goals and resolutions.

Stage 6. *Interpersonally evaluate the chosen resolution after a period of time.* This stage encourages people to recognize that resolution of a conflict in the past does not guarantee that the resolution will continue to be satisfactory. People change. Situations and their components change with time. The two people need to continually evaluate whether the resolution is working, whether modifications are needed, and when they will discuss the resolution again. The additional interpersonal communication skill needed is the ability to be honest with oneself and the other person.

PROFESSIONAL COMMUNICATION ON THE JOB

The primary difference between an informal speech encounter between two people concerned with the relationship between them and a transaction between two businesspeople is the **purpose** of the meeting. While both kinds of communication may take place on the job, professional transactions are directed toward achieving business goals.

In a one-to-one meeting, one or both people have a specific goal to reach. Think of the variety of one-to-one meetings existing in your life right now:

As a patient you visit your doctor for a solution to a medical problem.
As a client you consult your lawer for legal advice.
As a customer you return merchandise to a store and an employee serves you.
As a buyer you visit an automobile showroom and a salesperson demonstrates models.
As a consumer you call to discuss your bill with an electric company representative.

In each example, business is being conducted, and speaking and listening skills are important. Three specific business situations will be discussed in this chapter: interviews, business telephone conversations, and dictating or voice writing. Each requires special use of your skills.

INTERVIEWS

Formal **interviews** are conversations for a wide variety of business purposes ranging from information seeking to employee evaluation, from considering job applicants to explaining new policy. Let's examine the general characteristics of business interviews, consider the roles of the people involved, and then carefully examine a variety of types of interview situations.

Chapter 9   Communicating One-to-One

Characteristics of Interviews

1. Interviews have specific goals:

   To get information. ("I need to get a rundown on your plans for expansion.")
   To give information. ("I called to tell you about the services in your area for our new product.")
   To persuade the other person by changing that person's beliefs or actions. ("I'd like to talk with you about a possible transfer to our Dallas office.")
   To work together toward the solution of a problem. ("I've asked you to meet with me to iron out a problem in your department.")

2. Interviews involve two people (dyads):

   Both may be members of the same company with the same status level, such as two department heads.
   Both may be members of the same organization with different positions and status levels, such as supervisor and employee.
   Each may work for a different organization, such as a government agency employee and a company manager.
   One may represent a company and the other may be from outside the company, such as a personnel director and a job applicant.

3. Participants may play different roles:

   Directive Interview. One participant generally serves as the **interviewer** and is responsible for setting up the meeting, planning the goals for the meeting, and deciding how these are to be achieved. In other words, the interviewer may control the direction of the conversation. The other person, the **interviewee**, answers questions, provides information, and cooperates in achieving the goals of the meeting.
   Nondirective Interview. Both participants set up the meeting, define the goals, and work together to find ways of achieving the goals. Both dyad members provide the topics, explore a wide range of subject matter, deal in depth with some topics, and join in an ongoing relationship with each other. The leadership roles often shift back and forth.

4. Time and place may vary:

   Generally an interview meeting is set by appointment for a certain day and time. Often the meeting takes place in the territory of one of the participants. The physical setting (seating, temperature, lighting), social setting (nature of the occasion), and distance between participants affect the atmosphere of the meeting.

Types of Interviews

You will be involved in a wide variety of interviews in your professional life. We will discuss first the all-important employment interview, and then cover five types of on-the-job interviews—counseling, reprimand, complaint, evaluation, and training sessions.

Employment Interviews. This is the first one-to-one business conversation you will have. Your purpose is to secure your entrance into the job market. You will be the interviewee, and the personnel director or recruiter will be the interviewer. The event is important to you because your career may depend on it. However, you may not be the only one to feel tense during this meeting. Remember that the interviewer is pressured to select a person who will do well on the job, who will fit into the work team, and whose skills will benefit the company. The interviewer also is seeking a person with the required temperament (flexibility, dependability, stability, adaptability, etc.) for a particular job. It is important to the interviewer to select the right applicant so as not to be labeled incompetent by her or his supervisor.

As an interviewee, you should present yourself as favorably as you can because a part of your interview skill includes convincing the interviewer that she or he will not make a mistake in hiring you. This means you will have to answer some tough questions so that the recruiter can picture you in the job for which you are applying. You will have to do advance preparation. For example, how would you handle these questions?

"How do your abilities fit our job requirements?"
"What are your biggest weaknesses?"
"What can you do for us?"
"Why are you the best candidate for this job?"
"Where in the business world do you see yourself three to five years from now?"
"Can you tell me something about yourself?"
"What starting salary do you expect?"

Job interviews are based on successful communication. In an article that reported the speech communication behaviors of successful job applicants, the researcher described the following skills.[3]

Successful interviewees *showed great interest in the company and the position* by:

1. Identifying with the employer's interests and expressing career goals consistent with the position for which they were applying.
2. Emphasizing they wanted *careers*, not merely jobs.
3. Displaying positive attitudes toward the company to which they were applying.
4. Reporting research that they had done on the company through informed people, libraries, and in journals and brochures.
5. Being realistically informed about the responsibilities of the positions they were seeking.
6. Knowing about the specific qualities that employers were seeking, claiming to possess these desired qualities, and using evidence to clarify, amplify, and to support their claims as well as to overcome possible weaknesses in their backgrounds.
7. Asking specific questions about company policies, clientele, employee turnover rates, etc.

Successful interviewees *expressed themselves well* by:

1. Using language in interesting ways: concrete words and active verbs, terms that evoked positive connotations, colorful terms to make messages more interesting, and frequent use of technical jargon indicating their familiarity with the position for which they were applying.

---

[3] Lois J. Einhorn, "An Inner View of the Job Interview: An Investigation of Successful Communicative Behaviors," *Communication Education*, Vol. 30, No. 3 (July, 1981), pp. 217-228.

2. Elaborating on the information they provided by using specific evidence as well as by using a wide variety of supporting material to clarify and substantiate points—personal experiences, explanations, factual and hypothetical illustrations, comparisons, contrasts, statistics, and testimony from co-workers, supervisors, and teachers.
3. Speaking in short, simple sentences, making their referents clear, and adhering to accepted rules of grammar.
4. Speaking fluently and forcefully by varying their vocal rate, volume, and pitch as they responded.
5. Articulating distinctly, smiling often, gesturing meaningfully, and maintaining comfortable, natural postures while often leaning forward to communicate.
6. Maintaining direct eye contact while speaking and listening.

Successful interviewees *presented themselves effectively* by:

1. Appearing to sense what the interviewers liked and disliked from cues in the questions that were asked. When an interviewer phrased a question that implied a desired response, successful interviewees responded positively, forcefully, and without qualification.
2. Often wording questions confidently in the first person, such as: "What would be my duties and responsibilities?"
3. Talking 55 percent of the time and taking an active role in the interview by often initiating comments and expressing confidence in their abilities and a strong desire to work for the company to which they were applying.
4. Making summary statements in which they repeated their qualifications and interest in the position.
5. Trying to get a commitment from the recruiter as to when selection decisions would be made.

Thus, successful candidates communicated well and portrayed themselves as professionally competent and dynamic. These behaviors helped to establish positive identities which were reflected in favorable responses from the recruiters.

Counseling Interviews. When you reach a point in your work where you need special help, you may request an interview with your supervisor. Your purpose is to make the problem clear by careful analysis, to present your view of the causes, and to express your feelings. Your supervisor will then work with you to examine alternatives and review possible solutions.

Reprimand Interviews. It is possible that sometime you may be called into a one-to-one meeting where your undesirable behavior is brought to your attention. A private office with a closed door is usually the setting for this type of interview. No one likes criticism in public. In difficult situations of this kind, both the interviewer and interviewee may be ill at ease. A great deal of patience and skill is needed to tactfully disclose the problem, acknowledge the behavior, and together work out suggestions for improvement.

Complaint Interviews. These one-to-one meetings are often the basis for airing gripes and letting out hard feelings. If you should ask for this kind of interview with a supervisor, it is important to provide clearly worded explanations of the conditions which cause you distress. Rather than exploding with anger, it is helpful to propose solutions or suggestions for change. It is also prudent to examine your feelings from the other person's point of view. Empathy will enable you to say what you need to say and temper it with understanding of the other person's position.

Evaluation Interviews. Many companies evaluate their employees by conducting appraisals of employee performance. Rather than considering these interviews as threats to your self-image, it will help if you view them as opportunities to understand how your organization perceives you and your work. The interviewer will understand your feelings about being evaluated, and your open, cooperative attitude will make the interview easier for both of you.

Training Sessions. Once you are hired, you will be instructed in specific company policies and will be told what is expected of you on the job. This may be done for several new employees in a training class. But often you will be turned over to another employee, and the two of you will meet together in a one-to-one situation to go over procedures and to orient you to your new surroundings. Your purpose in this dyad is to learn; the other person's purpose is to provide instruction. It is important to ask questions and to repeat instructions to ensure your understanding.

Interview Preparation

"The lack of adequate preparation for an interview is the greatest single fault found in my studies of the interviewing process."

Samuel G. Trull

When you meet to talk with someone you know and like, the situation is usually relaxed, the atmosphere is warm and nonthreatening, and the flow of communication is easy and spontaneous. When the meeting is over, you have positive feelings because you have participated in a dynamic verbal encounter; both of you have achieved mutual goals. Such an interview requires planning and is successful only when both members are prepared. The following suggestions will help you become a more effective member of a dyad in a business interview—whether you are interviewer or interviewee.

1. **Know the purpose of the meeting.** Determine the *who, what, when, where*, and *why* before you make the appointment. If you are asked to meet with someone, go through the same steps.
2. **Learn what you can about the other person.** Seek information that will enable you to think of the other person as an individual. If you have not met before, dig up some background information: name, position, title, company and work the person does, location of office, etc. You are meeting with a person, not an antagonist. If you are interviewing for a position, it is essential that you know as much as you can about the company: its size, location, products or services, etc.
3. **Assure yourself of the time and place.** If you are requesting the interview, you will probably meet in the other person's territory. Be sure of the location, address, and how to get there. If possible, check beforehand. Try to visualize the physical conditions of the meeting. Allow yourself an adequate amount of time to get to the meeting. Try to ensure the wise use of the time available during the meeting to conclude it to your mutual satisfaction.
4. **Think through the interview.** Imagine what it will be like to sit in the meeting. How much distance will there be between you? Mentally sit in the seat of the other person and visualize how the person will see you.

5. **Plan the topics you want to discuss.** Write down the things you want to know. Leave space to jot down important answers as they are explained to you. Anticipate the questions you will be asked and think through your answers.

   If you are applying for a position, you will find some questions that are frequently asked of job applicants in the workshop activities of this chapter. You can prepare for an employment interview by familiarizing yourself with these questions. But don't just read them through. Answer each of these aloud in the privacy of your room at home. Do a few each day orally. Try tape recording them and then listen to your answers. Rephrase them to make them clearer. Don't memorize an answer. Give yourself practice in verbalizing clearly what you already know.

6. **Be physically prepared.** To know that you look neat and well groomed gives you a sense of poise. Investigate the appropriate clothes to wear by finding out what is worn by others in the company. Avoid buying something new for the particular occasion because you may be uncomfortable in something you haven't worn before. Bring with you the materials you'll need: a set of reference letters, examples of your work, your carefully prepared résumé, pencil, and notebook.

7. **Be mentally prepared.** If you are applying for a position, the more you know about the company to which you are applying, the more at ease you will feel. If you are expected to have certain information available, be sure you spend the time getting it together so that you can present it.

8. **Set the interview in the proper perspective.** Accept the fact that you may be somewhat anxious or apprehensive. This is likely to be the case if the results of the interview affect your future. Remember, however, that it is not a life-or-death matter but a simple transaction between human beings.

9. **Expect the interviewer to take the lead.** A speech situation cannot be diagrammed like a football play. You will need to be alert and aware as the other person gives you verbal and nonverbal clues. If you are the interviewee, the interviewer will indicate where you are to sit and what the interview style will be as well as when the meeting is concluded. If you are interviewing the other person (to get information for a report, for example) and are in the person's office, you are the guest, but it is up to you to take the responsibility for beginning and concluding the encounter.

10. **Carry your share.** Whichever role you play in an interview, the other member of your dyad cannot know what you are thinking if you do not speak. It is not necessary to volunteer information that is not requested. But it is important to be a responsive, involved, and active participant.

Supervisor Strategies

Someday you'll be on the manager's side of the desk and will be responsible for reviewing the job performance of your employees in one-to-one meetings with each person. That person will not like hearing some of the negative things that need to be said (perhaps alcohol or drug abuse, irresponsibility, etc.). You will not enjoy this part of your job. However, there are some things you can do to make such meetings less painful.

1. Remind yourself that your goal is to have a smooth-running operation with highly motivated employees. Set the tone of performance reviews (even negative ones) on a positive note by telling your employee that you are interested in his or her progress in the company and you are willing to be of help.

"We learn to do neither by thinking nor by doing; we learn to do by thinking about what we are doing."

George D. Stoddard

"I can give you a six-word formula for success: Think things through—then follow through."

Eddie Rickenbacker

2. Begin by making your employee feel less threatened and uncomfortable. Arrange the meeting in neutral territory; pick a convenient time for you both; be sure you will not be interrupted or rushed.
3. Plan an agenda: start by discussing the employee's strengths on the job, gently but firmly get down to the problems or weak areas in need of improvement, work together on suggestions for solutions.
4. Conduct the meeting as a dialogue—get the employee to talk about personal goals, immediate projects, and concerns. Listen as well as lecture. End on a positive note.
5. Set specific goals for changes in job performance and schedule a date three or four weeks in the future to meet again to discuss improvement.

BUSINESS TELEPHONE CONVERSATIONS

Most people cannot resist answering a ringing telephone! They will interrupt a face-to-face transaction (waiting on a customer, helping a co-worker fill out a form, explaining a procedure) to answer a phone.

"The shortest distance between two points is a phone line."

Bell System

The business telephone call is a tremendously important one-to-one speech encounter. It is speedy and direct. It can be a shortcut to securing information, setting up appointments, checking on potential problems or solutions, or maintaining goodwill with business associates. Because your telephone communication provides such immediate, direct contact, it is important to deliver a well-planned speech message.

Barriers

With all the advantages a telephone offers, there are some barriers in telephone communication. The instrument itself provides a barrier. Your voice speeding over telephone wires may not sound as you wish it to. Instead of the warm, responsive tones you deliver in person, the mechanical instrument may flatten your voice quality. Of course, if you are hesitant, fearful, or timid, these emotional states are revealed in your voice. Aline Thompson, former personnel director of the National Safety Council, says:

What I call the executive telephone voice-spoilers are dispositional traits. If you're a busy executive, daily tensions can cause you to become impatient, irritated, even hostile.

These unpleasant mental attitudes tend to prevent you from speaking with an open throat, and unattractively color and mar your voice, often giving it a robot-metallic quality.[4]

A second barrier is that a conversation by telephone has to be conducted without the help of nonverbal clues. You recall that your receiver skills rely on nonverbal messages—chiefly facial expressions. Since phonovision is not generally available, you cannot see the person with whom you are speaking by phone. You don't know what activity you have interrupted. You are not sure of the other person's receptiveness at the moment. You have none of the clues that help you read nonverbal feedback. The one-to-one telephone conversation depends on words and voice alone.

---

[4] Cathy Handley, "Get Rid of Your Bad Telephone Habits," *Nation's Business*, Vol. 63 (May, 1975), p. 82.

PHOTO 9-3

A business telephone call requires a well-planned speech message.

Skills for Answering the Telephone

Your voice on the telephone creates a picture in your caller's mind. This picture conveys a favorable image (or perhaps a negative impression) of the company you represent. The following suggestions will help you use the telephone to advantage on the job.

1. Speak clearly and distinctly. Answer by saying the company's name. Visualize the words as if they were printed on the wall before you. Carefully say, "Carlton Investments," "KDBC-TV," or "Brown-Root Construction Company." Separate the words with tiny pauses. Even if you say these words a hundred times a day, say them as if you were reading them.

2. Initiate the conversation. After you identify the company, it may be important to identify yourself. Say your name distinctly; again, separate your first name from your last name. Then say warmly and with interest, "May I help you?"

3. Smile as you speak. Your caller can't see your smile, but the quality of your voice changes when you're smiling. Listen for smiles. Note the fuller, pleasant tones. Consider each call a delightful surprise and smile as you speak.

4. Don't let the other person hang suspended. Tell the caller what action you're taking on the call. Explain, "Just a minute, I'll ring that office for you." Transfer calls only when necessary and when you know the third party will be able to help the caller. If you stay on the line, excuse yourself when the proper party has been found by saying, "Mr. DeKoatz is on the line and he'll be able to help you." When a call must be transferred, tell the caller, "I'll transfer your call now. One moment, please."

5. Take messages accurately. Keep a note pad handy to record key words and phrases. Repeat the message to ensure accuracy. Do not fail to pass on messages you take for others—who called whom, date and time, and the subject.

6. Use simple courtesy. Remember you represent the company who employs you. Use proper titles for the people to whom you refer. Include "please" and "thank you."
7. Be sure that the conversation is finished before hanging up. If you initiated the call, take the responsibility for terminating it.

Skills for Making a Business Telephone Call

When you are making a business telephone call, think about it before you pick up the phone to dial. Like other one-to-one encounters, a business telephone call must achieve a purpose.

1. Plan before you dial. Decide exactly what you want to say. Identify the specific information you need to know. Jot down the topics you want to cover.
2. Be physically ready to talk. Relax, sit back comfortably. Focus your attention on the telephone. Hold the mouthpiece about one-half inch from your lips.
3. Picture the other person in your mind. Drop your voice into warm, friendly tones. Concentrate on establishing vocal contact despite the lack of visual contact.
4. Structure your telephone message. Identify who you are and the purpose of the call in brief, clear statements. Try to limit your call to one major point. Discuss it descriptively and clearly. Support your proposal with an example or illustration. Tell the other person what you'd like her or him to do.
5. Develop a good mental attitude. If you are speaking to someone you don't know, keep your voice low-pitched and friendly. Say what you mean. Phrase it ahead of time if necessary. But beware of reading a message to the other person. If you do, you have taken the personal contact out of the call.
6. Gesture while you speak. Although the other person cannot see your face or movements, your head nods, hand gestures, etc., reinforce your vocal tones and add emphasis to your verbal message.
7. Remember the bonus of courtesy. The words you choose reflect your feelings. Wrap up your call with a summary, a plan for another call, and the phrases that cement relationships: "Thank you." "I appreciate your help." "It was nice to talk with you."

DICTATING—A ONE-TO-ONE ORAL BUSINESS SKILL

A great deal of business correspondence—letters, memos, reports, etc.—is dictated orally and then transcribed into proper written form. Secretaries are trained to listen, take shorthand notes, and transcribe these into written messages. Executives are rarely trained to deliver written messages in an efficient oral form. And messages look different frozen on paper than sounded out in the air. Dictating, then, is a team effort requiring the skills of both speaker and listener. Let's examine the skills of both members of the team.

A **transcriber** or **receiver** is a person who listens to and reproduces the dictated message. The purpose of dictation is for one person to speak *to* another person (the reader) *through* the person who is transcribing. The speaker must consider two people: the person receiving the live dictated message and the reader to whom the message is ultimately directed.

Speaker Skills in Dictating

1. Prepare to dictate.
   a. Organize your references—the letter you are answering, the order you are referring to, the topics you want to cover.
   b. Structure your message—jot down guide notes, number the sequence of ideas, plan supporting materials (dates, examples, etc.).
   c. Use principles of good letter or report writing; refer to appropriate models.

2. Plan favorable conditions for voice writing.
   a. Find a quiet room and close the door to avoid distractions and interruptions.
   b. Set aside an adequate amount of time so that you are not pressured.
   c. Be sure your transcriber is able to spend the time needed to work with you.
   d. Remember, your receiver is listening to the sounds you are saying rather than to the content of the message, so speak very clearly.

3. Give the person who is working with you all the information necessary to transcribe your message accurately.
   a. The number of messages you will be writing.
   b. The kinds of messages you will be writing (memo, letter, rough draft, report, etc.).
   c. Special instructions about the number of copies; how the messages are to be distributed or mailed; stationery requirements, such as letterhead or other type of paper, etc.
   d. Information about addresses, special or unusual spelling, punctuation, and paragraph clues.

4. Make any changes very clear by saying "correction."
5. Watch the rate of your speaking by checking nonverbal clues given by the transcriber's hands and face.
6. Picture your reader as you talk.
   a. Use simple, natural language.
   b. Refer to the reader by name.
   c. Develop each idea fully.
   d. Listen to how you sound as you speak.

Receiver Skills in Dictating

1. Limit the amount of feedback you give.
   a. Ask if there is something you do not understand, but try not to interrupt the flow of ideas while the speaker is composing.
   b. Familiarize yourself with your company—its function, departments, products, and terminology—so that you understand the company language.
   c. Keep a checklist of dictation procedures so that you get necessary information at one time.
   d. Be prepared to offer suggestions if they are requested.
   e. Be ready to "read back" if the speaker asks for this feedback.

2. Read the nonverbal clues.
   a. Pay attention to the things that are not said as well as to the verbal message. For example, if the speaker seems unsure of information, offer a suggestion.
   b. Sit so that you can see as well as hear the speaker.

Dictating to a Machine

Not far in the future are marvelous new computers that will recognize up to 10,000 spoken words and print them as fast as they are spoken. Executives will write notes merely by speaking into a computer. One such computer, called VoiceWriter, is now on the market, and industry experts expect the market for speech-recognition machines to explode. Such innovations call for clear speaking skills.

At present many executives deliver messages to a dictating machine (perhaps even through a telephone), and the message is then transcribed into written form to be sent to the reader. Careful pronunciation is particularly important when dictating to a machine, because the transcriber may have no opportunity to check back with the speaker if words are unclear.

Sometimes a transcriber's inability to understand what the speaker is saying can lead to a transcription that makes no sense. Can you figure out what the speaker intended in the following garbled message?

> "Our offer may seem meager to you; but if you'll end us your deep lot instead of your bee section, we made rum "up" business for your drill-in crews as well as our own. Shear in the profits with you is our so lame for this Lawn Guyland under take-in."[5]

Successful dictation involves clear speech. Practice aloud the following word sets to make the difference between them very clear.

seen—sin	tax—tasks
head—hid	be in—being
bell—bill	see in—seeing
pen—pin	do in—doing
real—rill	taken—taking
lips—lisps	cannon—canning
boats—boasts	garden—guarding
tacks—tasks	cash owed—cash showed
peaks—speaks	we'll own—we'll loan
pacific—specific	you'll end—you'll lend
caught—cot	will buy—wheel by
form—farm	we'll buy—will buy
bowl—ball	coal—call
ax—asks	on—own[6]

TEAM REPORT WRITING

Often a dyad of businesspeople has to put together written material (a report, the results of a survey, etc.), with both people composing the content of the document orally. For example, two engineers may together prepare a technical report on a project they have both designed, built, and put into operation. Together they share the ideas and organize the outline.

One member of the dyad may do the actual writing, while both contrib-

---

[5] Morris Philip Wolf and Robert R. Aurner, *Effective Communication in Business*, 6th ed. (Cincinnati: South-Western Publishing Co., 1974), p. 189.

[6] Ibid.

ute the words, phrases, and sentences that shape the report. It is truly a team effort, with both members of the dyad using their speech tools, such as perception, language, and speaking skills.

The team working as voice writers will need to keep the readers of the written material in mind. The writers must perceive the readers' level of knowledge of the technical subject, the need for a common language level, and the need for clear definitions of technical terms.

The dyad also will use listening, nonverbal communication, and feedback skills. As the two people talk together about writing the report, each will need to actively listen to the other—hearing the other person as the person wishes to be heard, feeding back to clarify the sentences they write, and checking nonverbally with each other to verify that they are in agreement. The result of this one-to-one meeting will probably be a rough draft of the report which can then be typed and edited to final form.

Finally, whenever you work with another person on a one-to-one basis, you must put your speech tools to work so that you will be a congenial partner in any dyad.

IMPROVING YOUR ONE-TO-ONE COMMUNICATION

No one of us engages in successful one-to-one communication encounters each and every time. Misunderstandings often occur in human relationships. Ideally we will learn ways to reduce problems so we can count on success more often. Since there is little we can do to change the communication behavior of another person, the secret lies in being responsible for our own communication. The following reminders can help as we work to improve our speech encounters with others.

1. Check your observations carefully and use all your senses to verify what you see and hear.
2. Recognize that your personal filters may distort your perception.
3. Admit the possibility of error and check again.
4. Report what you actually see rather than what you *think* you see.
5. Try to be open-minded and tentative in your conclusions by recognizing that other people perceive differently.
6. Look more carefully at the differences between people who are categorized as the same. For example, Customer 1 is not the same as Customer 2 or Customer 3.
7. Refuse to stereotype people by placing them in a rigid category with a label. Accept people as human beings who fill different roles and are different from all others.
8. Recognize that there are more alternatives than just a simple choice of either/or. Things are not clear-cut; a number of options are available.
9. Realize that you are fallible (can make mistakes), that things change, and that people and situations change.
10. Try being specific when you report what you see, rather than being general and vague.
11. Withhold your judgments until you have as much information as possible.
12. Refuse to display a know-it-all attitude and be aware that you cannot know all or say all there is to be said.
13. Verify your assumptions before you make positive statements or take action.

14. Refuse to prejudge. Permit each person or situation to provide new insights or information.
15. Maintain an empirical attitude (check perceptions in the real world when possible) and a symbolic attitude (realize that everything cannot be proven). Use the appropriate attitude to fit the situation.
16. Accept yourself with your strengths and weaknesses, and recognize that all human beings are a mixture of both.

CHAPTER SUMMARY

To be successful in the complex modern business world, you should be able to apply your communication skills to those frequent one-to-one meetings known as dyads. Two categories of communication on the job are "people-related" messages, which are vital in establishing and maintaining relationships between you and others, and "job-related" messages, which serve to get the job done. This chapter identified levels of personal communication, discussed business speech etiquette, and described the styles and stages in handling interpersonal conflicts. Professional communication situations covered in this chapter included interviewing, business telephoning, and dictating or voice writing.

ASKING QUESTIONS *(Dyads)*

Purpose: To practice changing "communication-stopper" questions into "door-opening" questions—communication promoters.

Briefing: Work with one other person. Read the questions aloud in the following categories. Discuss the questions in the debriefing section.

Communication Stoppers

1. Puts the other person on the spot.

   "You haven't held any job for very long, have you?"

2. Tells the other person the answer you want.

   "Nobody has anything to say, have they?"

3. Asks for either "yes" or "no."

   "Do you want the job or not?"

4. Probes further than necessary.

   "What do you think about the quality of that person's work?"

5. Arouses defensive behavior.

   "Are you responsible for the poor typing on this report?"

Communication Promoters

1. Open-ended questions.

   "How did you feel when that happened?"

2. Clarifies the purpose.

   "Because we are considering a promotion for Vicky, we'd like your opinion of her work."

3. Starts from common ground.

   "Do you know about our retirement policy or would you like a brief explanation?"

4. Comes from what the other person has already said.

   "Would you like to go into that aspect a little more?"

5. Focuses on what the person is feeling about what she or he is saying.

   "It seems you feel disappointed that your office staff does not appreciate your extra efforts."

Debriefing: In the list of questions below, put a check beside the number of a communication stopper. Circle the number of a communication promoter. Change communication stoppers to promoters.

1. What happened at work today?

2. How was your day?

3. What's happening?

4. What would you have done in this person's place?

5. What grade did you get?

6. Will you give me an example of that?

7. How are you feeling about your transfer?

8. Do you like that person?

9. I think the other employee is absolutely wrong. What do you think?

10. Do you love me?

REPORT ON A BUSINESS ORGANIZATION *(Individual Activity)*

Purpose: To improve research skills by investigating a company for which you might like to work. To report orally to the class.

Briefing: One of the skills that is most useful in seeking a job is obtaining information about a business organization to which you might apply for a job. Select a company for which you might like to work. Research to find answers to the questions listed below. Share this information by making a five-minute report to the class. Information other than the answers to the questions listed below also may be included:

Sources of Information:

Information-seeking interviews with employers, recruiters, or career counselors. Printed resources available in the public library, the chamber of commerce, or from the organization you are researching:

company advertising
company annual reports
trade periodicals
city chamber of commerce directory
state chamber of commerce directory
The Wall Street Journal
Business Week
Standard Directory of Advertisers (two volumes: classified edition and geographical edition)

Thomas' Register of American Manufacturers
Moody's Industrial Manual
MacRae's Blue Book—Corporate Index
Standard & Poor's Industrial Index
Standard & Poor's Register of Corporations, Directors, and Executives
The College Placement Annual
Dun & Bradstreet Middle Market Directory

Use these questions as a guide to determine the information to be included in your oral report:

1. What are the products or services of the organization?
2. Where are its plants, offices, or stores located?
3. What is its growth record?
4. What is its financial status?
5. How old is the organization?
6. What is the history of its development?
7. Are there plans for expansion?
8. How does the company rank in industry?
9. What were the company's gross sales last year?
10. If the company sells, to whom does it sell?
11. What kind of public image does the company have?
12. Who are the company's major competitors?
13. What is the organizational structure of the company?
14. What is the personnel turnover rate in the organization?
15. What are some job titles for entry-level positions in your field?
16. What kind of training do new employees get?
17. What kinds of salary ranges are offered by the company for entry-level jobs in your field?

PRACTICE QUESTIONS FOR AN EMPLOYMENT INTERVIEW *(Individual Activity)*

Briefing: The interviewer uses an extensive series of questions to obtain information about your personality, personal interests, goals, and educational and employment history. You must be prepared to communicate positive information about yourself and to present relevant information about your abilities. You can prepare yourself by thinking through the answers to the questions below. Then answer the questions orally. Try to clarify and amplify the information you give. It is helpful if you tape-record your answers and listen to them.

1. Tell me about yourself. (The interviewer may be assessing your poise and personal style. Select what is most interesting about your background, personality, and job interests, and phrase the information in three to five sentences. Talk comfortably about yourself in positive terms.)

2. How would you describe yourself? (The interviewer may be trying to determine personality characteristics and how you get along with other people.)

3. Tell me about your hobbies or what you do with your spare time. (Supply information about your activities that would benefit the company or relate to the job for which you are applying.)

4. What is your greatest weakness? (The interviewer wants to know if you can be objective about your shortcomings. Your answer should demonstrate that you know yourself well and have overcome some of your failings.)

5. Do you like routine work? regular hours?

6. What do you do to keep in good physical condition?

7. In what school activities have you participated? Which did you enjoy most?

8. Do you plan to continue your education?

9. Why did you choose your particular field of work?

10. What qualifications do you have that make you feel you will be successful in your field?

11. What jobs have you held? How were they obtained, and why did you leave?

12. What business and personal communication skills have you learned from some of the jobs you have held?

13. Which of your jobs did you like best? (The interviewer may be asking if this is the right kind of work and the right environment for you.)

14. Why do you want to work for this company? (This is a chance to show your knowledge of the company and how your skills and career goals can contribute to the organization.)

15. What interests you about our product or services?

16. Why should I hire you? (The question may seem aggressive, but it is designed to test your ability to sell yourself and handle stress.)

17. Can you travel or work overtime? (This is an indirect way of finding out if family responsibilities tie you down. Point out that you are flexible, yet set some limits on your availability.)

18. Where do you see yourself five years from now? (The interviewer is seeking a sense of how realistic you are. Keep your answer general and avoid discussing your personal life.)

19. Do you have any questions? (Be prepared to ask several specific questions which reveal that you have done your homework on the company before the interview.)

ROLE PLAYING AN INTERVIEW *(Dyads)*

Purpose: To assume the roles of interviewer and interviewee. To participate in a portion of a mock interview in front of the class. To answer questions orally which might be asked in an employment interview.

Briefing:

1. Select five questions from the list on page 311.

2. Before class, talk through the answers to these questions aloud. Determine how you would reply if an employment interviewer asked these questions.

3. In class, choose a partner. Give the person a slip of paper on which the five questions you have selected are written.

4. The two of you are to sit in front of your classmates and role play an interview situation. One of you is the interviewee. The other is the interviewer.

5. To start the one-to-one interaction, the interviewer may introduce himself or herself and ask the interviewee some simple questions to help establish rapport. Then the interviewer is to ask one question from the list of five. The interviewee is to answer as though in an actual interview situation.

6. The interviewer may ask other questions based on the answer (secondary questions). In fact, a skillful interviewer listens intently to the reply and pulls the next question from the responses. When you have completed your exploration of the primary question together, you may stop.

7. Terminate this brief mock interview in a skillful manner.

8. You and your partner may reverse roles and repeat the exercise.

9. Before you begin your mock interview, tear out and give the critique sheet on page 313 to your instructor. You will be evaluated during your turn as the interviewee.

Debriefing:

1. What did you learn about your poise in an interview situation?

2. What did you learn about preparation in advance of an interview?

Name _____ Class _____ Score _____

MOCK INTERVIEW CRITIQUE SHEET *(Instructor's Evaluation)*

Briefing: Tear out this page and hand it to your instructor before your mock interview.

POSSIBLE POINTS: 50

1. You did well in using these speech tools:

    a. *Perception*—understood the question, were prepared to present insight into yourself, were able to see the interviewer's point of view. (5 points)   _____

    b. *Language*—chose appropriate words, were fluent in expressing what you wanted to say, were careful to find a common language. (5 points)   _____

    c. *Speaking*—clearly audible to the whole class; seemed spontaneous, communicative, and enthusiastic; were descriptive and concrete in your answer. (5 points)   _____

    d. *Listening*—focused on the interviewer's questions, listened to and interpreted secondary questions well. (5 points)   _____

    e. *Nonverbal communication*—handled voice and body so as to appear poised and in control; paid attention to the nonverbal clues of the interviewer. (5 points)   _____

    f. *Feedback*—used paraphrasing to understand the interviewer's questions. (5 points)   _____

2. You seemed to participate actively in the one-to-one speech encounter. (10 points)   _____

3. You created a favorable impression through the way you presented yourself. (10 points)   _____

Total   _____

Instructor's Comments

Words of Praise:

Suggestions for Improvement:

DICTATION PRACTICE *(Group Activity)*

Purpose: To speak clearly so that the message can be written down. To separate instructions to the receiver/transcriber from the message itself.

Briefing: Work in groups of five or six. One person is to choose one of the paragraphs below and dictate it orally to the others in her or his group. The listeners are to write the message. Remember that your receivers are not necessarily trained in secretarial skills and probably will write in longhand. Watch for the nonverbal clues that indicate the speed at which you should dictate. Adjust your pacing. Include punctuation, spelling, etc.

Receivers are to close their books, listen to the oral message, and write only the message to be transcribed. When the speaker has finished dictating, the receivers are to turn in their papers to the dictator to be checked for accuracy. Each member of the group should have an opportunity to dictate one of the paragraphs or a message of his or her own.

Voice Writing Exercises*

1. This is (*give your name and spell it*) speaking. This is to be a short business letter of four paragraphs, correction, of three paragraphs, addressed to Higginbotham and Bowe Realtors, 775 17th and M Streets, N.W., Washington, DC 20036-1125. Ladies and Gentlemen:

2. This is (*give your name and spell it*) speaking. This is a three-paragraph letter. The address is on the letter that I am answering. First paragraph. Thank you for writing to us about your long-distance call to Dr. L. M. Thornell, 813-751-3478, St. Augustine, Florida. Second paragraph. In view of the facts as you have so well reviewed them, we are promptly canceling the charge of $4.60—the unpaid balance shown on our records. Please consider the matter closed. Third paragraph. You have our gratitude for your prompt and courteous replies to our inquiries. Your cooperation helps us to keep our service standards high.

3. This is (*give your name and spell it*). This is a three-paragraph letter. The address is on this letter. First paragraph. Please send me a new, compressed-air closing device for the Luxe-Art aluminum screen door (Model 27D) that I ordered from you on August 3. Paragraph. After fitting the door into place, I found that the automatic closing device did not operate, apparently because of a defective compressed-air valve. Paragraph. I shall appreciate promptly receiving a new compressed-air valve and instructions for installing it.

4. This is (*give your name and spell it*). This is a three-paragraph letter of adjustment. It goes to the address on the letter which I will give you. First paragraph. Thank you for your thoughtfulness in writing on September 7 and for sending in the package of dull blades. You will receive some of the keenest blades in the world to replace the ones you returned. Paragraph. Enclosed is a package of 25 blades. We are giving you five super stainless steel Omnibus blades for each one you returned. These are yours with our compliments. You will enjoy new shaving luxury from the feather-honed, high-chrome, polymer-coated, Swedish stainless steel edges. Paragraph. Please let us know your reaction to your new Omnibus blades.

5. This is (*give your name and spell it*). This is the final paragraph of a letter I dictated this morning to a customer. Please take this down and correct and retype the letter. Third paragraph. This is what we are doing (*colon, capital "F"*). First of all (*comma*) we are asking the shipping clerk to send a brand

---

* Paragraphs 2-5 are adapted from Morris Philip Wolf and Robert R. Aurner, *Effective Communication in Business*, 6th ed. (Cincinnati: South-Western Publishing Co., 1974), pp. 396, 402–403, 410.

(*hyphen*) new book (*comma*) and heaven help her if she doesn't. (*That's apostrophe "t."*) (*New sentence.*) Then we are going to say this (*colon, capital "Y"*). You can have your money back in addition to the new book (*comma*) or we will do any other thing that will convince you that we are a fairly decent lot of folks here.

Debriefing: Collect the papers from your listeners. Circle errors by reading them against the paragraph that you dictated. Use the following self-analysis to determine which of your speaking skills you need to improve. Ask for feedback from the others in your group.

Name _____ Class _____ Score _____

SELF-ANALYSIS OF SPEECH SKILLS *(Individual Activity)*

List below the words missed on more than two of the papers written from your dictation.

1. *Check your speaking errors:*

    a. I did not articulate clearly. (mumbled) _____

    b. I was not loud enough to be heard over other distracting noises. (failure to project) _____

    c. I spoke at too rapid a pace for my listeners to write accurately. (failure to adjust rate) _____

    d. I did not phrase clearly. (pauses and inflection patterns not accurate) _____

2. *Check your communication errors:*

    a. I failed to read the nonverbal clues of my transcribers. (did not spell words, indicate punctuation, etc.) _____

    b. I did not permit enough feedback from my receivers/transcribers. _____

HOOK-UP SPEECH COMMUNICATION *(Dyads)*

Purpose: To participate with a classmate in a one-to-one discussion of a problem. To use empathetic listening, thoughtful feedback, and open-ended questions to stimulate interaction and sharing.

Briefing: Choose one of the following methods of dividing into dyads after reading the instructions below. One person will play Role A and the other Role B.

1. Pull numbers from an envelope and find your partner by the matching number.

2. The instructor may arbitrarily assign the dyads.

3. Students may select a partner.

Like electricity, communication sometimes needs a conductor. Your instructor will give you and your partner a piece of string about two feet long. Each of you will simply hold the string as you talk. Think of it as a two-way connection between you, and then forget it as you interact with each other.

Role A: Think of a problem which has been bothering you recently. You are to share this problem with the person playing Role B. Start right in and tell the other person about it. If you are not comfortable about sharing what you are really concerned about, you may select something not so personal. However, you will have a listener who will really pay attention to you as you talk honestly about your problem. Note if there is a change in your feelings by the time you have finished. Do not release your hold on your end of the string!

Role B: You are to play the role of a good listener as your partner talks to you. The first ground rule is to keep your attention focused on the other person as an individual. As Role A talks, think to yourself, "How does it really feel to be you?" Reflect to your partner your thoughtful attention. When you feel moved to talk, ask open-ended questions (those which cannot be answered "yes" or "no"), focus on feelings, and feed back your sincere interest. Be careful not to judge, evaluate, or advise. Your role is not to provide solutions but to help your partner go deeper into the subject. Encourage your partner to extend his or her thinking and see the topic in a new light. Keep holding on to your end of the string!

Debriefing: When the time is up (approximately 20 minutes), answer the questions for the role you have just filled. When you both have completed the questions, reverse the roles. The person who has just played Role A will now listen, and the person who just played Role B will share a problem. Take hold of the string again. At the end of the second discussion, fill out the evaluation sheet on the back of this page.

Name _____ Class _____ Score _____

HOOK-UP SPEECH COMMUNICATION EVALUATION SHEET *(Individual Activity)*

Role A

1. Did your feelings about your partner affect the topic you chose to discuss? Did you deal with a problem of real concern to you? Did you switch topics when you found out who your partner was?

2. What kinds of things did Role B do that made it easy for you to share more deeply?

3. Describe your feelings at the beginning of the 20 minutes. How did you feel at the end of the time? Did the string make a difference?

Role B

1. Do you think it was easier to share with Role A after hearing Role A discuss his or her problem?

2. What things did you do that made it easy for Role A to talk to you?

3. Do you think the string hook-up made it easier for you to listen to Role A?

PRACTICE IN FEEDBACK *(Individual Activity)*

Purpose: To practice the skill of paraphrasing (feeding back what you understand the speaker to say). To restate speech messages to check your own understanding.

Briefing: Before you respond to another person's speech message, you often need to verify that you have received the message accurately. To feed back the content of a message, begin with such phrases as, "Do I understand correctly that you said," "Are you saying," "Am I interpreting that you mean," or "Do I hear you saying." For example:

Message: "I want you to tell this person there will be no more charges to this account."

Paraphrase: "Do I hear you saying this person is not to charge again until the balance is paid?" *or*

Paraphrase: "Do you mean you will not approve any sales on this account until the customer reestablishes a pay record?" *or*

Paraphrase: "Do I hear you saying that regardless of how the customer pays on the account, there are to be no more charges on this account?"

Restate what you think the message says. Do not parrot the words. You are not *repeating* but rather *restating*—either more generally or more specifically. Remember, you are checking your *understanding*, not whether you believe the speaker to be right or wrong.

Message One: "We're closed."

Your Paraphrase:

Message Two: "This is for authorized personnel only."

Your Paraphrase:

Message Three: "For true efficiency in business management, observe the most prosperous organization near you."

Your Paraphrase:

Message Four: "We are looking for a mature individual who can learn new procedures quickly, adapt to others easily, and assume a responsible position in our company."

Your Paraphrase:

Message Five: "Thank you for taking care of my April 26 order so promptly. But I found, upon opening the shipment, that one of the items—the slotted spoon rack—was unsatisfactory."

Your Paraphrase:

FURTHER PRACTICE IN FEEDBACK *(Individual Activity)*

Purpose: To practice the skill of feeding back to determine the intent of the speaker's message.

Briefing: It is often important to restate the message received from a speaker in order to check your understanding of *why* the speaker is saying those words or in order to verify the speaker's feelings. This is called feeding back for *intent*. This type of feedback often begins with the words, "You feel . . . ?" "Do I hear you expressing the feeling . . . ?" The speaker, of course, is the only person who can tell you if you have responded correctly. For example:

Message: "The concept of human rights is in the air, and the U.S. is *the* dynamic force in the world that will advance progress toward social justice."

Response: "Do I understand you to feel that the United States must lead the other nations in establishing an idea whose time has come?"

Message: "The sun dress you are wearing does not project the image of a banker."

Response: "Do you mean that you would rather I not wear this dress on the job?"

Write a response focusing on the intent of the speaker. Restate what you perceive as the speaker's intent. Do not just repeat. Do not challenge the speaker's motives or feelings. You are feeding back only *to check your sense* of the speaker's intent.

Message One: "Our company does not have many more copies of our *Advertising Designs* left, but we will let you take one of the few we have."

Your Response:

Message Two: "I know that you are an extremely busy person with extra assignments that you recently received, and I know that you are bothered a great deal by people who ask for favors."

Your Response:

Message Three: "Just as I began to dictate a letter to you, a co-worker told me about your promotion and new title. Your company has picked the right person for area supervisor."

Your Response:

Message Four: "The package with my birthday present in it just arrived. Thank you for remembering me. The vase was shattered in a million pieces, but I could see it had an attractive shape."

Your Response:

Message Five: "Would a high-grade, complete, personalized telephone answering service right here in Coronado Towers help you solve your office problems?"

Your Response:

PLAY THE MARKET* *(Group Activity)*

Purpose: To work together in dyads within a larger group. To discover what factors create competitive patterns of behavior.

Briefing:

1. Choose a partner and form a dyad. You and your partner are brokers who buy and sell goods on the open market.

2. Join three other dyads and number the dyads 1, 2, 3, and 4. Sit in this position:

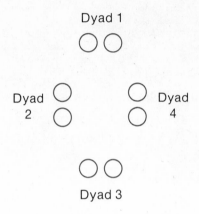

Dyad 1

Dyad 2   Dyad 4

Dyad 3

3. This is a *timed* exercise of ten rounds. You and your partner are to make a secret decision for each round. Choose to either "buy" or "sell" as you bid each time.

4. Begin with round 1. Circle your bid on the score sheet on page 322. Do not reveal your circled choice until the timekeeper tells you. Do not change your bid.

5. After each dyad has declared its bid orally, use the table on page 322 to determine whether your dyad won or lost money and record your amount for each round. Keep an accurate record of your balance.

6. Proceed through ten rounds with the timekeeper indicating when your group of brokers must announce your bids. Opening bids will be rotated clockwise around the dyads. Each dyad must have the opportunity to be first, second, third, and last bidder.

Stock Exchange Floor Rules:

1. You may not talk to the other dyads.

2. You may not signal nonverbally to other dyads.

3. You must keep your decision secret until it is your turn to announce it.

4. These rules will be suspended for three minutes before each bonus round (rounds 5, 8, and 10).

---

* Adapted from an exercise developed by William Gellermann, Ph.D., in J. Pfeiffer and J. Jones, *Structured Experiences for Human Relations Training*, Vol. II, published by University Associates, Inc., 1974.

Stock Market Results (Table for Scoring):

If there are 4 "sell" bids	. . . .	Each dyad loses $1,000
If there are 3 "sell" bids	. . . .	These 3 dyads win $1,000 each
1 "buy" bid	. . . .	This dyad loses $3,000
If there are 2 "sell" bids	. . . .	These 2 dyads win $2,000 each
2 "buy" bids	. . . .	These 2 dyads lose $2,000 each
If there are 1 "sell" bid	. . . .	This dyad wins $3,000
3 "buy" bids	. . . .	These 3 dyads lose $1,000 each
If there are 4 "buy" bids	. . . .	Each dyad wins $1,000

Score Sheet: Each dyad should use only one book to keep score.

ROUND	CIRCLE ONE	AMOUNT WON	AMOUNT LOST	TOTAL
1.	Buy or Sell	_____	_____	_____
2.	Buy or Sell	_____	_____	_____
3.	Buy or Sell	_____	_____	_____
4.	Buy or Sell	_____	_____	_____
5. (3 times amount)	Buy or Sell	_____	_____	_____
6.	Buy or Sell	_____	_____	_____
7.	Buy or Sell	_____	_____	_____
8. (5 times amount)	Buy or Sell	_____	_____	_____
9.	Buy or Sell	_____	_____	_____
10. (10 times amount)	Buy or Sell	_____	_____	_____
			FINAL TOTAL	_____

Debriefing:

1. How did you feel during this game?

2. What did you learn about your classmates and your interaction with them during this activity?

3. What factors are built into this game which create a competitive spirit (a win-lose situation)?

4. What did you do to persuade other dyads to bid your way?

5. What did you do and how did you feel when others would not listen to you?

BUSINESS COMMUNICATION PROBLEMS *(Group Discussion)*

Purpose: To discuss a communication problem in a business case. To use the problem-solving method.

Briefing: Work in groups of four or five. Choose Case 1, 2, or 3 as the basis for your discussion. Follow the steps of the problem-solving procedure listed below.

1. Read the case aloud.

2. Role play aloud the feelings of each person in the case. Do not role play a confrontation between individuals in the case, but rather permit each person to tell how she or he sees the case as if speaking to a good friend.

3. Discuss the communication barriers that you recognize in the case. Do not discuss solutions. Discuss the problem. Whose problem is it?

4. Identify any other factors in the case that cause barriers.

5. Role play again, expressing each individual's idea of an ideal solution.

6. List all the practical solutions that are available for each person in the case.

7. Make a recommendation. Who should initiate the action toward a solution? What action should be taken? How should the person go about it? What results may be expected?

Case 1: Transfer Interview

Maria Sainez, 32, is a supervisor of twelve employees at the Regional Telephone Office. Eleven of the twelve people under Maria's supervision are female. The twelfth person is 22-year-old David Newhaus. Maria has been employed by the telephone company for ten years. David has worked for the company for two and a half years. Maria has worked in the analytical office for the entire ten years of her employment. She was promoted to supervisor ten months ago. David transferred into the office five months ago. Before his transfer, he was a telephone operator in both the long-distance and directory-assistance departments.

The policy of the telephone company regarding transfers is as follows: when an employee is hired, the employee must stay in that position for six months, after which she or he may fill out a transfer form and be moved to another department. Of course, there must be an opening in the department requested.

The purpose of the analytical office at the telephone company is to conduct studies on businesses that want either larger or smaller telephone systems and to determine how the change in the system affects the businesses' income. The twelve employees in the analytical office work together in groups as they compile and analyze the data.

David has stated that he is dissatisfied with his work in the analytical department. Although he has been in the department for only five months, he has already filled out a transfer form and requested the next opening in the coin-collection department. The other employees have stated openly that they will be glad when the transfer comes through.

Case 2: Employment Interview

Data-An is a data processing company that provides computer services for businesses. Its services include bookkeeping, balancing accounts, and writing payrolls. It hires both full-time and part-time keypunch operators. Within the next month, the company will need two temporary employees to work full time during the period when two of the regular employees will be on maternity leave.

One of the employees who will go on leave is Ann Armstrong, a 23-year-old black woman who has been employed at Data-An for three years. She knew that her friend, 22-year-old Betty Moody, also black, had just completed a course in data processing at the Technical Institute and was a certified keypunch operator looking for a job. Ann telephoned Betty and suggested that since there would be a temporary opening at Data-An, it would be a good idea to apply for the position.

One of the policies at Data-An requires that all applicants be interviewed immediately after filling out an application. When Betty went to the Data-An office, she filled out the application form and returned it to John Smallson, age 48, the white receptionist for the firm. He thanked Betty for applying and said that the firm would call her. Several days later, Betty learned from Ann that her application had not been mentioned at the office. Ann spoke to Marlene Richards, the president and personnel director of Data-An, who indicated that she did not know of the application. By the time that Betty got this word from Ann, Betty had not received a call from the company, and Marlene Richards had left the city for a vacation.

Case 3: Reprimand Interview

Reiko Yoshino and Gary Dunn work together in customer relations at the Craft Leather Company. Both of them are clerks who take orders and complaints over the telephone. Reiko Yoshino has worked for Craft Leather for two and a half years, and Gary Dunn has worked there for nine months. Stan Stein is the manager who hired Reiko and Gary.

One morning in August, Martha Cummins, the supervisor, came into the office and discovered that Gary was away from his desk. She looked around and found that the other five clerks were on the telephone with customers. During the next three hours, Martha came into the customer relations department three times. Each time she noticed that Gary was not at his desk. On the third visit Martha questioned Reiko about Gary's whereabouts. Reiko reported that she had seen Gary at his desk earlier, but that she did not know where he was at the time.

The following morning, Martha called Gary into her office and spoke to him about his behavior. Martha stressed the company policy about the clerks' responsibilities to the customers and the incoming telephone calls. Gary said he understood and Martha excused him to go back to work.

During the next two weeks, Martha observed Gary's absence from his desk on four occasions. On one occasion she found Gary in another department talking with another employee. Another time Martha saw Gary in Mr. Stein's office making a personal phone call. On two other occasions, Gary was not to be found at his desk.

One day when Martha came into the office to speak to Reiko, she noticed that the telephone light on Reiko's desk flashed ten times during their conversation and that no one answered the call. Martha checked the clerks and discovered that Gary was reading a magazine at his desk while each of the other clerks was on the telephone taking incoming calls. Martha notified Gary that she wanted to see him at 3:00 that afternoon. Before the appointment with Gary, Martha went into Mr. Stein's office and told him that she would appreciate his action in dispensing with Gary's services. She stated her reasons to Mr. Stein. Mr. Stein told Martha that he would handle the problem but that he did not feel that such drastic action was necessary.

CHECKLIST OF COMMUNICATION TERMS *(Quiz)*

Check your understanding of the communication terms presented in this chapter by writing the number of the correct term in the blank preceding its definition. Note there are more terms than definitions.

Definitions

a. _____ One-to-one meeting in which an employee is judged on behavior and job performance.

b. _____ Two people meeting to talk together.

c. _____ Unwritten rules of behavior and speech communication on the job.

d. _____ A level of communication exemplified by nodding or saying "Hello" to another employee.

e. _____ Messages concerning the task to be done.

f. _____ A "lose-lose" approach to a solution, often leaving both people dissatisfied.

g. _____ A one-to-one meeting in which both people set up the meeting, define the goals, and decide how these are to be achieved.

h. _____ A level of communication at which a great deal of self is invested, trust is built, and personal concerns and feelings are shared.

i. _____ One of several steps during which the conflict is defined interpersonally.

j. _____ One-to-one meeting in which one person presents himself or herself to another person to be considered for a position in a company.

Terms

1. dyad
2. job-related messages
3. people-related messages
4. interview
5. interviewee
6. interviewer
7. recognition level
8. chit-chat level
9. minor investment of self level
10. major investment of self level
11. styles of conflict management
12. confrontation
13. competition
14. accommodation
15. compromise
16. avoiding
17. stages in conflict management
18. purpose of meeting
19. business communication etiquette
20. directive interview
21. nondirective interview
22. employment interview
23. counseling interview
24. reprimand interview
25. evaluation interview
26. business telephone call
27. transcriber/receiver

CHAPTER 10

Let's Talk About the Business of Work Teams—Communicating in Small Groups

This chapter will help you understand the dynamics of group communication that operate in the workplace. Through your understanding of how groups operate, you can adjust your behavior to serve as a successful group member. After you have studied this chapter, you should be able to do the following:

Chapter Objectives

1. Identify the dynamic factors found within the group and those outside factors that affect the group.
2. List types of task-oriented and process-oriented behavior and how each contributes to group discussions.
3. Explain three factors that must be attended to if a group is to be successful.
4. Discuss two methods by which a group may organize its task.
5. List the ways that groups arrive at decisions.

"One can do worse than think of a business organization as a hierarchy of committees."

John Kenneth Galbraith

Human beings like to gather in groups. They meet together to talk and laugh, to play and work. But a businessperson may sigh, "I have a meeting this afternoon. There goes another three hours when nothing gets done." You probably have felt the same way and chuckled knowingly when you heard the definition, "A committee is a gathering of the unfit, appointed by the unwilling, to do the unnecessary." Or perhaps, "A conference is something at which, after all is said and done, more is said than done." If group meetings were always productive, there probably would be fewer jokes about them. Perhaps many business meetings do waste time, money, and talk, but not when employees understand the dynamics of group communication. That is what this chapter is all about.

In recent years U.S. business organizations have begun to use the Japanese approach to management to increase efficiency and productivity. This approach is to reduce the barriers of job status levels and provide opportunities for workers and managers to cooperate to solve problems and make decisions. It is interesting to note the benefits derived by business organizations who shift to small task-oriented groups for some decision making:

1. Input from a number of organizational levels can be gained in face-to-face meetings.
2. Information and feedback from a number of sources are readily available.
3. Decisions made by groups are often easier to put into action than individual decisions.
4. People participating in work groups learn to appreciate the capabilities of their fellow workers.
5. Employees who are involved in work groups feel a sense of responsibility and loyalty to their organizations.

Both employees and organizations benefit from group meetings in which people interact. Meetings can be improved if people have realistic expectations about goals, group dynamics, and the contributions each one can make.

It would be a lonely business world if people did not interact in conducting business. People have to work together. It should not surprise you to find yourself employed in a position where your manager expects you to be a member of a problem-solving or decision-making group working out matters concerning your job. When this happens, you can be armed with some knowledge of how work groups operate. Two things are important to remember. First, business meetings have a job or **task** to be accomplished. Second, the work is achieved through a social **process** or interaction between people working together as a team. Both the task and the process are influenced by a number of factors that create changes in the task and process.

GROUP DYNAMICS

A **work team** may be defined as a collection of individuals interacting for some specific organizational purpose. **Group dynamics** refers to those factors that affect the way the group operates. Some of these factors are found *within* the group itself; others are forces from the *outside* that affect group interaction and decision making, such as group size and the time and place of the meeting.

Outside Factors Affecting Group Dynamics

Group Size. A work group is generally fairly small, five to seven members. There are several reasons for this:

1. Each person can interact with each of the others face-to-face.
2. Each person, even the shy and less assertive members of the group, has an opportunity to share views.

3. The odd number permits majority decision making while encouraging clearly recognized dissent.
4. The work load can be distributed evenly among a few people.

Group size also affects the kinds and number of interpersonal relationships possible within a group. In a work group of five individuals talking together, there are ten possible interpersonal exchanges. The number of people in the group multiplied by the number of people that any one person can speak to—divided by two—equals the number of possible lines of communication within a group. (See Figure 10-1.) The number of communication lines possible in a work group of six people would be 15. The more people, the greater the number of possible lines of communication. This means that the people in a small group, if they interact with the others, are constantly adjusting their thinking and message responses to others. Clearly, then, communication problems within a group can increase with the size of the group.

FIGURE 10-1

A work group of five members has 10 possible lines of communication. With only one more person added to the group, the possibilities jump to 15.

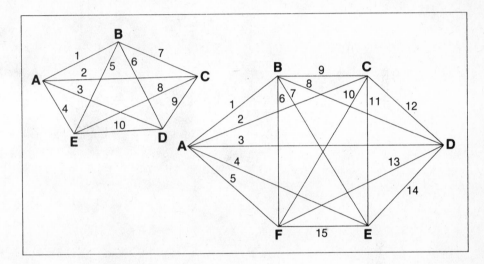

Time and Place. Where and when a group meets is important. The time, place, setting, occasion, and space arrangements affect working relationships. Consider the importance of time. Work groups need several hours to accomplish their tasks. Each person must be freed from other responsibilities to spend the time working with a group.

The meeting place for a work group also affects the group members. People need to get to the meeting place easily. Whether the meeting is held in an office, in a conference room, or at a work station, it should be within reach of the members. The location of the meeting area should provide easy access to reference materials, reports, and a telephone if these are needed for a group decision.

The physical setting and arrangement of space are critical in developing a climate for interaction. If the individuals are meeting as equals (same status level within an organization), each should sit at an equal distance from each other. In a leaderless group, the physical environment must draw the members together. Each should see and hear easily and should be close enough to feel a sense of unity.

In a meeting room where people sit around a table, the individual who elects to sit at the head of the table, rather than next to someone else, may be regarded as the leader or chairperson by the other members. Often this seat is taken by the person who called the meeting or by a person of higher status in the organization. When there is no leader, however, where a person chooses to sit may indicate the person's feelings about others. An individual who selects the seat at the head of the table may be indicating a "loner" position. Because the shape of the table itself may detract from the unity of the group, some groups use a round table for meetings to ensure that no one is sitting apart from the others and everyone has equal status.

One other factor that may affect the work of a team is the presence of other people who are not involved in the discussion. These "other" people can change the group interaction. For example, a secretary may be present to take notes, or someone may be sitting in just to observe the meeting. To be overheard by one who is not involved in the discussion may distract some members of the group and limit their participation.

PHOTO 10-1

Using a round table ensures equal positions for the participants in a meeting.

Factors Within a Group Affecting Dynamics

Participants. The group members themselves form the greatest force affecting the dynamics of a work group. Besides the task to be done, there is also the process of maintaining the group of people as a functioning unit. Attention must be paid to how the group members feel about the task and about each other. And each person arrives at a meeting with his or her own set of individual needs:

$$\frac{\text{Individual}}{\text{Needs}} + \frac{\text{Group}}{\text{Process}} + \text{Task} = \text{Work Group}$$

All three aspects are important to the work group.

People work well with some people and not as well with others. This is not surprising! People are complex. While we like to believe that our decisions are logical and analytical, based on sound reasoning and factual evidence, this is sometimes not true. While people are creatures of logic, they are also emotional, subjective, sensitive, and whimsical. Their motivations often revolve around self-interest and unconscious needs and drives called **hidden agendas**.

These hidden agendas often affect our interactions. Messages are heard in terms of personal needs. Responses spring from emotional reactions. Messages that seem logical to a speaker may be loaded with hidden meanings. And speakers cannot always predict how each listener will respond. Imagine the complexity of a maze of interactions between five individuals talking business.

If group members are aware of the opportunity, four specific needs can be met for individuals: the need for security or safety, the social need of belonging to the group, the ego need of recognition by others, and the need for self-fulfillment. Low group morale results if individual needs are ignored. Clearly, then, communication problems within a group increase if the people do not know each other and concentrate merely on the task. When members of a work group have different status levels in an organization, the hidden agendas may be even more complicated. For example, when a business group meets, it does so for a specific reason. Yet each member has private needs—for inclusion, for control, for recognition. Because of differences in status levels, members of the lower-status group may hesitate to speak out and, therefore, may feel uncomfortable. Members of the higher-status group may compete for leadership roles, and thus use the group for their own personal needs. It may be difficult to communicate when personal agendas get in the way of the group's designated purpose.

Cohesiveness and Climate. Two other factors affect the dynamics of a group. A **cohesive** group is one in which the people work well together. In this case, the individuals influence each other, get personal satisfaction from being a part of the group, recognize their dependence upon each other, and are willing to assume specialized roles to accomplish the group task. The atmosphere produced by this cohesiveness is known as **climate**. When the climate is right, group members:

1. Exhibit high morale within the group.
2. Discuss questions with lots of give-and-take.
3. Have a sense of involvement with others.
4. Use disagreements to extend their interaction and to clear the air.
5. Show a commitment to company goals.
6. Contribute to the group without commands, threats, or pressure.
7. Move the task forward in an organized fashion.
8. Maintain a sense of humor.

The camaraderie established by members of such work groups develops positive attitudes toward the organization and helps shape a sense of worth and integrity for each member of the team.

"If men would consider not so much wherein they differ as wherein they agree, there would be far less of uncharitableness and angry feeling in the world."

Joseph Addison

MEETING STRUCTURES

Organizations rely on subgroups of people to meet together to do a variety of tasks. These group meetings are called by various names: committees, conferences, business meetings, seminars, forums, executive sessions, task forces, etc. Each one may have a different number of people. Each group may meet one time or several times, or may exist as an ongoing group, such as a regular departmental meeting. Nonetheless, each group will meet for a specific purpose related to the work of the organization. For example, there are:

1. Staff meetings for fact-finding or information.
2. Production meetings for problem solving.
3. Committee meetings for policymaking or decision making.
4. Training meetings for informing or instructing new employees.
5. Task-force meetings for brainstorming.

These work-group meetings are of two general types: (1) one-way meetings where people have little opportunity to interact, and (2) give-and-take meetings where people are expected to interact.

One-Way Meetings

Often a meeting is called by upper-level people to pass on information. Such a meeting is:

1. Structured with a specific agenda (list of items to be discussed is prepared in advance).
2. Conducted with a designated leader who presides.
3. Arranged so the leader sits or stands in a focused position.
4. Limited as to the amount of interaction between group members.
5. Guided by questions and answers directed through the leader.

Some one-way meetings are very formal, with members required to raise their hands to speak. Others are less formal, with members sometimes speaking directly to one another. However, there is always a group leader who takes charge and manages the discussion.

Give-and-Take Meetings

More frequently, though, businesspeople meet as work teams in less structured situations. They come together to bring their expertise to a job-oriented situation. They are expected to provide give-and-take interaction. At these meetings, the members:

1. Identify the common purpose but do not set up a planned agenda.
2. Communicate on a horizontal level with each other.
3. Develop leadership from within the group.
4. Work out individual roles within the group itself.
5. Contribute ideas and information.
6. Handle the discussion by creating methods of proceeding.
7. Make decisions based on the group discussion.

More than ever, organizations are using **task-force** groups which are composed of individuals with different skills and knowledge to handle problem-solving or trouble-shooting situations. Within such groups one may find a variety of status levels and positions. The common goal is the task to be done. Managers, engineering specialists, operation researchers, and executives may meet in direct consultation with workers and ground-level technicians. In such meetings, the group is productive only as opportunities exist for each person to:

"You no longer have strict allegiance to hierarchy. You may have five or six levels of hierarchy represented at one meeting. You try to forget about salary level and hierarchy, and organize to get the job done."

Frank Metzger

1. Interact with others.
2. Give and receive information.
3. Contribute to the decision making.
4. Find and fill a useful group role.

ORGANIZING GROUP TASKS

If a work team of employees is charged with the responsibility of solving a problem in a give-and-take situation, how does the group approach the job to be done?

A work group is a social process. Let's say a team is meeting together for the first time. There must be a time for social speaking and listening, for action and reaction. On the surface, the individuals appear to be discussing the task. Actually, they are setting up group **norms** (patterns of behavior) and discovering their relationships to each other. If there is to be interaction in a comfortable climate, people must get to know each other. Each must have some idea of what to expect from other team members. It takes some time before the basic climate is established and the group can move into the task in earnest.

There are generally two ways in which a discussion can be handled: one is a logical and analytical method known as problem solving; the other is a freewheeling, creative procedure called brainstorming.

Problem-Solving Method

The **problem-solving** approach requires the group to follow a step-by-step procedure in discussion. It is important to have a leader who is willing to take a dominant role in moving the group through each step. Obviously the group will follow this method more successfully if each member is familiar with the pattern. The problem-solving pattern usually follows this series of steps:

"A problem is an opportunity in work clothes."

Henry J. Kaiser, Jr.

1. **The problem is identified.** It is helpful to state the problem in question form. There are three kinds of questions:
   a. **Questions of fact** ask whether a statement (condition, proposal, issue, etc.) is true or false. "Is our recent advertising campaign paying off in terms of increased sales?" Thus: "The problem is that our advertising campaign is not increasing our sales."
   b. **Questions of value** ask that the subject be judged in terms of worth (good/bad, reliable/unreliable, superior/inferior, etc.). "Are our hiring practices effective?" Thus: "The problem is to develop more effective methods of hiring people."
   c. **Questions of policy** require decisions on future actions. "Shall we introduce our newest product through a national advertising campaign or a regional door-to-door promotion?" Thus: "The problem is to determine the best method to introduce our product."
2. **The problem is analyzed.** After the problem is clearly stated, the basic issues must be considered. At this point the members of the group specifically consider all the "who, what, when, where, why, and how" data that relate to the problem. These questions are asked and answered by the group:
   a. To whom does the problem belong?
   b. What are the basic causes of the problem?

c. How do we know something needs to be changed?

d. What are the symptoms of the problem?

e. What effects is the problem creating?

3. **Criteria for judging solutions are decided.** People in groups often disagree about the solutions to problems. It is helpful, therefore, to take a few minutes to discover what each person wants the solution to do. Rather than discussing any one solution, the group at this point should describe a set of goals that an ideal solution should achieve. These standards—or **criteria**—will serve as a basis for judging the strengths and weaknesses of the practical solutions. These criteria should be listed on a chalkboard. Perhaps agreement on such criteria as these can be reached:

a. The solution will satisfy everyone involved in the problem. (This certainly would be an ideal standard to achieve.)

b. The solution will not create problems greater than the problem it solves.

c. The solution will be practical to put into effect.

d. The solution will not cost more than the present problem costs in time and money.

e. The solution will reduce the major causes of the problem.

4. **Possible solutions are listed.** Now the group is ready to list all possible solutions that members can generate. Three or four solutions are selected from this list for discussion.

5. **Solutions are evaluated.** Each of the solutions will have merit. Each will have some disadvantages. No solution will meet all the criteria on which the group has decided. By checking every solution against the criteria, the group weighs the pros and cons of each.

6. **A decision is reached.** If the problem has been analyzed carefully and if the group agrees on the most important criteria that the solution should meet, a decision can be made. One of the solutions is chosen. Remember, each group member must be free to discuss and share ideas during each step along the way to the decision.

Groups move slowly through the problem-solving process. It takes time to contribute information, struggle with issues, and describe the criteria. Problems have no easy solutions. Because of the investment such decisions involve, company work groups that are entrusted with decision-making powers proceed carefully through the problem-solving method.

Brainstorming Method

Another pattern that groups use to solve problems attacks the issue in a different way. **Brainstorming** sessions are unstructured meetings designed to stimulate creative thinking on a particular problem. Members of the work group give free rein to their ideas. This is how the discussion operates:

"Imagination is more important than knowledge."

Albert Einstein

1. There is no tightly knit structure, no pressure to arrive at a decision; each participant is encouraged to take an active part.

2. Individuals are encouraged to think aloud and speculate. "Off-the-top-of-the-head" ideas are welcomed and considered.

3. Members agree in advance that no one is to judge, criticize, or put down another person's views.

4. Individuals can express ideas that may or may not be in accord with their personal viewpoints.

5. Members are free to role play different viewpoints. One might take the role of the customer, while another represents the company. One may represent management; another, labor, etc.

Chapter 10   Work Teams—Communicating in Small Groups

PHOTO 10-2

Brainstorming stimulates creative thinking by permitting the free flow of ideas from all members of the group.

6. The group controls the discussion and the decision making, and the leadership may change several times during the meeting.

In this kind of brainstorming session, people spark each other. They catch fire spontaneously from the ideas of others. From these free and open discussions evolve new and creative approaches to problems.

"Creative ideas do not spring from groups. They spring from individuals."

Whitney Griswold

MAINTAINING THE GROUP PROCESS

Three things must be paid attention to if a group is to be successful: the task, the maintenance of the group process, and individual needs. Maintenance of the group process depends upon (1) the kind of leadership provided, (2) the roles the members use in their interactions, and (3) the types of decision making used by the group.

Leadership Responsibilities

There are several reasons that a group may have a designated leader: (1) because of that person's status in the company; (2) because that person is perceived to have more knowledge about the topic than other members of the group; or (3) because of certain qualities of personality. If there is a designated leader, that person has certain responsibilities to perform:

"A great leader never sets himself above his followers except in carrying responsibilities."

Jules Ormont

1. Prepare an agenda or list of the topics to be discussed.
2. Inform group members of the time, place, and length of the meeting.
3. Arrange for appropriate meeting space.
4. Prepare background information on the topic.

During the meeting, that leader has a number of jobs to do:

1. Introduce topics; stimulate discussion.
2. Keep the group to the agenda.
3. Ask for information and opinions.
4. Keep group focused on one topic at a time.
5. Clearly state purpose of meeting; help group set goals.
6. Assist the group to set criteria to evaluate ideas.

7. Summarize to help group clarify issues.
8. Ask, "Are we ready to agree . . . ?"
9. Encourage participation.
10. Work to resolve conflicts.

Good leaders watch for cues that tell when to pull the group back to the agenda or when to relax the rules of procedure to permit free discussion.

Leadership Styles

People who lead groups use a variety of styles that range from strong control of the process to very little control at all. These may be identified through the leader's behavior:

High control. The leader decides and then tells the group what to do.
Persuasive control. The leader decides and then works to persuade the group to accept that decision.
Equal control. The leader joins the group as an equal and accepts the group decision.
Low control. The leader allows others to make a decision and agrees to support that decision.

In some groups, there may be no leader designated. The leader or leaders may arise from the group process. For example, you may evolve as a leader in a particular group because you are highly motivated, enthusiastic, and willing to take responsibility. The leader in this case derives power from the group and remains responsive to the group to continue as leader.

You can see that the kind of leadership a group has often determines how the group process will operate. Perhaps you will recognize the following descriptions of different groups:

1. **Autocratic style** (one person in charge). The individual who exhibits the "commander" type of leadership (because of position or knowledge) is likely to tell the group members what to do and how to do it. This is, of course, an efficient method of getting things done. It cuts down on wasted time (people do not interact as much), provides a tight structure for the meeting (an agenda is set up in advance), and makes it easier to assign work. A group operating with an autocratic leader may appear harmonious on the surface. Often, however, resentment and disagreement are not voiced in the meeting. Dissatisfaction may result.

2. **Democratic style.** A group operating under this style of leadership expects members of the group to initiate discussion, suggest procedures, and make final decisions. One person may take the lead in starting the discussion while another person leads in helping the group determine its goals. Members are free to decide on their common efforts and to evaluate the results. This style of leadership permits members to participate actively and requires them to take responsibility. Members generally find themselves involved in the discussion and often satisfied with the work accomplished.

3. **Permissive style.** In some groups, a leader never develops. The group may never decide on common goals and, as a consequence, the discussion drifts without direction. If no one person accepts a leadership role, and if the members are unwilling to make decisions or accept responsibility, little work is accomplished. Members often feel the meeting time is wasted.

In concluding this discussion of leadership, let us note that groups often work well with several leaders doing different things. For example, one leader pushes the task along and keeps the goal for the meeting in front of the group, while another focuses on the group needs. In this way, both the task and the process of group interaction are managed simultaneously.

Membership Roles

The behavior of group members is as important as the leadership roles. How members act determines whether the job gets done and whether the group feels satisfied with the meeting. To be successful as a group, each person must find a place on the team. Specifically, a person must feel that she or he has something to offer in terms of know-how and enthusiasm. Each one needs to be recognized for the unique contribution he or she can make to the team spirit or to the task.

Let's examine the ways in which individuals contribute to a group effort. People have special abilities. Some like to organize, initiate, or coordinate ideas. Others have a special knack for making people comfortable. Through empathetic listening, responsive feedback, or sociable behavior, these people set a relaxed climate for group work. Both roles contribute to a team effort.

People get to know each other during the initial meeting or the first part of a longer association. For example, people recognize that "Bill has good ideas" and that "Sarah is willing to summarize and ask for a decision." As the group recognizes the role of each member, the individual knows what the others expect of him or her. Each person finds a useful role in the group. As these behaviors become stable (recurring and predictable), they are accepted by the group. At this point, group members feel more at ease with one another, and the work of the group moves ahead.

When speaking about roles, we are referring to the behavior of individuals who work to get the job done (task-oriented roles) or those who concern themselves with how the members get along together (process-oriented roles).

Task-oriented behavior centers on the task to be done. The **task** is the purpose of the meeting or the specific goals to be achieved. The goals, which will be different for different types of meetings, may be to:

1. Collect information
2. Establish policy
3. Identify a problem
4. Solve a problem
5. Change behavior, etc.

For a group to operate successfully, each member must understand the task. When someone in the group talks about the job to be done, that person is working on the task and is focusing the discussion on the subject. Presented here are some examples of **task-oriented roles** that people may assume in group interaction:

Information seeker—one who asks for factual material based on knowledge or experience.

"Mr. Watanabe, you are our accountant. Do you have those figures handy?"

Information giver—one who provides factual information based on an area of expertise.

"Our records show we send 1,100 pounds of documents to Caribbean Data Services daily."

Opinion seeker—one who asks questions to see how members think or feel about a topic.

"I'm not sure of the extent we should get involved with foreign data processing at this time. Do any of you have thoughts on this?"

Opinion giver—one who states opinions based on experience and qualifies them as opinions.

"Well, it is my opinion that these skills are available at considerably lower cost than here in the U.S."

Initiator—one who is willing to start speech communication, set up procedure, define terms, organize ideas, suggest solutions, etc.

"Why don't we suggest all the possible solutions and then try to narrow them down?"

Summarizer—one who pulls together the various ideas, restates general points, tests group opinion, etc.

"As I see it, we have discussed two major solutions to this problem. Are we ready to make a decision at this point?"

Coordinator—one who speaks to clarify ideas by rephrasing, giving examples, showing relationships between different ideas, etc.

"Jack's idea is similar to the suggestion Billie made earlier—but it sets a time-table for getting it done."

Please understand that these task roles are not *assigned* to people in order to get the job done. Rather they are descriptive names for the kinds of behavior that people engage in when they are seeking to do a job by interacting with others. One person may play many roles or serve in a variety of functions during the course of a meeting.

You too will fill a number of these different task roles as you work with a group. You can be an information seeker as you ask questions, and an opinion giver when you share your experience. You can be a summarizer as you accept responsibility for structuring and organizing group thinking. You will be a contributing team member as you take various roles in the discussion.

The second type of behavior—**process-oriented behavior**—refers to the way that members maintain their relationships with each other. Conflicting ideas are bound to arise. Disagreements spring up. These must be resolved somehow. So, some group members take process-oriented roles to help group members get along with one another. These individuals develop two important attitudes within the group:

Cooperation—willingness to work agreeably with others and to view the outcome as profitable for all.

Collaboration—willingness to share and to learn from the ideas and experience of others.

Often you will serve your group successfully in a process-oriented role. You will work to maintain friendly relationships between members of the group. You may also speak to increase group spirit, to fill interpersonal needs for recognition, and to provide positive feedback. Here are some process-oriented roles that people may assume in group interaction:

Harmonizer—one who speaks to avoid conflict, to patch up misunderstandings, or to reduce tensions.

"Both Yu-lan and Sandra have offered excellent suggestions. I think we can work both ideas into our solution."

Climate maker—one who speaks to create a friendly, encouraging group atmosphere.

"I'm looking forward to hearing your ideas at this meeting."

Gatekeeper—one who speaks to bring others into the discussion, asks about feelings or reactions, etc.

"I'm not sure how you feel about this suggestion. Sue, what's your reaction?"

Standard setter—one who speaks to keep personal feelings out, to keep the group's objectivity, to maintain the momentum, or to set the model for good listening.

"I feel we're really making progress on this plan. Could we hear that explanation once again, Lucia?"

In short, as a good working member of a team, you can make a contribution with both task-oriented and process-oriented behaviors. You will carefully avoid roles that are destructive to the group or obstructive to accomplishing the task, such as:

Withdrawing—acting indifferent or bored.

Competing—clowning for attention, distracting the group from its purpose, aggressively blocking the ideas of others, monopolizing the conversation, etc.

Sidestepping—refusing to stick to the topic, interjecting personal topics, arguing on minor points, rejecting responsibility, etc.

Remember, a work group is a team effort. The behavior of the group members determines the group's success.

Decision Making

The way groups arrive at decisions is a third means of maintaining a successful and effective group process. Group members are often not aware of the ways by which groups reach a decision; they only know how they feel about the final result. Decisions range from rejected suggestions, on the one hand, to full and open discussions and a willingness by all members to support the solution, on the other. Often members will not all agree, but if they have the chance to express themselves and to listen to others, they will often be willing to give the decision a chance.

Decisions are made in a variety of ways:

1. **Plop**. One member of the group makes a suggestion and the other members ignore it. There lies the idea before them—exposed and unsupported—while the originator of the idea feels rejected and alone. This is negative decision making. The idea loses by default . . . plop!

2. **One-person decisions.** One person may volunteer to record the notes of the meeting. The group may agree. Or an individual with recognized authority or prestige may announce, "I think that we should use a tightly structured problem-solving method in this meeting." Because that individual is respected for his or her knowledge, leadership qualities, likability, trustworthiness, or status, the members of the group may voice no objection and the decision is made.

3. **Two-person decisions.** One person may propose an idea that is warmly supported by another group member. For example:

"Let's try the brainstorming method of solving this problem. It works. What do you say?"
"Good idea. I've never been in a group that permitted everyone to express any and all ideas without fear of being rejected. Besides, I like the idea of not following any structure."

Because of the enthusiasm of these two members, the rest of the group may go along with the idea and the decision is made. If, however, there is an objection, the decision may be lost.

4. **Majority vote.** A decision made by a show of hands or a voice vote will finalize a decision quickly. The majority of votes "for" or "against" an issue rules. As acceptable as this method is in reducing conflict (after all, the losers had a chance to express their views through the vote), people do not like to lose. A member who is constantly outvoted may withdraw from the discussion.

5. **Consensus taking. Consensus** means an agreement reached in harmony. Before a consensus can be reached, each member must be able to present her or his point of view, provide additional information, question other members, and use persuasive arguments. If the decision permits both sides to win in some areas while each compromises in areas of lesser importance, a wholehearted agreement may be reached. It is most important that individuals not feel threatened or rejected on the basis of the decision. A feeling of cooperation between members is essential.

Groups do not arrive at every decision the same way. After a two-hour meeting, it may be easy to arrive at a consensus to adjourn. But it may be difficult to arrive at a decision as to when to meet again. A majority vote may be taken to decide. But there may be disagreement about whether another meeting is needed. Further discussion takes place before a decision is made. Frequently much can be learned about a work team through its approach to decision making.

"It's not a sign of weakness to bargain as hard and as fairly as you know how, and then compromise in the interests of both sides."

Anonymous

IMPROVING WORK TEAMS

By now you understand something of the complexity of working with a group on a task. With this understanding, you are ahead of the game, for you will have some realistic views of what to expect in your small group meetings. The work of these task-oriented groups can be valuable to business, but these groups work best when its members know something about group dynamics.

Unrealistic Expectations

People who have had little experience in the study of group dynamics may condemn the whole process as unnecessary, inefficient, or a waste of time. Because they may not understand the process, they blame outside forces or the personalities of some members for what they consider failures of the meeting. And because the meetings do not proceed as they believe they should—efficiently following a planned agenda, everyone speaking clearly and to the point, all members involved, eager, and contributing equally, little discussion but rapid voting—these individuals feel thwarted by group meetings.

Realistic Expectations

You know better. You understand that group work requires considerable time as people try to understand each other as well as the topic for discussion. You recognize that people have short attention spans, speak from their own individual needs, seek recognition or fight for control, do not always cooperate or contribute. You know that some people are uncomfortable if the meeting is not tightly structured, and yet you realize the freedom to "kick ideas around" is important for building a relaxed climate. You are also aware that groups do not always approach problem solving directly; they may approach the issue in a circle beginning with solutions, then discussing the problem, setting goals, and arriving at consensus—all without a formal vote.

Using Your Skills

Because you remember that groups must operate at three levels—the task itself, the maintenance of the group process, and the filling of individual needs—you understand what is going on. If you are task-oriented yourself, you will assist by:

1. Helping to set goals.
2. Asking task-oriented questions to move the group along.
3. Summarizing when needed.
4. Helping to reduce conflicts or misunderstandings when they arise.

If you are naturally people-oriented, you will help the group by:

1. Showing sympathy and understanding.
2. Praising the efforts of others.
3. Urging harmony or unity.
4. Reducing tensions.
5. Expressing appreciation.

As you become more skillful in group work, you will become more and more comfortable in moving from one kind of role to another whenever it becomes necessary to keep the three levels of group work in balance. And when the leader of your group has problems in structuring the task or delegating work effectively, you will recognize the problem and carefully offer task-oriented suggestions. Without arousing resentment, you will assist the group to move forward by your willingness to serve as gatekeeper or harmonizer. Your understanding of group dynamics will make you a valuable member of the group.

Whatever your role in the group process—as the leader or as a participant—you will constantly practice your good communication skills:

1. Sharing ideas and feelings openly.
2. Listening to the content of messages as well as to the feelings that lie beneath the messages.
3. Feeding back what you are hearing so that message senders can verify your understanding.
4. Separating statements of fact from statements of inference while speaking and listening.
5. Keeping arguments centered on issues rather than on people.
6. Changing roles—shifting from task to process or vice versa—whenever a dynamic change is called for.

CHAPTER SUMMARY

Chapter 10 has listed the benefits of work teams in business and has identified the levels of group work as the task to be done, the group process by which the task is accomplished, and the individual needs of the group members.

Factors that affect the group come from outside the group and within the group and are known as group dynamics. Outside factors are such things as group size and the time and place of the meeting. Factors within the group are the participants themselves and the cohesiveness and climate of the meeting. Meetings are structured to be formal one-way meetings or informal give-and-take sessions.

Problem solving and brainstorming are two patterns of organizing the group task.

The group process is maintained by the role of the leader, the behavior of the members, and the decision-making process. Suggestions for improving work groups are offered to the student.

WORKSHOP ACTIVITIES

COMPETITIVE AND COOPERATIVE BEHAVIORS *(Individual Activity and Group Discussion)*

Purpose: To identify different individual behaviors as "competitive" or "cooperative." To discuss situations in which each of these behaviors is appropriate.

Briefing: Complete this exercise individually first. In the blanks at the left headed "INDIVIDUAL," mark the item *O* if you consider it a cooperative behavior, *X* if you consider it a competitive behavior, or *?* if the behavior seems to be neither cooperative nor competitive. Then join a group of four or five classmates. Review the entire list with them and check in the right-hand column those items on which the group does not agree. Discuss situations in which the behavior would be appropriate. Remember that different situations call for different types of behavior.

INDIVIDUAL   GROUP

1. _____ Wants to beat someone else at a particular task.   1. _____
2. _____ Enjoys winning.   2. _____
3. _____ Doesn't hesitate to ask questions if the task is not understood.   3. _____
4. _____ Can change own mind without loss of self-esteem.   4. _____
5. _____ Is considered friendly, good-natured, helpful.   5. _____
6. _____ Has high self-image.   6. _____
7. _____ Is willing to discuss the views of another.   7. _____
8. _____ Listens well and is interested in others.   8. _____
9. _____ Can pull ideas together to make them work.   9. _____
10. _____ Is receptive to new ideas.   10. _____
11. _____ Often puts profit, prize, or position before people.   11. _____
12. _____ Will point out errors to others.   12. _____
13. _____ Loves to receive praise and encouragement.   13. _____
14. _____ Is willing to talk, lead, and take responsibility.   14. _____
15. _____ Works to eliminate communication barriers.   15. _____
16. _____ Trusts others to do their part.   16. _____
17. _____ Can follow directions.   17. _____
18. _____ Accepts group decision when different from own ideas.   18. _____
19. _____ Feels the need to live up to the expectations of others. 19. _____
20. _____ Is ready and able to challenge.   20. _____
21. _____ Feels the need to be superior.   21. _____
22. _____ Doesn't admit defeat but tries again.   22. _____
23. _____ Puts group goals before personal achievement.   23. _____
24. _____ Takes deep satisfaction in accomplishment.   24. _____

Debriefing: Report any items on which your group could not agree. Identify those on which you agreed after discussion.

COMPETITIVE CONTAINER CORPORATIONS *(Group Activity)*

Purpose: To cooperate with others in a small group that is competing against other groups. To identify behaviors developed in a win/lose situation.

Briefing:

1. You will need one set of the following materials for each group: five sheets of heavy construction paper of various colors; two pairs of scissors; glue or paste; stapler and staples; cellophane tape.

2. The class elects three classmates to serve as judges. After they are chosen, the judges withdraw to a corner of the room to read the rules of the game and the Instructions to Judges that start below. The judges are to confer with each other to verify their understanding of the rules.

3. The class members divide into groups of seven to nine people. Each group selects an observer who then moves outside the group and follows the Instructions to Observers on the next page.

4. The instructor distributes a set of materials to each group and reads the following aloud:

   Each group will function as a corporation that produces and sells its product. The task of each corporation is to design and build "The World's Best Container" made of paper. Use only the materials provided to construct the best possible container in 30 minutes. Before beginning construction, each corporation selects a sales representative from among its members. The responsibility of the sales representative is to sell the finished product to the class (who may represent either consumers or industry). The container will be judged on the basis of four criteria: (1) capacity, (2) aesthetics (design elements and attractiveness), (3) sturdiness, and (4) sales pitch. The timing begins now. Proceed.

5. The instructor writes the four judging criteria on the chalkboard as a guide while the corporations begin to work.

6. At the end of 20 minutes, the instructor warns the corporations of the time limit by announcing, "10 minutes before judging time." The instructor also gives a 5-minute warning.

7. At the end of 30 minutes, each sales representative brings the container made by his or her corporation to the front of the room. Each representative has 3 minutes to present a sales pitch and show the product to the class and to the judges.

8. While the judges add the individual scores and compare notes, the observers move into their groups and report their observations to the group members.

9. The judges announce the results of the competition.

Instructions to Judges

You have been elected as an impartial panel of judges. Try to be as fair and objective in your decision as you can. Judge each container on the basis of (1) capacity, (2) aesthetics (design elements and attractiveness), (3) sturdiness, and (4) sales pitch. While the corporations are building their containers, meet with the other judges and decide what proportional value each of the four criteria will have. You may give the sales pitch more value than capacity, for example, or rate them the same. Consider how you will determine each container's sturdiness.

Each judge will rate the containers individually. Then compute the total for each category. If there is a tie, resolve it through discussion. The corporation receiving the highest total from all the judges is the winner. The judges must announce their decision to the class.

Instructions to Observers

Use these questions as a guide for observing your group. Make notes on a separate sheet of paper as you observe. Try to answer most of the questions. Be prepared to make an objective oral report to your corporation after the sales speeches.

1. What kind of group decision resulted in your selection as the observer (one-person decision—you volunteered or someone suggested you; two-person decision; majority vote; general consensus of the group)? Speculate on why you were chosen. Ask for feedback from the group on this point.

2. What kind of decision making did the group use to choose its sales representative?

3. What types of leadership did you see displayed in the group (autocratic, democratic, permissive)? Who emerged in leadership roles? What behaviors did you note in the leaders?

4. What behaviors did you observe that indicated group cohesiveness (ability to work together)? Were there tensions? Was there withdrawal?

5. Which students pushed to get the container designed and built (task-oriented roles)?

6. Which students took on the process roles of helping others, repeating good ideas, supporting suggestions, creating a friendly climate, etc.?

7. Whose ideas were used for the basic design of the container?

8. What kind of behavior helped in the creative aspects of the task? Which students contributed this way (imagination, artistic ability, physical dexterity, etc.)?

9. Observe the behaviors your corporation exhibited after the announcement of the winner by the judges. (This is not to be reported.)

Debriefing:

1. What effect did the time pressure have on your group?

2. What kinds of behavior produced the actual container made by your corporation?

3. What methods did your corporation use to resolve conflicts and lead to more effective production?

4. How did your corporation discover individual talents that could be used in designing and building your container?

5. How did you feel about competition between corporations?

6. What were your personal feelings about winning or losing? How did you feel toward the judges?

QUESTIONS OF FACT, VALUE, OR POLICY *(Individual and Group Activity)*

Purpose: To develop skill in identifying the line of argument in a question up for discussion.

Briefing: Your ability to help a work team clearly identify the type of problem being discussed will be an asset to your group. Study the examples below and then identify each of the numbered questions as a question of fact (*F*), question of value (*V*), or question of policy (*P*). Join a group of four or five others and discuss your answers.

Question of Fact: "Are our defense procedures against shoplifting working?" The discussion presents evidence and reasoning that will determine the truth of "Yes, our defense procedures are working" or "No, our defense procedures are not working as well as we had hoped."

Question of Value: "Would it be more effective to add two-way mirrors or to hire a security guard?" Facts and reasoning are essential, but the discussion must add criteria for judging the effectiveness of each, such as: "Is it efficient?" "Is it cost effective?" "Will it work in our store?"

Question of Policy: "Shall we take further measures to reduce shoplifting?" The discussion must estimate the consequences of putting into effect the change suggested, must offer facts that provide a sound basis for making a change, show probable results, and determine whether these would be desirable or undesirable. Such points include: "Is there a need for a change?" "Can we set up a plan that meets our needs?" "Would the benefits outweigh the cost or harmful effects?"

Mark each of the following questions *F, V,* or *P.*

_____ 1. "Is our product selling as well as our competitor's product?"

_____ 2. "Shall we change our vacation schedule by closing the store for two weeks, or shall we continue to alternate our time schedule as we have in the past?"

_____ 3. "Is packaging our product costing us more than it formerly did?"

_____ 4. "Is doing the customer's job rapidly more important than taking the time to do it well?"

_____ 5. "Is it better business to hire more licensed hairdressers or to update the decor of the salon?"

_____ 6. "Shall we ship by Meritex Express because it is the fastest?"

_____ 7. "Shall we develop a new line of sandwiches or continue to offer only the old favorites?"

_____ 8. "Will a 10¢ tax on every can of spray paint provide the millions of dollars needed to clean up graffiti?"

_____ 9. "Shall we drop our existing level of research and limit ourselves to just two product lines?"

_____ 10. "Shall we enter the price war by dropping our current prices and cutting our profits?"

_____ 11. "Are we top-heavy with administrative personnel in advertising?"

_____ 12. "Are we making more money this year than last?"

Debriefing: Discuss your answers with your group. Try to reach consensus on each answer.

GOALS FOR OUR TOWN *(Group Activity)*

Purpose: To participate in a group discussion in the role of a citizen of your town. To present "The Three Most Important Goals for Our Town" in this citizen's opinion. From the goals presented by the citizens, to arrive at group consensus on the top three goals.

Briefing: Roles may be selected or assigned several days before the class discussion is scheduled so that students have time to research attitudes for the citizens they represent.

On discussion day, the class will be divided into groups of 10 to 15 members. Each group will conduct its own discussion at the same time in different corners of the room. Each student should wear a name tag to identify which role he or she is representing. Each representative will make a brief statement to the group by introducing herself or himself in the citizen role and then will present the three goals that the citizen perceives to be most important.

After each citizen has spoken, members of the group are to consider all the proposals made. The group is to decide which three goals it will recommend to the city council. These should be listed in order of their importance to the group. One member will report the decision (three goals only) of each group to the entire class.

Citizen Roles of Our Town

1. The president of a local utility company.

2. A teacher representing the public school teachers.

3. A militant person from a minority ethnic group.

4. An active member of a labor union.

5. The owner of a small business in the downtown area.

6. A senior citizen over age 65.

7. A middle-aged, lifelong resident of the community.

8. A foreign student (short-term resident).

9. A retired military person.

10. The manager of a chain store located in a suburban shopping area.

11. An agricultural or environmental representative.

12. A representative of the town's biggest industry.

13. A social worker who works with people in a poor housing area.

14. The director of the local symphony orchestra.

15. An elected official or any other representative of a group that exists in your town.

Debriefing:

1. Did you find it difficult to step into the shoes of another person and present views different from your own?

2. Who in your group did you feel made an excellent presentation? Why?

3. How did you structure your discussion?

4. How did you arrive at leadership roles in your group?

5. What kinds of behavior helped your group arrive at a consensus decision?

IDENTIFYING TASK-ORIENTED AND PROCESS-ORIENTED ROLES *(Individual Activity)*

Briefing: Some statements made by group members are task-oriented and help to move the job along. Other statements are process-oriented and help involve members by building team spirit and group unity. Read the statements below. Mark a *T* before the task-oriented statements and a *P* before the process-oriented statements.

_____ 1. "You haven't said anything, Ann. Do you agree with us?"

_____ 2. "That's a good idea, Juanita."

_____ 3. "We have considered the problem carefully. Are we ready to set up criteria for the solution?"

_____ 4. "Pete, will you write these suggestions on the board?"

_____ 5. "Lola, I don't think you have given Sue a chance to make her point."

_____ 6. "Are you saying that these are the long-term goals we should consider?"

_____ 7. "Mr. Roberts, will you give us the sales figures for the past six months?"

_____ 8. "I am inclined to go along with Andy on this issue."

_____ 9. "You sound as if you are unhappy with this suggestion."

_____ 10. "I can think of several solutions to this problem, but they will not meet any of the criteria we have set."

_____ 11. "What was that statement from *Business Week*?"

_____ 12. "Are we ready to make a recommendation?"

_____ 13. "What do you think, Ms. Andreas?"

_____ 14. "What a great idea, Jerry! I never thought of it like that."

_____ 15. "Are we ready to vote?"

_____ 16. "Are you saying that there are two separate and distinct causes of this problem?"

_____ 17. "It seems as though we all agree on these two points. Right?"

_____ 18. "You seem to be supporting John's idea, George."

_____ 19. "Should we start by discussing the third point?"

_____ 20. "Wait a minute, Henry. I don't think that is what John means."

_____ 21. "Let me rephrase what we have said so far."

_____ 22. "How are we going to tackle this issue?"

_____ 23. "I don't know if we could start the plan that soon. What would the shipping department say, Noriko?"

_____ 24. "You are suggesting that we put the plan into effect at the same time we inventory the warehouse?"

_____ 25. "Let's move on to the next point."

SELF-IMAGE DIARY *(Individual Activity)*

Briefing: The statements you make to others often reveal how you feel about yourself. Listen to your own comments for several days and check the categories into which they fit. Is your self-image low or well balanced?

Low Self-Image:

1. Unable to accept praise or to give recognition to others: "Oh, think nothing of it." "It was really nothing." "Do you really like it?" "Anyone could do that."

   _____

2. Defensiveness about accepting blame: "It's not my job." "Nobody would help me." "Mary started it and then walked out." "It's not my fault."

   _____

3. Cynical attitude: "Well, it's not bad, if you like that sort of thing." "I've heard better ideas."

   _____

4. Putting yourself down: "I'm a natural klutz." "I've never been good at math." "I blew it, as usual."

   _____

5. Sneering at others: "Oh, he was just lucky." "She got the job because her mother works here."

   _____

6. Pessimistic attitude: "I don't know why I go. I always have a rotten time." "I won't enter; I never win anything."

   _____

Well-Balanced Self-Image:

1. Focusing on others: "If it wasn't for you, Joe, we would have never made the deadline." "Jane has a good idea. Will you explain it to the group, Jane?"

   _____

2. Honest apology: "It was my fault. Please forgive me." "Sorry, my mistake. You were right." "I was wrong. What can we do?"

   _____

3. Able to handle different relationships: "The boss and I play golf, but I always call her Ms. Gray at work." (To the custodian): "I've made a mess at my desk. Let me help clean it up."

   _____

4. Able to take risks: "I really don't understand. Will you go over that once again?"

   _____

5. Able to empathize: "I'm not sure I agree with this decision, but I can certainly understand why it is important to you." "I'm upset about the error, but I can see why you did it that way."

   _____

DISCUSSION PRESENTATION *(Group Presentation)*

Purpose: To participate in a group discussion as the class observes. To follow the steps of the problem-solving method in discussion.

Briefing:

1. The instructor will divide the class members into small groups. Each group will conduct a 30-minute discussion on a selected topic by using the problem-solving method.

2. The class assignment will be made a week in advance of the first presentation so that group members will have adequate time for research.

3. A 20-minute period will be set aside during class time for the groups to meet, to decide on a topic, and to share ideas about sources of information. Each member of the group will prepare independently for the discussion. The topic will be worded in the form of a question and submitted to the instructor.

4. On its presentation day, each group will have 30 minutes to discuss its topic. The group should not discuss the topic before class time. Members of the class will observe the discussion, but the discussion will be conducted as though it were not being observed. Members may sit together around a table in the front of the room. A chalkboard or flip chart should be available to record information during the discussion. Names of group members should be listed on the board.

5. Groups may select from the topic suggestions on the following page. Before the discussion begins, one member of the group will hand to the instructor the critique sheets on pages 353 and 355.

6. Follow the suggestions below and on the following page for your presentation.

Task

1. Write your topic question on the chalkboard so that it can be easily seen.

2. Use ten minutes of the time to discuss the problem. Define terms, identify causes, symptoms, and effects of the problem. Be specific as to why the issue is a problem. For example:

    It causes danger and suffering to those who experience it.
    It is recognized as a problem by those authorities whom your audience accepts as credible.
    It causes other problems.
    It keeps a business from operating as well as it should.
    It directly or indirectly injures the audience or business.

    Be sure to identify whose problem this is.

3. Use five minutes of the time to set up criteria for the ideal solution. Each member should be prepared in advance to contribute to the list of criteria or standards. One group member may write these on the chalkboard or on a flip chart. Remember that you are describing an ideal solution. Think of how you would like the problem to be resolved if the ideal solution existed.

    Some examples of criteria for an ideal solution are:

    The ideal solution will guarantee that everyone will be satisfied with the solution.
    The ideal solution will not create greater problems than the problem being solved.
    The ideal solution will be easy to put into effect.

4. Use two minutes to list all the possible solutions the group can generate. Record the solutions rapidly on the board so the audience can keep track of them.

5. Use ten minutes to decide on two or three of the possible solutions that group members believe to be best. Compare these solutions to the criteria for the ideal solution. Discuss the strengths and weaknesses of each solution. No solution should meet all the criteria. Indeed, it cannot; if the perfect or ideal solution existed, we wouldn't have the problem. Our criteria for an ideal solution merely describe how we'd like the problem solved.

6. Use three minutes to make a group decision as to which solution the group will recommend to the audience—even if the solution is not ideal.

Process

1. Communicate with other members of the group as if no audience were present. However, speak loudly enough to be heard by the entire class.

2. Sit around a table so that all group members face each other.

3. Establish a comfortable climate.

4. Share the recording of information on the chalkboard with other group members rather than having just one person doing it.

5. Try not to make negative judgments about others' ideas without first stating a positive attitude.

6. Paraphrase each other's statements to check understanding.

7. Try to move the discussion along, but give everyone a chance to contribute. Draw out the quiet group members. Recognize the ideas of others. Listen to each other.

Suggested Topics

Word your topic as a question. Some suggested topics are:

1. How can communication barriers be prevented between the worker level and the management level in business?

2. What can be done about the problem of pay discrimination between men and women in American business?

3. What is the best method of dealing with the problem of petty theft by employees?

4. How can a company handle the problem of layoffs so that the employees maintain their self-esteem and retain a good attitude toward the company?

Name _____ Class _____ Score _____

INDIVIDUAL CRITIQUE SHEET—DISCUSSION PRESENTATION *(Instructor's Evaluation)*

Briefing: One member of the group should tear out this page and give it to the instructor.

Each individual will be rated from 1 to 10 points for each of the following items:

1. Did the student seem well prepared?
2. Did the student contribute to a good group climate?
3. Did the student show growth in speaking and listening behavior?
4. Did the student seem to understand the problem-solving method?
5. Was the student willing to change his or her normal behavior in the interest of a good discussion?

NAME	NAME	NAME
_____	_____	_____
1.	1.	1.
2.	2.	2.
3.	3.	3.
4.	4.	4.
5.	5.	5.
TOTAL _____	TOTAL _____	TOTAL _____

NAME	NAME
_____	_____
1.	1.
2.	2.
3.	3.
4.	4.
5.	5.
TOTAL _____	TOTAL _____

GROUP CRITIQUE SHEET—DISCUSSION PRESENTATION *(Instructor's Evaluation)*

Briefing: Tear out this page and give it to your instructor before the group discussion.

SUBJECT OF DISCUSSION: _____

POSSIBLE POINTS: 50   (Each category: 10 points)

Knowledge and Thought Content:

Stated topic clearly.
Presented adequate and relevant information.
Gave thoughtful consideration to topic; cited sources.
Stayed close to the topic.
Had a sense of direction in handling material.   _____

Emotional Climate:

Animated and lively when speaking and reacting.
Good verbal and nonverbal interaction.
Clashing ideas with satisfying resolutions.
Positive attitudes toward others' contributions.   _____

Involvement and Participation:

Shared the speaking roles evenly.
Cooperated in leadership and participant roles.
Was interested in presenting and supporting ideas.
Asked questions, paraphrased, listened to each other.   _____

Use of Time:

Moved the discussion along.
Kept within the limits of time but was not pressured.
Differentiated between problem and solutions.
Used the criteria as a basis for judging solutions.   _____

Achievement of Goal:

Understood the group goal.
Prepared to participate and discuss.
Arrived at a solution through consensus.   _____

                                                    Group Total _____

Instructor's Comments:

SELF-DISCLOSURE QUESTIONNAIRE *(Individual Activity)*

Briefing: Recall any of the class group activities from this chapter. Check your understanding of groups by answering these questions:

1. Identify the class activity or the group task. _____
_____

2. How long did it take before you felt comfortable in this particular group? _____
_____

3. How many people were in the group? _____
List the group members: _____

4. How did you feel about speaking out in the group? _____
_____

5. How did you feel about others' reactions to what you said? _____
_____

6. Did one person speak more than the others? _____
If so, was this person regarded as the group leader? _____

7. Did everyone speak at some time during the meeting? _____

8. How did others seem to listen to you? _____
_____

9. Did you paraphrase the comments of another person to check your understanding of what they said?
_____
Did anyone paraphrase your remarks? _____

10. Toward which person in the group did you feel most responsive? _____
Why? _____

11. Was your behavior primarily task-oriented or process-oriented? _____
_____

12. Name some roles you filled during the discussion. _____
_____
_____

13. Were you satisfied with the group's accomplishments? Why or why not? _____
_____
_____

14. What suggestions do you have for improving the climate or the way the group worked on its task?
_____
_____

CHECKLIST OF COMMUNICATION TERMS *(Quiz)*

The following terms were defined in this chapter. Check your understanding of the communication term by writing the number of the correct term in the blank preceding its definition. Note there are more terms than definitions.

Definitions	**Terms**

a. _____ Describing a group that works well together.

b. _____ A freewheeling, unstructured type of discussion in which members are stimulated to provide creative thinking on an issue.

c. _____ Factors within a group and outside the group that affect the way the group operates.

d. _____ One way of stating a problem in which the issue is defined in terms of worth.

e. _____ The name given to a person who brings others into the discussion and checks the feelings of other members of the group.

f. _____ Negative behavior of a group member who acts indifferent or does not actively participate in the discussion.

g. _____ Standards by which solutions are evaluated in the problem-solving method.

h. _____ Decision making that results in a harmonious agreement by all group members after there has been an open discussion.

i. _____ A style of leadership in which the leader tells other members of the group what to do.

j. _____ A group of individuals interacting together for some organizational purpose.

Terms

1. group dynamics
2. task
3. process
4. hidden agendas
5. cohesive
6. climate
7. norms
8. criteria
9. brainstorming
10. autocratic style
11. permissive style
12. democratic style
13. task-oriented behavior
14. process-oriented behavior
15. roles
16. cooperation
17. collaboration
18. one-person decisions
19. two-person decisions
20. plop
21. majority vote
22. consensus
23. information seeker
24. gatekeeper
25. harmonizer
26. opinion giver
27. withdrawing
28. climate maker
29. sidestepping
30. question of fact
31. question of value
32. question of policy
33. work team

COURSE QUESTIONNAIRE *(Individual Activity)*

Purpose: To give you an opportunity to evaluate this speech communication course. To provide feedback that will help your instructor increase the effectiveness of this course. *Do not sign this questionnaire.*

Check one for each question

1. Compare this course with others you have taken.

   a. Was this course: more time-consuming .... _____

                         less time-consuming .... _____

   b. Was this course: more valuable .... _____

                         less valuable .... _____

                         about the same...................................... _____

   c. Was this course: more interesting..................................... _____

                         less interesting .... _____

                         about the same...................................... _____

   d. Was the grading in this course: too easy .... _____

                             too hard .... _____

                             about right .... _____

   e. Was the grading fair and consistent: yes .... _____

                             no .... _____

2. Use this rating scale to answer the questions below:
   1—poor; 2—fair; 3—average; 4—good; 5—excellent

   Circle one for each question

   a. How clear were the goals of the course? 1 2 3 4 5

   b. How useful were the assignments in helping you to achieve the goals?......... 1 2 3 4 5

   c. How useful was the course for your professional needs? 1 2 3 4 5

   d. How useful was the course for your personal needs?....................... 1 2 3 4 5

   e. Was the textbook clear and interesting? 1 2 3 4 5

   f. How useful was class discussion? 1 2 3 4 5

   g. Did you feel free to participate in the class activities? 1 2 3 4 5

   h. Was your instructor knowledgeable, interested, helpful, and enthusiastic? 1 2 3 4 5

   i. Was your instructor concerned about your development and achievement in the course? 1 2 3 4 5

   j. Rate the value of this course to you. 1 2 3 4 5

3. On the back of this form, write any additional comments you may have concerning the course, the textbook, or the instructor.

INDEX

through overt body movement, 185–186
through personal appearance, 184–185
tips for improving, 191
and verbal communication, compared, 182
Norms, defined, 333
Note cards
as delivery aid, 254
sample, 255
Nylen, D., 203

O

Objects
defined, 127
as visual aids, 257–258
Observation, example of inaccurate, 43
One-to-one communication, 290–291. *See also* Dyad
suggestions for improving, 307–308
Opaque projectors, 264
Open-door policies, 48
Opening remarks. *See* Introduction
Oral cavity, 156
Oral presentations. *See* Business presentations
Ormont, Jules, 335
Outline form, for speech presentation, 226
illustrations of, 227, 229, 232, 233
Output, defined, 2
Overhead projectors, 264–265

P

Paralanguage, 7
Paraphrasing, 80–81. *See also* Feedback
Parent ego state, 85–87
Peale, Norman Vincent, 80
Pearson, Craig, 103
Perception
classification system in, 34–35
defined, 29
and effect on communication, 42–45
and effect on feedback, 44
and effect on listening, 44
example of distorted, 43
filters in, 39–42, 125
organizing and labeling in, 34–36
physical senses in, 32
process of, 30–39
selective, 32–33
suggestions for improving, 44–45
techniques in checking, 37–39
Permissive style of leadership, 336
Personal appearance
as an aspect of communication, 7

as a nonverbal message channel, 7, 182, 184–185
Persuasive presentations
arrangement patterns for main points in, 228–230
examples of, 209–210
strategies for, 215–216
types of, 215
Pharynx, 156
Pictorial graph, 260
illustration of, 261
Pie chart. *See* Circle graph
Powell, John, S.J., 292
Powers, Jimmy, 39
Prather, Hugh, 187
Presentations. *See* Business presentations
Private lines, 48
Problem-solving method, 333–334
Problem-solving pattern, in persuasive presentations, 229–230
Processes, defined, 127
Projectors, for visual aids, 263–265
Pronunciation, 158, 163
errors in, 158
Public Affairs Information Service, 224
Public speeches
and oral business presentations, compared, 211–212

Q

Questions, types of
answer-seeking, 268
getcha, 267
message, 267
Question-and-answer sessions
advance preparation for, 267
suggestions for responding in, 268
types of questions asked in, 267–268
Quintilian, 186

R

Rankin, Paul T., 73
Readers' Guide to Periodical Literature, 224
Reality
and distortion through language, 125–126
and personal differences, 30
Receiver, 6
defined, 5
role of, in communication, 79–80
skills, 80–82
Referent
defined, 120
illustration of, 128
using common, 126–128

Toffler, Alvin, 31, 36, 189
Topical order, in informative presentations, 227
Training sessions, 300
Transaction
  business, 296
  description of, 6
  face-to-face, 7
  limited, 7
Transactional analysis, 85
Transceiver, 6
Transitions, in speech outline, 230
Transitive verbs, 125
Transparencies, 264
Trull, Samuel G., 300

V

Values, defined, 40
Vertical structure in business, 47
  communication channels with, illustrated, 48
Visual aids, 233, 256–266
  advantages of using, 256
  factors to consider in planning, 256–257
  guidelines for using, 265–266
  handouts as, 265
  methods of projecting, 263–265
  types of, 257–265
  ways to display, 262–263
Vocabulary building, 162–163

Vocal characteristics
  enunciation, 162
  pitch, 159
  quality, 162
  rate, 159–161
  volume or intensity, 161–162
Vocal cords, 155, 156
Vocalizing process, 156
Vocal messages, 158–159
Voice box, 155
Voice writing. *See* Dictating

W

Wall Street Journal Index, 224
Weider-Hatfield, Deborah, 295
Whiting, Percy H., 211
Whitman, Walt, 129
Wiener, Norbert, 154
Winans, James A., 216, 251–252
Windpipe, 155
Wolf, Morris Philip, 169, 306, 315
Words as symbols, 126–129
Work teams in business, 327–342
  benefits of using, 328
  expectations for, 341
  factors affecting operation of, 328–331
  improving, 340–342
  maintaining group process in, 335–340
  organizing tasks of, 333–335
  skills needed for, 341–342